WHAT THE CRITICS ARE SAYING...

"I couldn't put this book down! — it would levitate from the poolside table I put it on and open to the next page to read and my glasses would, on their own, fly up and attach to my face!"

— Emery Larson, Director of Jacuzzi Enterprises, Inc.

"Well, I, it was, uh, it was, oh! Wait, I can explain, I mean, I mean, okay, so, like it, it can't be, uh, don't! Where! Will you, oh no! So right now, it would, uh, it would help if, if, if, but stop, just, just a minute, just wait; let me, let, not now, but, well, listen to me?"

— Allen Childs, Professor Emeritus of Linguistics, Aleutian Trench University

"In order to understand the book it's best you go to all the places mentioned and stay in each location while you're reading about them — give it three months"

— Maria Johnson, Docent, Leisure Planet, Des Moines, Iowa

"Memorize this author and then his somewhat awkward style may be gotten used to so that one is then not distracted from the interesting underlying message"

— Lulu Ann Oribello, Readiness Clinics, USA

"Read it in one sitting when the prostitute didn't show up — it was better than sex!"

— Arnold "Easy" Maiterlink IV, Director of Project Bonobo

"Whaaaaaaaat? — Where's Stockton?"

— Carol Sadler with California Marijuana Grow House Collective

"I taught him all he knows and then he stopped answering my texts and emails when he blew up with the publication of *Stockton* — guess fame has messed with his memory and gone to his head — still, the book has a place on my shelf."

— Guy Fergussen, Writing Coach, Cannon Beach, Oregon

"A.I. might have played a role in the creation of this volume, as the writer's block this author has been suffering from for the past thirty years could well have pushed Arntson to drastic measures — notwithstanding such a possibility, go and get this book if you can find it!"

— Maureen Latimer, mountain lion whisperer, Breckenridge, Colorado

"It was an angry read, then a happy read, and after that a questioning read, followed by a teasing read, a relevant read and then an angry read again — I just couldn't decide!"

— Oliver Staples, M.D.

"I just love camping but the author refused to answer any of my questions — he did however show great interest in my answers."

— Candy Felicia Smith, geologist

We'll Always Have Stockton

by
Steve Arntson

Last Laugh Productions
Walnut Creek, CA
2023

Copyright 2023 by Steve Arntson

ISBN: 979-8-9875209-2-5

Library of Congress Control Number: 2023912821

This book may not be reproduced, in whole or in part,
without written permission from the author.
Reviewers may quote brief passages.

To contact the author:
cozzy2424@gmail.com

Photos:

Front Cover:

Moshe Harosh from Pixabay.com

Back Cover:

Stefan Keller from Pixabay.com

Interior:

Badge icon by Bing Image Creator

Cover Design by Deborah L. Fruchey

Preface

This book was originally intended as the first part of a trilogy. After I wrote *The Year of the Fox*, which was about Burning Man of 2016, I thought to revisit the subject. The previous effort was loosely structured: it was about experiences on the way, on arrival and after.

When COVID came and Burning Man was canceled in 2020, a smaller number of enthusiasts still came out to the Black Rock Desert to party anyway — not sure of the numbers — maybe a couple of thousand arrived and spread out. Unlike the usual Burning Man, there was plenty of space, and small planes were landing here and there. I thought to amplify — why not repeat? — but take the near-nothingness of 2020 and celebrate it! The planned trilogy would be greatly expanded: travel to, a similarly magnified Burning Man review and, lastly, a detailed account of Wyoming, Colorado and other states I went to after the week on the playa; the whole conception to explore sparsity and how it encourages imagination. Just as some of the isolated communities of eastern Oregon invoke the basics, and the vast tracts of public lands lead to reflection, just so a spread-out Burning Man, greatly downsized and discovered with binoculars, seemed the perfect prompt for imagining. Similarly, the post-Burn regions, driven to, could also make a case, not just for sightseeing, but for amateur philosophy.

Okay so far, I thought — then I realized the project might be too ambitious. With this in mind I completed the first book and tried to look ahead. We'll see! Meanwhile I hope you enjoy the present volume.

I have many to thank for assistance — Mel C. Thompson, who was always willing to hear certain passages and who encouraged —my publisher, Deborah Fruchey, the easiest person to work with ever and who always has good suggestions — my friends and supporters, Marvin Hiemstra, Julian Mithra, Nancy Margolies, Betsy Mueller, Tom Stolmar, Jan Steckel, James Cagney, Jr., Richard Hack, Jocelyn Mikolka, Linnea Arntson (whose name I stole 35 years ago!), Tim Donnelly, Anna Wolfe, Mel Vapour with East Bay Media Center, Bruce and Ruth Harteneck, Kris and Shannon Dyszynski, the Waverley Writers, especially Mary-Marcia Casoly, who has kept the flame going for Waverley, Richard Loranger, special thanks for all you do for others, and Loie Johnson for years of love.

Steve Arntson, 2023

Table of Contents

1. Red Mystery...1
2. "If You're Not The Guest"....................................2
3. Hillman Ascended—From the South....................5
4. Big Hole—With Fallen Timber..............................9
5. Let's Start Down..10
6. Connections—Loie—Marvin..............................12
7. Return to Fort Twilight.......................................13
8. The Gate..17
9. The Cop in the Water..19
10. The Softness of Certain Waters..........................23
11. Always Abroad..25
12. Too Cold So Two Bags..30
13. A Dream with Richard Loranger in it.................31
14. "Can I See some I.D., Please?"...........................35
15. The Caves Road...37
16. Don't Enter or it's Hanta for Sure!....................42
17. In the Paisley Booth..46
18. That Cop for a Third Time..................................47
19. The Walls of Abert..50
20. Cindy's Scenery...56
21. What's Strewn..59
22. Wagontire..67
23. Valley Falls Junction...73
24. The Burns Swing...75
25. Riley, Oregon...77
26. No Smoke...77
27. The Sundowner..84
28. The Missed Concert Dream................................85
29. The Republicans..86
30. The Round Barn with Xena................................87
31. The Owl..89
32. The Scent of Weed...92
33. The Round Interior..95
34. Red Cinders...99
35. The Otley Brothers..103
36. With Hay and Lava..105
37. Severity, Austerity...108
38. Frenchglen's Mercantile Store..........................113
39. The Alkali Lake Disaster...................................114

40. John, Hotelier..117
41. Spirit..121
42. Companions on the Precipice of Kiger.............122
43. A Brand New Brink..124
44. A Certain Beautiful Bonobo.............................128
45. The Many Moons Till Now...............................135
46. A Windbreak with Stones................................139
47. Suicide by Wind...145
48. Loranger Long Distance..................................149
49. The Lost Car Key...155
50. That Frenchglen Green....................................157
51. The Grey House with the Red Roof.................158
52. A Cow in Command of the Others...................160
53. The Distant "Gunsight"....................................166
54. Slanted Trees..167
55. Bright Trees...171
56. Lago Tranquilo...174
57. Lake Stones and Tan Hills Deserted................178
58. Ordination at Kiger..181
59. Why You Went...188
60. Moon Perfect...190
61. Those Millions of Years...................................190
62. Fast-Forward...193
63. Call Back...195
64. Not Someone Who Makes a Living..................197
65. Alvord, Below the Airplane of Land.................198
66. It's a Mile...202
67. The Blue East..202
68. Alpine Places to Come....................................207
69. Ships...210
70. Distance..212
71. Tufts..214
72. Grey and Green...219
73. Dream of an Argument....................................221
74. Venus Casts a Shadow....................................223
75. Three Hours with the Wild Horses...................226
76. Little Blitzen to Page Springs..........................229
77. The Riddle Brothers..235
78. Catlow's Creeks and Farms.............................238
79. Barrier...244
80. History's Structure..246

81.	Lava's Summit Foregrounded by Trees	249
82.	The Best Picture	252
83.	Farms Unseen	255
84.	The Stone House	257
85.	A Yearning for the Alvord Spring	261
86.	Dog Food Deluded	265
87.	Slats and Postcards	270
88.	That Steens Couple, a Reprise	272
89.	A Fields Lecture on the Barn	273
90.	The Denio Piano	277
91.	140 and its Escarpment	284
92.	The Ponies at Adel	286
93.	O'Keefe Lane	287
94.	The Black and White Porch Pup Bow-Wow	290
95.	Adel to Plush	294
96.	Supplies in Plush	298
97.	Additional Bulls	301
98.	Layers of Light	305
99.	Hart's Hazy Distance	306
100.	The Duned Shore East	307
101.	Junipers' Slopes	308
102.	The Dark Blue that Pulls You Over	312
103.	What's Horizontal's Left to Enthrall	319
104.	From the Wet Shoreline	321
105.	Shaded Trees and Future Groves	325
106.	The Golden Line	329
107.	Sunstones	330
108.	Small Houses, Big Country	334
109.	Slave Ship	342
110.	The Revolutionary War Spreads to Oregon	344
111.	"You're Set"	351
112.	Dinner Bell Cafe, "The Octagon"	352
113.	Where's Goose Lake?	353
114.	That Shifting Borderline	356
115.	Fandango Pass Abandoned	363
116.	New Pine Creek	364
117.	Red Jeep and a Pepsi	370
118.	"Keep Out and Keep Away!"	374
119.	The Hollow Barn	379
120.	The Cedarville Corner Store After 6,200 Feet	382
121.	The Wagons at the Cedarville Garage	390

122. The Station..393
123. Woody's..396
124. In Eagleville We are Wearing Black..................................397
125. The Green House So Pale..399
126. Weathering's Wavelengths..402
127. Those Bells in the Churchyard..408
128. The Tower..412
129. Bales..415
130. The Burnt Land...417
131. The Sheep..424
132. Nevada, Entering..424
133. Franck's Quintet at the Crest..425
134. Parsing "Squaw Valley" and the Encampment There........427
135. Wrong Turn to Bivouac...434
136. Mosquito Glen...434
137. An Eastern Wind...438
138. How Easy it was For Evil..441
139. Happy Fourth of Juplaya!...448
140. Laura...452

About the Author..465
Other books by Steve Arntson...466
Other Offerings from Last Laugh Productions..........................467

We'll Always Have Stockton

for the
Cafe Babar Poets
with love

1. RED MYSTERY

It was to go wrong I took it
Highway 16
    prior to 505
        the shortcut freeway lanes

16   while 16 was east and not west of it

And so the sun was thought to be out of place
The sun was wrong and not myself

And it was red as well because other things were
        not right
            like football without the ball

And having no direction
        the roads would take you far away   weirdly
Somewhere without the word "orient" spoken
Somewhere the Indians would not have gone

While the driver   hapless   imagines
        that red sun will set in that east and confound

A traveler
        not trusting signage   trusting only himself

The fire's haze in support of illusion
        wanting everything lost
Those smudgy pastels a good art
      in the service of the red, red sun
          that had to be west but wasn't

A sun longing for the infrared
        not satisfied with *visible* light
            wishing to rule the darkness
                    in a drunken hangover

Sweet 16!
I'd thought to see the coastal mountains
      close to the lake they called the "Clear"
Then loop some distance returning

Never mind
It was geography unlearned by the smoke
Going haywire
     right where the wire
          and the hay bale's bundles
              broaden the valley and all its silts

505   the shortcut miles   *accepted* finally
Due south for due north still playing tricks
Nature having fun with infrastructure
     a ball in the hall of Reversal rolling

The color red like a crime without any passion
     save for the satisfaction of overthrown reason
        the last three notes
        those low-down Ds
            clanging Chopin's last Prelude of 24

The mystery
The mystery of a red sun replaced
     but lasting long enough to unsettle assumptions

The taste of it
Like the finest ash of poison oak
     that lingers
        informing true south
            even to the border with Oregon

The wrong way persisting
Like a negative print
     in the red of the darkroom
        refusing to develop

2.   "IF YOU'RE NOT THE GUEST"

The Lodge had given notice:

"If you're not the Guest you can't be inside!

The rules are very strict!
No!   you can't work the puzzle!
Leave the Crater Lake picture puzzle *be*!
Don't touch the table it's on or anything else!
Don't sit in the chairs or the sofas
No writing postcards!
Don't ask any questions!

"You're not The Guest get *out*, understand?!
No gawking!
       no dawdling!
              no breakfast!
                     no lunch!
                            no *nothing*!"

COVID had come to the Lodge
The only   Guest
      who checked in with a *rural* identity
        one that was assumed
                      after assuming so much already!

Finding fault while it sought to spread
Complaining the sun was too bright and the Lake too deep

It argued and bullied
Told the staff it wasn't leaving   *ever*
Told the *maitre d' it* was now in charge
Sent the five course meals back to the kitchen

Cried "Freedom!" over and over
               like a deranged Mel Gibson

Started a fire but not in the fireplace
Commanded carpenters to fix what wasn't broken
      make squeaky the *furnishings* of the Lodge
Took down pictures and replaced the blinds with itself
Admired the mirrors
      but stole their reflections
            like a creature of *Hoffmann*

And if you're a lower case guest it'll know
For its nose is exclusive
    a dog's dream of detection

The manager's in hiding
His mask is no protection
The gates of the mountains have closed
And all the doors of the Lodge
        yet the capital Guest
                is everywhere a virus *can* be
                      and still do damage

Still be a bully

Motors   all machinery   goes on
The shutdown's for humans
     all pronouns and genders

Wuhan perfection!

The virus says,
     "I am yours and you are mine
         in bright scenery's restricted forests
            where we chase the rodents together"

If you're not The Guest   you don't get it
You don't go   *anywhere*

If you're not The Guest
     it doesn't matter you brought toothpaste
     and blades
     remembered suntan
     packed the pep pills and vitamins
        brought reading
           or thought to write something yourself

There's a brainier bug   and *much* smarter than you
If there's learning to be done
     it will say just where and when and for how long
        until you graduate to coughing   and
        all the symptoms the bug has packed
            and prepared to share

If you're not The Guest of Crater Lake's Lodge
     it means you must be a *guest* of The Guest
       the *only*
And so will undergo *that* sign-in

    that registration
        that card   accepted or declined

One whose postcards cost the price of a ventilator
Whose souvenir cups and gifts
        are terminal flirtations with nurses

The Lodge is a tourist trap trapping heat
High temps held in the heart of Mazama
    itself bemused by all the destruction
        and thinking Kali *too* is a kind of contagion
    that the Hindus can handle
        so the good times can roll
           immunity
           resorts
           volcanoes
           RVs
                and yappy dogs

3.   HILLMAN ASCENDED   FROM THE SOUTH

Hillman Peak   from the south   barely
It's called "Hillman"
    a name   someone from history
        from the Crater and posterity to come

And he's the highest point
What's left of Mount Mazama
    and a volcano in its own right
        a sub-vent   split   in the larger collapse
All the plumbing seen as cross-section

And there was a desire to "summit"
Say the verb despite objections
Scramble *to* that craggy place
Come at it from the *tricky* side
    with happy thoughts of coming back

Climb the sunny side   the southern side
Harder   steeper   hotter
     where the rocks say you're not at home
         and make you wonder if fear plays poker

Start from the beginning
     and parking   and tourists milling   indecisive
        unsure of what they see

In the pale blue of the forest smoke
     perhaps they wonder why they came at all
        to be so dimly rewarded
        those six miles of vanishing lake
A canvas muted   barely comprehended

Follow for awhile the trail to false summits' sandy inclines
Trace a path approximate
The best way
     to stay acquainted
        with the edge and finish of the mountain
           where it plunges acutely
           damaged by subsidence

The best trees to be shade and remembrance
Reenacting another try
     so long ago the story ended

But it *was* the Hillman
Same spire   same south
     in a storm
        in the night with rain   and even fog!

And it couldn't be done
Blindly   slowly   the flashlight useless
You remember stopping
     the wall of darkness
        the wall of steepness
           left for another day

This day!
In the smoke and the sun
     waiting to see if the south was possible
        if seeing made any difference at all

Now   higher   the danger's restarted
The lanes to the lake cleared by rockfall
        and slides of a palest coloration
              down chutes to scalloped shores

Now   so close   the butterflies swarmed
Steal calories for themselves
So close that climbing was fearful

A circumspect scramble around and over
What sea level said was easy
       become perilous gambles
           and gaming acrophobia
Shaky caution not up to height *above* and trembling

It was amazing
     how quickly can't-climb-up and can't-climb-down
         were joined in a quandary
         an essay of guessing

What key?   what moves?
What discoveries for hands and feet?
What means of escape
     the way away from Hillman's vertical
        the route *around* to secure a confidence!?

You *abandon* the edge and seek the west
Where Mazama was a more gentle giant
     yet sloping still
     as if the cataclysm had been one big lie
              told too often

There   in the jumble of andesite
     struggle with assurance
        that ankles *only* were at risk
        and one's life is saved for later

Hillman Peak   the highest   the hardest
That has no path in any brochure
Just an "X" marking   and numbers
     eight thousand feet and more
     the start of nine thousand
        as Mount Scott is the end

The hot stones and their random sculpture
    want nothing more than mountain-building
      building *back*
        to be a "strato" once again
With the LIke filled in
And the volcano higher than ever before

The *homo sapiens* has   other ideas
   likes to "be here now"
     in a "see ya' later" landscape

And one of them reaches the uneven ledges
    that would topple and render balance impossible
      the pay-attention slabs
Everything seen that *can* be seen
      while dancing ballet
        tiptoeing the creases
        and sharpened slate

There's sufficient blue for a sky down there
Crater Lake   blue laid flat
  a full page of Euclid to offset chaos

Concentration   sobriety
What's needed to stay on top
     and take pictures of below
All that zen asking "Why?"   but not *too* insistently

Why was Hillman so honored
   he managed "ultima thule"
     made a fool of Superman
       and raised the bar for BCE?

The ancient ash   imagined   inherited

Soon the diamonds
Diamond Lake and Diamond Junction!

A bowtie to go with some achievement
As long as you don't try to tell it with words
For the solo ascent
    like the antioxidant
       is taken best internally

4. BIG HOLE   WITH FALLEN TIMBER

It was another way to see the pit
The steam explosion's mighty work
So long ago a forest's filled it
                many, many times
          another maar   bigger   better

Its bowl a vast depression's hidden walls
Secret places a dirt lane circles   discreetly

In the center of it all   an openness
     some trees taken
     maybe unlawfully
          maybe with blessings

And there were wood piles too down there
Branches stacked
     you could wander freely
          with lines of sight assisting

But I sought the higher ground surrounding
          the perimeter to see another way
Big Hole from above
Another way   entranced by the pines
     being careful
          that the race across time
               is slowed to a walk

Your best self
     in a gallery of fallen timber
          logs' treasures taken seriously

Dead fine-grained grey
Or black where the charcoal lies
     a campfire's tomorrow
          entertaining   exhausting

The rim is somewhere the sun has traveled
              a one-time Spanish star
          the end of an afternoon
         a dimming such
       the maar's balcony seats

        could not be found

Though the forest's rows were begging
                             for discovery
                                 and mourning

Beyond the borders of imaginary parks
     a liberty is taken with their attractions

5.   LET'S START DOWN

How are you feeling?
Just dozing?
Hungry?
Wanna' descend?

There'll be the moon
Don't mind the children
      they'll be getting sleepy them*selves*
                   and our neighbors here
                   are very good parents!

It's a place for the family
      no matter one's income
           for the orange smoke has leveled

Why not   start down the sand?
To the intermittent fortress go?
See the remains of the day
      that Hole-in-the-Ground was made!

The great explosion
      when the dead lava was rent
           and the pulse of the planet taken

We'll get to the bottom
Where the road from the west concludes
           with bullet holes and target cans
Dead-center's dance floor

      where we get the crater's goat
          and defy a volcano's plans to repeat

It's a relief to be believed
In the realm of Newberry's shield
      the rough circumstantial evidence serves

For twenty-four hours let us linger
         sharing the austerity
        in the split basin
            whose faults are our own
Our study and school of thought
     concerning Earth's heated announcements
       its attempts to resurface
       turn things inside-out

"Hole-in-the-Ground" is what it's called
But you and I will rename it   say it's more than that
Rename it for something of value

The way its shape is the shape of understanding
       and enclosure
How love is like that broken depth
          being closest then

And, dearest
     the pastel painting we've entered
     wants to warm us with cascading light

Bright brazen exchanged
        for the nineteenth century's afterglow
A balance of power
     between the day and the night
       the quickest   the easiest   satori

We've been somewhere else in the Outback
Saying where and when we deserve to live
          our worst moments confined to the cities
Getting right with resolve to go elsewhere
Making camp where the trees have sheltered

It couldn't be easier!
The end   all endings   needed
    these many years of caring deeply

                    deep down as magma

To visit's to reside
Your best price of freedom   selected
                    in a moment of clarity
    and respect for the many coercions

How are you feeling?   still drowsy?
Stay lovely awake
There's the Moon
      where it triangulates with Jupiter and Saturn!
The conjunction to satisfy even Wallace Stevens
                    and his "bauds of euphony"

All is revolution   but fear is not an issue
The twilight may enfold
      uncorrected   unreported
           except in news from the heart

Not everyone will know that *together* we pause
On the level ground
In the overall comfort that Oregon's brought

Hole-in-the-Ground
           awaiting further geology

6.   CONNECTIONS   LOIE   MARVIN

You   be   connected
Though the wheels roll
Though distance would have it otherwise   and when

That phone   those towers
And speed day and night
      as now   hurtling
          passing and braking
Technology traveling too   and making allowance

Softly tethered

Ever so slightly
The dim voices while forward rushing
     to that vanishing point in the headlights

Just think connected
The adjective made a loving noun
          the best medical care provided
     in a mobile hospital

The way you like it
The Fifties enwrapt in fresh white sheets
     prior to bedtime
     or searching for breakfast
          some stretch of a two-lane

Connections   so easy
You think the road should be the best part of every day
     with a consequent metabolism
          racing like an engine

Salt water competing with fresh
Christmas without its solstice
Every good thing a sorrow in the bones
     until your voices are heard
          and long-distance settles down
               to be a passenger
               one who helps with the driving

The names of intimates said in August and September
Thinking those months   of all of them
     those months away
          is fondness sufficient
          for a calendar entire

7.   RETURN TO FORT TWILIGHT

Though the sun had ceased its publications
Let the ink dry thoroughly
     thanked the sky for its press

                      and hospitality the while
Another paper made bold to print

Began a story concerning twilight's rocks
And how they silhouette so nicely
      all the orange west
           world literature leaving

The Fort *too* is written   the proverbial stone
The book is finished
      but gone missing is the postscript   the epilogue
         what the censor washed away
                   with Ice Age waves

Letters eroded
In a valley needing that volume especially
    the rarest
        a novel of the maar
           having crisp hieroglyphics
              and a plot of shadows

I said, "Nothing doing! it must be closing time!"

But Carnegie's gift was unlocked
    the caretakers   fast asleep
        in their state-of-the-art motor home
Best I browse in the perfect time allowed

Today it's "Fort Twilight"
    that was simply "Fort Rock" before
And we'll say it's a depository of braille
A chance to speed-read the biographies
    the Dewey Decimals
        the reference
           and children's

Be where the alcoves and cubicles
    save for later the faults of earlier
        in every crack and fissure of the tuff
      the lapilli tuff ring   volcanic
The record magnificent!

Here may darkened research conspire
Join with once-softened ash

        secretly   slowly   as befits a thesis
Ancient classics sequestered
Bestsellers the book clubs missed
                                        preferring pulp

Carefully climb   as if with a ladder
               the teetering stacks
                      to remembered tiers
Your doctor gave the go-ahead

The moon has amazed the ghost writers all
       who'd been   till then
              content with gothic romance
                       her intrusion   and mine
              a boon to writer's block

There will be no checkout
         for the balconies would detain
I am slow-dancing the aisles
               immune to any dyslexia for once

Understanding   albeit with a certain fatigue
         the collected works of 100,000 years
             brought forth
             when ground water ruined
                       the path of eruption

First alarm that something was wrong
                     with the sediments
The back issues of papers past   engraved

First editions explored
      with a tactile attention
      to what's believed to be a lapidary truth

The flashlight save
There's moon enough to light your way
      with footwork sure   and dust jackets plain

The delicate Egyptians have been consulted
Their priests informed
       they must make ready the chisels
                    for basalt autographs
                    for mysteries and sci-fi

For prehistoric travel
    both ways on the land bridge

The night   and its book review
    await a readership
        expect bestsellers
            prepare release parties
                practice Chopin Nocturnes
And look forward to crowds in line for signing

Fort Twilight as reason why
    an education can take as long
    as a lonely planet wants to keep you company
Or help with that book report on Luxor

The Fort   like a flawless vault of carvings
The reason I came to its twilight
    the better to earn its Stone Age letters

Tomorrow made to wait awhile

Those clear-and-present dangers
    summarized   and modestly retracted

The Past is serious
        and its short stories and editorials
            eagerly seek
                to inform of fight or flight

Each footstep assimilates
Each handhold communicates the contents
    of Fort Twilight becoming Fort Midnight
                    Nijinsky in the shelves

The librarian's said every patron's an agent
They search for blockbuster encryptions
        sure a payday's nigh
            but *ghostly* they go
Transparent   to collect imaginary royalties

I am scattered as the scent of sage
        across threshold layers
        and near-invisible corrugations

Suddenly remembering I'm due elsewhere in Oregon
        Summer Lake Hot Springs

I may not linger   and so
Before any morning editions
    may tell of trespass
      or fault Rachmaninoff
        for leaving his country
          prior to the full flowering
              of Socialist thought
Return to the KIA   parked so stealthily

Close the distance to Summer Lake
Those restful alkali pools
    trusting the pages to stay here   still unturned
      and air- conditioned
        by interglacial breezes

Go with some reluctance to the 31st highway
            passing Silver Lake
Ask once more
    if the farmers are willing to hear a city boy recite
      as much as may be easy
      urban obsessions concerning country

All his scrolls read in plain sight of green circles
Those well-watered discs of agriculture

I will not tell a soul
Their well-disguised epics are safe
World literature left to find out for itself
            with once-again sunrise

8.   THE GATE

It was a fierce and formal clanging!
    relentless!   startling!

Never mind the mechanism

Its simple latch and proven purpose
The cattle gate could not be learned!

In the silent night   arriving lately
        delay's narrative was told to Summer Lake
        with a plea for understanding

"How does it open?"
"It's never closed!"
"Uh, okay…"

So I made more noise than ever
And entered   finally   after a fashion of strange

The whole Hot Springs alerted to intrusion
The pricey cabins beset by noisome
And those who thought to retire
        roused from their sleepy vacations
            to wonder what drunkenness survived a journey
                        to pester their repose!

What apologies in the night were due?
And would there be another like myself?
A crasher to follow
        for whom the gate was a mystery also?
Might the guests expect more of the dungeon
            its heavy percussion to resume?

Having entered   I was furtive
        and sought to be silent
            as before I'd been calamitous

Sneaking past
        with a minimum of "whoosh" once inside
Thinking cleverly   farm-ignorant no longer   I hoped

The manager had said,
        "You can pay in the morning
                    that is all…"

And it was
        his voice a little ghostly with late night
        and even sounding sorry
            the gate had confused

> the metal being stiff

The clangs persisting   prison echoes
Like a concept full of percussion
There in the afterwards
    while I searched for explanations

I'm like the cattle with no understanding
No wonder the gate is enough
              to thwart their escape

Those who were awakened
    return to unconscious saturation
    forgiving   forgetting
        holding together as a species

The corral has possibilities
                the prelude didn't imagine
Now I'm longing for onomatopoeia
    to match the banging bells of admission

For   though they may have stressed the herd
        still   they were something beautiful
                brought to solitude

9. THE COP IN THE WATER

There was a cop in the pool
I'd helped him start a conversation
    and he had done the same for me

Nobody's painless
That's why the waters
That's why the barn of Summer Lake
    whose pool is also a plan for acquaintance

                  and dipping done
                  as if for religion

Summer Lake Hot Springs!
A most successful resort
Yes!   say "resort"
      though it's a humble affair

And that barn?
Well, maybe it isn't exactly that
There's the big pool inside
            and changing rooms
                    oh, and showers of course

But it sure *looks* like a barn on approach
Think it *should* be   and one with a customer base

It was late
It was after I thought I was alone with all that timber
      those beautiful rafters like a geometrical reverie
           nothing dangerous even imagined

For the first few minutes we might have been deaf
The shared pool was all
But someone spoke   someone started
    as if we were suddenly family
    with no preliminaries needed
Someone said, "Why, out of all destinations, *this* place?"

And, "Why now?"

It was easy for us to talk   I didn't think too much
Our conversation was screenplay
      the exchange of two chronicles
          two partial biographies
              wherewithal history spoken fluently

He didn't say he was a cop right away
When he *did* I asked, "A cop *where*?"
"I work out of Stockton"
"Really!"

The town I dreaded   made fun of

Being not sure why
Maybe it's a town you get stuck in
        town with a flat grid
            not responsive
                its EKG a steady line
                    the Valley taken off life support

Of course it's unfair
My ignorance had built a case
A case against Stockton   *laughable*
        and I had seen to it
            that law enforcement was impossible
                in my   "alternate" Stockton

I guessed it was time
        I learned how hard the hardest job in the world is
            but I didn't go there right away

We had the smoke to parse
Had to breeze the day
        and where the fires went
And they'd been everywhere that *he* had been
And everywhere I'd been as well

Oh yes!
He had been motorcycling
        with just three days to go before Stockton again
            just that trio of midnights left

Might he find time for Steens?
Motor over and go right on up   the loop to enjoy?
Sure, Steens Mountain maybe
                so I said so

When he found out I'd left California
        he sought a reason why
            but there was no right way to answer
              no smart way to summarize
                  for my disaffection was profound

While the hot water flowed
        and baptized   with its unique pH
While I wondered how much should be said
                      or recommended

What role reversals might ensue
        when I could see Stockton *differently*

The talk had surpassed expectations
And a third condition of politics found us
      while splashing absent-mindedly
          and the environment got attention paid
         a topic too important for crackpot denial

He took time out to say he'd been undercover
Said he'd run down thieves and once rescued a cat
I told *him* there'd once been a "Fred"
A three-legged tabby you'd see in the manager's office
An orange ball on the counter   and purring
        while the Springs ran your credit card

"Cool!"
"Will it be difficult to leave the open road
              for the confines of Stockton?"
"No, for the getaway's again as soon as I say"
"How's that?"

We'd swum to the central fountain   pouring

"My partner's a marine   a mentor and friend
He said any time's the right time to go
     and he had my back
         knew the right people
         knew service to the community begins
               with wanderlust!"

He was a cop in the water
And I   his partner in the crime of escape

10. THE SOFTNESS OF CERTAIN WATERS

When showers are never ever over
For imaginary soap seems to keep you there
      trying not to feel slippery
        as if there were something wrong with that
And soap's sensation does not go away
                        for a long, long time

Then it's a new season of slippery
      with a mind of its own to thoroughly clean
So that one *lingers*   disinclined to leave
Fact-checking the shower for squeaks
      not believing the rinse
      not ready to exit the stall

How many past hotels possessed this same!
A softness offered   a watery documentary
        concerning the Springs
        and all their minerals
What the Earth has always gifted

A qualified ablution
      feeling brand-new and scoured
          but at the same time conflicted

There's doubt   persistent
However much you wish
      stockpiling cleanliness
          there's an obsession almost   to stay
                flooded
The downpour to cleanse past what's required

And those who may assemble to see
        note the results   suspecting sin
          the softness of a morality play
              enacted as surprise

The suds   a case made for conditioning
              for invisible shampoo

Something taught
There's always time

Softness like a memory
        of *wrongdoing* perhaps
                leading to more of the same
                in spite of the lesson

A serious smoothness slick with implications
        not to one's liking exactly
Warning's copyright that strays into bathing

Imagination lives to see the sun
However bright
                it's another must-see episode of light
              no matter the darkness
                    that may have befallen

Still   the *noir* is soothing
A kind of shampoo in its own right
        employed to lather sin's originality

There is no price to be paid
Just prolonged reminding and clinging
As if one is enrobed
        in another skin than blameless

And a catholic steam cloud gathers
Taking upon itself the task of making me see differently
For the duration of washing away transgression
        a psychic sauna
Nothing the law would understand
                being the merest vibration!

Feeling the heat of inscrutable no-no's
I wasn't happy until this sudden chance
To level   even start again
        as if it were the forties
        and strange music is heard

With downbeats stolen from baseball organs
        that intermittently swell on game day
A decade never over   like the shower
Though Bing Crosby himself is abandoned

And you wish the softness would go on forever
The lyrics of that surrey

        the one with the "fringe on top"
For there's so much to account for, you know?
Children are a part of it   they always are

Think of the shower as a warm rain
      prepared for a robbery
           where nothing's stolen

A crime as punishment
      that only the criminal discovers
Soaking wet and saying hello to the past

A third degree given solo
      with a splashy soundtrack
      a peculiar score
           while you're being naked
           in a filibustering cascade

The alkali Niagara
      like an insistent healing
           of the material world
                  hoping Madonna's relented
                      somewhat

There's a calmness to all of this
I'm left alone to consider miracles
      and new life for even half an hour
As long as illusions delay the squeak
                of ordinary washing

What part of the story's straight
      to be decided standing drenched
      till   wrinkled with wisdom
                        one's faith is updated

11. ALWAYS ABROAD

It is only necessary to be Interstate
Only a rental's required

The square states wait
        to be considered as foreign
                part of America but really abroad
                being over seas that are dry oceans

"Faraway" is a choice of nearby geography
Where someone says, "Welcome back!"
        before you've even left

One roof   and hospitality's confirmed
Like showing up for a party
        wide open
                fighting infection in a foreign land
                fighting depression

In Wyoming and Montana
        you don't need to know who's catering
        or what ghosts there are
                of European aristocracy   hovering

There is no artificial heart to break
                      with spurious homesickness
Just a few allergens
The sage and certain plants
        with unpronounceable Latin names

Traveler as travel *agent*
        knowing that deal's best that's lickety-split
        and needs no passport
Just a full tank and a decent highway

That deal's best that's under the stars
                and nighttime stripes remaining

The monster of xenophobia strapped down
Given medication   told to chill
        even if the border crossed is Colorado's
A holiday with customs   costumes
                              and currency

A living room
        when the next day
                and the day after that
                      one's involved as a local

                              living legendary lifespans
                                      in brand-new buildings
The scenery suspended by puppet masters
        well-off enough to do it for fun!

Am I exaggerating?
Am I too old to do so?

Nah! drive on!
The world
        with a mild case of nostalgia
        converts a piece of the continent
                to a religion based on a fighting spirit
Oh, don't worry!   24/7, no one's going to war!

The West as ersatz Europe and more
And coming back and repatriation
Time-lagging and every resumption
The forty-hour week still being abroad
        because gravity and air are the same

Still a matter of motels and tents
Every breath an aspiration
        the inland parts of the biosphere
                their multiple refugia found intact

How much longer will illusions befriend?
How many times will the square states rescue
        and be amenable to bygone honeymoons?

The exchange rate of escapist longings
Every time machine dying to be of service
Respected scientists incredulous
        in a warm London house in Missoula!

What's wrong is resolved a little at a time
The happiest brides and grooms
        entrusted to the Swiss Alps
                of Jackson Hole

Some things well-known are easily blended
Their notoriety merging   with helpful guides
In the uncertain world
        the Rockies dissemble

     built to last and locked in
        to the poetry of place
How a place may be anything you say it is
   with souvenirs, even!
     with raw video feed

Party of one
   to dine with the bison in downtown Tokyo

It's all right it's decades since your birthday
Pure silver in the hills! and gold!
All of it to stay in place
   for the riches of geography
   its maps alone supersede the metals
        with zero dollars down
      on the paradox

How the cities and towns of elsewhere
   settle in all the ravines and valleys
   in the open deserts unlit in the night
Something seen before
An identified dreamscape
   with a number and recurring

Just as the season turns the aspens yellow
      and chills the air with history
Cairo has come to the lower Colorado
      where it empties past pyramidal stone
And every culture is tucked away
Some time ago tomorrow

Abroad where the wars were many
   is safely installed next door
     where I can keep an eye on it
And hope out-of-context may do its work

May it stun the aggressors
     when they settle down
       like pioneers shorn of Empire
A strict limit on arrogance

In the provinces of the coyote hide away
        in plain sight for spaciousness
Calamity's diluted

        and the crowds go home
                in the back seats of Hondas
            Toyotas, too
                    and now this KIA

They are anxious to be of service
Somewhere abroad in Utah
Or Colorado again   lovely Idaho
                        with its wealth of calderas

The KIA at top speed through "Deseret"
The Mormon region hard upon Pakistan
A Nevada bordered with finding out
      with good explanation
The "loneliest highway"
          peopled with hitchhikers
                    stranded in Mongolia

The music was everything!
Music made it happen
The oceans closed   the climates converged
      and the peace of Tchaikovsky
          overwhelmed the unthinking
Made its own bed in the Basin and Range

A school of Russian suffering attended
Religion tested for cutout priests
Analyzed for loopholes
      calling on all the saints
        to continue their stories
           till beginnings are preferred
          and borders enlarged

All I can see is you
And the fountains
      set in motion by abundant caring
        for lands already known
               and known to be habitable

That may be visited without a Titanic crossing
Or taking a flight of fancy with Amelia Earhart

The right risk is right here
Wondering

        if Steamboat Springs is likely to cool
            in the middle of a marriage proposal
          and honeymoon conceived
                    in Fontainebleau

12.   TOO COLD SO TWO BAGS

This Oregon moment
      has a nighttime attached to heavy metal

Cold when the winds push past walking speed
      touch on running and all-out elopement
            in full flight to the Outback!

Our careful survival depends on the bags
     packed   dry   dependable down
        waiting to be useful against this cold

Is Rachmaninoff still playing the piano?
That's important   more batteries
Take the time to fumble

Sleep is the prize   albeit smoky
The orange bag and the blue
      the former reliable to five degrees
        get both
           overpaying for warmth
                and to be sure

The car camping easy then
You contour snugly   reclining
The windows just right
      for as much of the westerlies
            as may be needed

Tonight no radio's white noise reception
Now the music's lost and its perfect plan
The cocoon of midnight's enough
     and international

        in the sense that everyone would like this
Well, if they knew to *do* this

There are no hospitals or discotheques
Yet Summer Lake's *fermata* adds time to time
        that the sands had somehow missed

I could hunger-strike and not notice the pangs
Whatever that plural actually means
        Rachmaninoff means everything
          his choruses for women's voices
And they have made going and coming so easy

Though now we are so wonderfully stopped
        it is nothing to wait in the night!

13.   A DREAM WITH RICHARD LORANGER IN IT

Like a memory he flexes
        before he's even agreed to use it
Because comedy and tragedy needed a mic
        one that's open to the open air
        that slaps your face
           despite your innocence

There he was   over his head by choice
Because he knows nothing gets done
              if it's done otherwise

One more time he'd forgiven my clumsiness
And for my part
        I had to believe in the dream
              for the dream is always a message
              a therapy refused until that snoring

I talk about what I want
To be "dancing with the stars"
          of which he's one
        where he lives in a firmament

Where all pay close attention to the universe
And laugh off all that interstellar nothingness

My own memory is strengthened
A contact exercise done
The safe money of mind-body spent
      opening the heavens
Comedy and tragedy enacted after dark
                with squawking extras

According to a study made
      the dream was an exceptionally lucid one
And those who did the study
      wished only that the dream
          might be their own somnambulism
        when mortality's arrested
            with specific symbology

Why is this important?

There he was is why
Teaching handicrafts to slackers
      hampered by thousands of years
                of indolence

Helping
Though it meant nothing doing
      in the realm of science
        while thus tutoring the supernatural

There were no sofas
Only dirt floors and thatch
Not even a hammock
      until a shipload from the waking state

It was hard to make out the lesson
But it seemed to be about "anyone can make it"
Even if what is made is a faulty slingshot

Though he'd given up cigarettes
      Richard smoked because we did
I had to hide our supply

Nothing in the night oppressed

For his excellent commercials were a type
      where nothing is sold
           but the barter needed
                to energize a commune

He said we were lucky
      not to have a Stalin skulking
      the kind of bad guy
           that comes with crowding
                    and Revolution

There is poetry in smaller numbers
And that explained Richard's presence
He didn't mail it in
      but hand-delivered
           the most delightful eclogue

A bucolic gathering
When the mysteries of Spoken Word
      deepened with impromptu
      the novelty of Thought Word
           with telepathy at large

I'm being honest
He even played the guitar for us
      on top of that
      he wanted to dance the Argentine tango
Just to be amazing!
Just to be sure!

It will take a week of staying awake
      to parse the charisma
           or decide to make it my own
Yet the dreams in line may not wish to wait
The subconscious an embarrassment of riches

The dream took commitment l'd promised
Promised him?   maybe
Whatever the obligation
      wardrobe was involved
It was not enough   those street clothes

I wanted to be Ralph Kramden
To have a day-job driving people crazy

There were others
They too had found some costumes
It meant a clean break from "who's next?"
        the worn-out question asked
                at every ordinary poetry reading

Richard put a premium on premium
Every day of the dream
Because that's how long it lasted
                            prior to sunup
                              I was out-of-it
                                    until

Out-of-it before
Then   like a medic
       a man called Loranger came
       saw to it I entered in once more
In a poetic moment unchecked by stage fright

He said. "Here's the deal…"
And   for once
       this meant a pack of cards
               strewn for a whirlwind of poker!

Then cupcakes were served   improbably
               but whoever made them stayed away

It was a toss of the coin
        whether underneath language
                        entailed side-effects
But we spoke it anyway and gladly

There was the scent of lavender indoors
Even though we were certainly outdoors
Defeating COVID   the signup lengthy
It took method acting
       to get my way
       to get a grip
A summer's doings enacted in autumn

And it was time to go home
Many did not and ran after him
It was a tactic of learning
       learning more

          about whatever it was
                  that Richard was teaching

And they made a kind of Christmas wish
                to be gifted again for the thrill of it all

The dream would recur
      and what was left of previous poetry
          assigned to a waiting list
              with makeup to make it better
Perhaps to guitar music played
                by a master of more than mere ceremony

14.   "CAN I SEE SOME I.D., PLEASE?"

With morning and packing
With prospects good
      for unopposed travel east and north
The Japanese moved me to get on with it
Gave me a samurai tug   serving tea the while

It was good they shadowed
Seeing to it the journey was disciplined

And there was the cop again
His own Spartan batteries charged
           as he went about departure too
              loading his Mad Max bike and gearing up

And because we'd talked so much already
And could have gone on
        we did a little more of it
And I said, "Can I see some I.D., please?"
He loved it   wishing each of us adventure

Summer Lake directing traffic   nothing to it
"Can see some I.D., please?" a valuable phrase
A concept that disagrees with complexity
Listens patiently

       while complexity babbles

The cop in the water
       was now the cop in the grass
Still badgeless
But little-by-little returning to the force
       to Stockton
              to be happy but vacationless again

He had his own minders   his own samurai
The ghosts of marines
       supervising pushups
       and close-order motorcycle maintenance

So by-the-book was our mutual exit!
              albeit staggered

My KIA first   creeping
A respectful five miles-an-hour
       through the sleeping encampment
As if it were a playa's strict enforcement

He would follow
On how much sleep
       to be determined by rest stops

The slanting light   the early clock
The curiosity of puppies
The angle of the roof
       that shelters the spring!

All of this informed a second "Good luck!"
And "See you later!"
       the idea of casual acquaintanceship
              tested for encores

Strangers to be trusted
       before the wicked ways of lifelong knowing
The odd encounters to stand out
Non-partisan
       before even a first impression
              has had time to sink in

15. THE CAVES ROAD

It was the turnoff to the caves I sought

One looks for the telephone poles
There can't be that many
Drive slowly   go accordingly
Do yourself a favor   don't be in a rush

The access road is rutted
You remember at last
      and take it   continuing
      slowly   towards the wonderful caves

There's plenty of time before it will be too late
In the heat relax   that's what it's for
The heat that follows the Chewaucan River
      prior to Paisley
           the town that named the Pleistocene caves

Five Mile Point!   there it is
The smoke couldn't hide it
      the darkest ridge of all the rest

Search as if you were hired to do so
Or be military   and no mistakes!

Ah!   the dirt track!
      and you've found it and turned as before
          to weave your way northward
          through the gullies
          taking those little detours
             where the rains had ruined

Staying true to the route
Saying hello to the rangeland
      so dry it needs a doctor
      so empty the jackrabbits left
          to avoid depression

Being back here's the right thing
      though so much of the West is still wrong

Yesterday is undecided
The lives of First Peoples are inscrutable

But their hiding places are known
Those ancient Hiltons
          shelters scattered
The pluvial lakes
          lapping everywhere allowed
          in the Basin and Range

Where the lava rocks were weak
     and wore to recess suitable for safety
     and being cozy, even

Right now
With theoretical greenbacks
          stashed to thwart thieves of credit
With polarized sight to see
With wax removed for better hearing
     my help is on the way

Just who I'd help is yet unknown
For they lived before and may not be found

But across the prairie go
To what is wrong somehow
     and needs scoring by Max Steiner
      its colors made a black-and-white movie
               of uncertain worlds

Definitive cinema
     traveling slowly to the caves
         with motion sensors   set
       for any ancestral ghosts
           in their ancestral sandals
Their slightest move
     beyond a reasonable doubt

Impeccable prehistory!
How unique was every thought and feeling!
What comes to mind in the aromatic sage!
How complications
     may take their first trip in the air
                 and vanish!

Pray the caverns are still there
That they were not illusion
      but the sustained vision
           of fourteen thousand years
         not lost to the clanking
              the twenty-first century
And its creaking future of no memory at all

Though we are entitled to know

This day could be a holiday
A secret holiday declared by a solo explorer
Giving up and giving in
      a performance on foot
        once arrived on the stage of a shore
        which the waves of Lake Chewaucan
                    had terraced

What long evenings there must have been!
What extra hours
With a wife who wanted to belong
        to another clan than her own
           so that it was all arranged for her
A clan where she imagines
        she'll never catch cold

I'll keep on
      careful myself in these COVID days
And reach the springboard clearing as before

It was the turning that takes you back
The very meaning of "backroads"
And J.J. Schultz once sang a song
      one I'd like to hear again
      because the lyrics had a verse
          with these words:
              "that means something to me"

There is no deadline for discovery
It is the ages taken that were taken away
      when the Holocene happened

And the lakebed is saying

>   "Talk to yourself
>   as you would talk to others
>   slowly   as befits isolation
>   like a slow refilling of the Basin"

Detour as beautiful distraction
As mood swing   and guided decision
    for one who's haggard
    and cross-eyed with nostalgia
            for times out of time

Did they really murder the mammoths?
The rest of the megatheres?
After all   so few had come to the lake
            to anywhere survival had a chance

It is still a pleasure to see it all
And the tour will be one that takes as long
    as the Paleo-Indians took
            to discover habitat

Dare to stay through winter   would you perish?
Dare just one season of privation!

This short journey
    to spend the night
        in the middle of the day

I'll hide away myself and let it happen
The mysteries surrounding   including
    the precarious present
    still all right for now

If there were a court
    what a case for Luck could be made
        for "Being Here Now"
        in a Sixties sense of belonging

Counting caves as before   unhurriedly
With thoughts of ascending past them
The whole assemblage of stone
    seeming to wait upon your steps
    as you walk the length
    of its extravagant spine

Collecting for later the samples of earlier
Always trying to do the right thing
      in spite of the crimes of the hominid

The smoke pretends there's no destination
And wishes to veil the distance
    with impressionist grey
But this will be investigation
The same previous as surmising

"*Dona eis pacem*" always
      trying Latin first
And only after all conjugations are learned
And the Roman vocabulary mastered
        seek other languages than human

Nature's rhetoric says:

"As you know
  my caves had proven useful to indigenes
But am I done? I am not
The caves are for you to live in too
      albeit briefly
      they will shelter
    as before
And be that personal retreat
Where the years since their discovery
      are reimagined history"

Well, okay
We're back to that
Having turned off the main road
  it feels so fine there'll be more turning
    and stealing only what's necessary

Real estate
A home that needs no repairs or furnishings

There's no dot-com anything
And solitude whispers sweet nothings
  like a Vegas virgin
    assigned to you special

Someday
      the other caves   and even excavations
Someday
      the same species that crossed the bridge
            Beringia called
Someday they'll manage interstellar crossings
To stars still in their prime
      with worlds suitable for life in *their* caves

Until then I'll sit in *this* sun's acres
Getting warmer a little at a time
This sun   whose heat is like a slogan said:

"Do more!   at least in principle"

Think of a drive to take us elsewhere in Space
As hunting brought us here
      right-turning south from Beringia
           and relocating to the future

16.   DON'T ENTER OR IT'S HANTA FOR SURE!

Don't do it!
Don't enter!
      for it's hanta for sure if you do!

You've heard of it   that hantavirus
That's right   the one the rodents have
      and you can get   oh, yes!

And you've seen them, haven't you!
The rats in and out of their holes
      furtive and quick like a fast-motion flic!

Shocking they were there
      culturally appropriating
          moving in without asking
The caves are now unsafe
For the air is still and perfect there

        perfect for disease
              and why should not disease abide?

The one that's spread by *rattus rattus*!

So don't do it!   don't enter!
It's airborne, it's dangerous!
The symptoms?   there are many
      this and that
          it takes time
              might be weeks
                  fever
                  headache
                  chills
                  dizziness
                  one's breathing affected

Hang on, it gets better!
More unpredictable
      you might not know it's hanta!

But the Latin is so lovely
Want to hear it said?   the scientific names?
Oh, it's a virus bad as it wants to be
        and wanting to spread
        with the energy of COVID

Inspecting the caves would need some caution
Going one to the other a worrisome thing
And rats that had scurried
      from careful footfalls
          were grey as the walls
          were a menace belied
              by that neutral shade

With alacrity they've tunneled deeper
Their sudden motion
      like the random impulses
             of wayward buddhists

I didn't want to let on
I tried to think straight
      in the presence of crooked
The work of archaeologists to resume

Managing the layers
      the stratigraphy returned to hanta

An electron micrograph's required
To clearly see into the realm of the *ribovirus*
Explore the kingdom come
      of the *Orthornavirae*
          the specific phylum *Negarnaviricota*
          be in the same class as *Ellioviricetes*
          take the order for *Bunyavirales*
          meet the family of *Hantaviridae*
And of course its sub-family
            Mammantavirinae

And finally join the Orthodox

There is a way to do this
And so many will   wandering
        as candidates for change
The culture of hunter-gatherers
      to resume forthwith
      and be welcomed back
          as a perfect communism

Something only possible with smaller numbers

In a moment of honesty
      deciding to follow to its end
          the precepts of a stateless existence

The rats will quit the caves at last
They were never really cozy there
They won't know how to act at first
          though they will do well in time

For the present the caves are a question
One of health
      a question asked in the heat of the day
      growing older each hour
          of reconnaissance

My name is of no importance
      in a hospital vast as Oregon
          where the mysteries of migration

are subsumed

It's downright creepy   here at the caves
Still wary of rats   the tour's cut short
After cautious peeking and persistent faith
Waiting to find out the courage it takes
              to enter the dead air of stony estates

Did the actual scientists
        and their student assistants
              worry too much while digging
              and meticulously sifting
              transitioning lower and lower
                    to the DNA that mattered?

Were they concerned at all
        or did they make pets of the critters?

I was not knowing or noticing before
Those other times   less aware
There was just the counting of the caves
How many might qualify as such
              how many mere recess

There was the after-the-fact furnace
                    of vision questing
As close to Indian knowledge as I'd ever get
              and conspiring with unseen spirits

Although the rats had made a home
        it was health-related
They did as they were told by evolution
They did what was best for themselves

But my visit's a benefit
The danger so worth it
The perfect antidote to politics
There *are* no politics!

There's a planet spinning only
        with the town of Paisley a detail to the west
              worthy of inspection in its own right

Though entering the caves isn't possible

       for entry means sickness
Yet a collapse of will is possible
One may not care
       that *Orthohantavirus* lives its half-life
              among the dust motes

I'll specialize in learning the symptoms
       by contracting the thing
       as if it were a Thanksgiving gone missing
         till now
              the devil eager to play a part

A high-quality demise
       if full of eventual suffering

But when something feels truly different
       then is knowledge had
Entering   leaving
Then staying the night   not so bad
       at first

Looking forward
Fatefully involved in a pathogen's mission
Testing positive for pests because you *could*
             for the sake of experience

17.   IN THE PAISLEY BOOTH

It was recovery and seance in the Pioneer Saloon
And thinking of the Oregon Outback's version of an Octoberfest
       to come

A caution sign above the bar:

"Don't drink and drive
       you might hit a bump and spill it"

And some advice:

"If you can't say something nice to someone
    go ahead and lie!"

The Paisley booth   and cream of mush
The breakfast tab a repair bill
        with books opened and closed
            and a waitress not letting anyone leave
                    lest they leave the town of Paisley
                and miss out on small town peacefulness

A river runs through it also
Like that movie
        but no one's famous   not yet

Raised their kids and guessed the rest
It's quite all right
        and they dance in the snow
            at twenty below

How much of the city
        can come to the country
                and start all over again?

18.   THAT COP FOR A THIRD TIME

Since it was the third encounter
            and we were not having as much to say
                    as the other two occasions
                        I took the cop's information
                    as if writing *him* a ticket
            careful to get it right

Too bad the little poem of his email address
            was later lost
                like other   longer   poems

"When you're not here," I ask him
        "do you think there's enough enforcement
                or will Paisley have to rely

                      on impromptu vigilantes?"

There should have been guitars
Like in "The Good, The Bad and The Ugly"

Or opera excerpts
A record collection concerning honky-tonk

If I could change anything it won't be Paisley
                        not with the serendipity it fosters!

So a third exchange
A light bulb went on
      though the sun was bright and early

There was his bike   sounding good
There were the further plans he had for it
He was talking to others but I took him aside
        to say that synchronicity
                was now a destiny to follow
                like the highway to Steens
                or the pasture path to the caves

Turned out he was going there
On his own   without my urging or mention
It was a fitting finale
        seeing him off and onward

A man from the Valley
Fair-enough flying
        to who-knows-where the mountains are!

I'm thinking he could end up late for work
Late for civilians   for life back on the beat
                    with that sergeant marine
                    mentoring
          protecting
      spending all the time that's needed
                      to help him be a good cop

And though I got it right
Stayed tuned sufficient
        to copy his email
           phone and Stockton precinct

                    nothing would come of it
                                no tracking at all

A fourth meeting was not to be
Our clumsy present was all
The love of strangers
        not lasting beyond the time it takes
        to take down names
        as one does at a crime scene
                comprising good intentions
                become matter-of-fact forgetful

It was generations talking past themselves
        but it was fun
Old enough to be his chief
Yet I sat in his youthful class
        and listened well to the lecture
                while planning for a Model T

We never learned each other's names
There was too much shooting
Too many cases to solve
It would have taken more instruction
        a crash course in police work
                        and hurry-up Chopin

My dedication to *his* art
        and his own practice keyboard
                to get *my* drift

So easy to conceive of better friendship
Surer bets than chance encounters
Better health care than superstition

We never got around to proper restraint
        and what you do to de-escalate tensions
Could not discuss why I hated haiku
        but the cop made sense and he shared it

And that was enough for now and later
Like friendly banter between two adults
Rolling before a *tête-à-tête* could matter

Read the trip notes later

        and knew that once more
        I'd lost the clues to a casual identity

Though everyone was safe
                      everyone was sorry as well

19.   THE WALLS OF ABERT

There had never been a barrier like it
One of foreboding   one kept in mind

And   perceived at some distance
       as it's a false horizon
             higher than expectations

The walls are rampart
       whose profile's stone imprisoned
            sheer upper
            slanted lower scree
The "angle of repose" a *questioned* scree

It falls down slowly   even as it rises
Its many parts in tandem with uplift
Cells with soft mattresses
         sturdy and level-lain
              coming to conclusions jagged

The blessings of free fall learned
And nothing to it to plummet
             flying as if it's a birthright

All the miles past Lake Abert
       the walls are an oppressive border
Your loved ones kept beyond   above
The close preferred   delayed by commands

A for-heaven's-sakes place
And over the edge
      halfway to Wagontire

The walls are the curse
       of a crustal spreading
              and all the names it's called
            for the sake of science
                      and one upsmanship

The darkened lava started knowing things
That it was not alone
       but a partner of the magma

The upsides offset by the lower
The walls a gift of the Miocene
                      one wishes to have seen when given

But I have to settle for Valley Falls
            and even *searching* for those falls
            stretching the legs
            formulating reasons
                to abide at the junction
The highways joining
       giving up their separate routes

Maybe conjure the hotel there was
And that dance hall of yester

It's possible to be a little delayed
Awed by Abert's so very grand mansions
       and the sight of bighorn sheep
The Ferruginous Hawks
            tumbling through the thermals
            paragliding down
                to hurry the critters along
                in those golden acres

There's a supplement of ponds
                filling prescriptions for habitat
            calling for John   John C. Fremont
                to share his impressions
                      when he passed by the walls

And let's hear from Mister Abert himself
The man-for-whom
       John James Abert

                    to say him completely
The escarpment his alone
       among the wonders of the intermontane

The hard shell of the mountain is breached
             my own carapace stubbornly in place
                       as long as the fairie shrimp persist
                              and the beauty of migration

Let's be after the sunstones, too
        the chatoyant gem with the feldspar
Perhaps the end of desperation
And following rarity's suggestions

The flight of the inland plover to its nesting
The safe arrival of the eared grebe

We've imagined the listric curve
       where the walls enter the ground
              flatten down below
                    to be a cousin of the horizontal

It's said the lava cooled quickly
Though a flood   it froze
                 a wealth of plagioclase crystals

It is geology but also flight perceived
               those hawks especially
               can you say "Ferruginous?"
In high school you'd have never heard of them
Here at the walls
       one's close to the truths
              and unboxing resolve to find it out

Look what happens in the fresh air!

No money   no plans but Juniper Creek
                       the route to the top
     three miles north of lichened rubble

I'm ready
Been ready since a first acquaintance
       with the barrier

        the dangerous scree of reconnaissance
              when each rock of the talus slope
                      might teeter and shift
                      and imperil footing

The ankles at risk
    and nearly hurt
        with every step   up or down

It was not knowing the balance   the repose
    kept exploration to a probe of uncertainty
        and no expectation of a summit toast
With no one in particular
to nothing in particular
    except all that's arduous

The porphyritic basalt
    to come straight home to my heart
    whenever I can't do well at anything

In sunshine or shadow   the walls remind
Like a project of memory
    when responsibilities devour

The amazing creatures easy to tame
Make pets of
    the rattlesnakes that manage surprise
        in whatever scenario of discovery

Let's do it!
Fill in the blanks on our personal topo
    twirling thumbs with the contours of it
We know what's good for us, finally

Abert's fortress a beautiful incarceration
    to include the flight of Wilson's pharalopes
        and the red-necked version
Like odes to constancy
The rituals of every season observed

There'll be a half century more of this
The best part saved for marriage
    when I ask,
      "Will you help me

                    master the Walls of Abert?"

For this is the place you were taken to
First visit for both   and yes
           it is possible the basalt noticed
                     felt something for you as well

The colorations enlivened
           knowing they'd catch your eye
Gently, even   for the outdoors

Maybe we'll find the petroglyphs
They won't say where they are
                         it's taboo to tell
Fine   we're on our own anyway
                    been self-reliant from the start

There are clues   hints   instincts
All you need to chase the inscriptions
           hearing muted violins
                the while a search is made
                     for those incised expressions
                          of serpent love
                          lizard love
All the game you could ever go after
                         and leave *alone* after

Alone-together   in public wilds
Needing Abert's echoes to improve the hunt
Chess-mind put to rest   made peaceful
         by the edit of solid rock
            going all-out   outdoors

Hoping the next crustal shift
          is this time zone's very special quake
Building and relaxing the walls to new heights
The hundreds of former jolts celebrated then
          the perfect seismic gift

You'd think there'd be a penalty for wanting it
The Walls of Abert
           to keep your journals and mine
                     sequestered
                     the Walls' possessions

for safekeeping

What's within them to stay unrevised
Our "Prelude, Aria and Finale"
      to sound truthfully
           all the unused cleverness of children
           all the pets they'd wished for
      with obvious intensity
              naming names ahead of time

This is every playground   sandpit jumpoff
King-sized
      playing on the road
           to a tie with the kit fox

Let's remember fighting
When the struggles were harmless
      and pretend
           star-studded with extras

Abert like a scrim
Soft-lit   weather-resistant for bionic youth
      following footprints to amazing grace
                  without interference

What we always desired   like vitamins later
Getting close to
      and taking care of
           all the emptiness
           since the birth of the Universe

What am I talking about?
That which we will say together
              with assurance

A love letter to the cities still standing
           that will prove there's no ill will
What time it is to be   subjective
Attuned to epochs

Their many parts made a deathless clockwork

You will find out   embarrassed it took so long
Yet feeling privileged

      to behold geology's soft machine
                in slow enough motion
                        to thrill with understanding

20. CINDY'S SCENERY

Just when she called

Highway 395's something-for-everyone route
     was some way north into Oregon
        north past Valley Falls
             but not by much

Just when she reached me

The scenery had changed
It was amazing   the remoteness
     a stretch of reimagining
     a manipulated View Master's take

It was allied with magic and improbability
A cartel of images
     and I enjoyed those three dimensions
        while Cindy's voice was heard

At the same time she asked, "How are you?"
     the expanse of Lake Abert
        said to tell the truth
        flatten the curve of exaggeration
        make a donation
            to candid discussion

During the q and a she filled the blanks in
Was acutely informative
Summarized the moments
     since last we spoke like this
              a record interim

Ah!   the many numbers needed

        to recount the hours to reunion!

The fires figured in all this
Her daughter's home destroyed
      at a fixed rate of conflagration
A movie out of the Book of Flames
          with bonus chapters
             on the principality of Loss

The mild complexity of discourse
      welcome in the zen simplicity of travel

And to make sure the call got through
To ensure we continued
      found completion
         no one breaking up
            I stopped right away
It was unplanned   I did a good job of it
              caught off guard
            by the ringing

Audience of one reacting
The film sudden   with no title, even
             starting with a turnout and parking

The real story of this year's Burning Man
     to have this highlight
       of getting there   and beyond

So attuned to the cell
     I'm like the pets of childhood
             begging for scraps
Parallel lives that really happen

And congratulations are in order
     their critical moments
        part of a viewpoint's administration
       now a story of tumbling down

Those boulders from the Rim
     rolling out afterwards
       to qualify as sculpture's *objets trouvés*
         in a gallery of miles to go
And wanting critics

Just when she called

Everything came to a stop
Was vista with a voice-over
       in a land not so far away
              that seemed far away indeed
Was saying the right thing
                a crucial conversation

I wanted to thank her!
Welcome her to the road trip!
Describe the sights of this intermission
       scenes that save lives
       and update perception
All its days and ways learned
          to musical accompaniment
          and taken seriously

Like the environment itself

Didn't stay at home
Had to get out in it
Accept the professional counseling
       of Cesar Franck
           playing his Eclogue in E Flat Major
                that murmured in the many silences
                            between small towns

Valley Falls and what's to come before Burns
Smooth-running like imagination
       her words and mine imprinted
                in biblical lands

Where "How are you?"
       and "It's been so long!"
           is flexible language
           chapter and verse
Both Cindy and myself customers
                      of the Cosmic Sounding Line

Both of us qualified for a discount sadness
For *noir* in broad daylight
Discussing the fire that came to her daughter's home
       still Becca was safe

        and it was safe to celebrate
Knowing out-of-control doesn't always win

It will take more actors
      and actresses
           than the drama requires
                for deception
                    was always the spark

When you're determined to go on
And feeling forward-slash
      yet someone may call
      it might be Cindy
A very early Christmas present of endurance
Her voice fastened
      to the perfect kindness
           of open spaces

21. WHAT'S STREWN

A shallow lake
A job done finding it
One turns one's attention to the birds
      and all that's lying about
      all that's strewn
           for the sake of random appearance

And there's a way to go to the very shore of it

Though it's unfamiliar strolling it's free
The admission was a willingness to go

There's no one, of course
Just yourself   wondering if quicksand waits
And whether you'd remember
      what the Book of Quicksand says to do
          while unhurriedly lying flat

But don't worry   the shore's a white pillow

Walk on   be emotional
      because Lake Abert wants it that way
        and makes so much sense in the sunshine

The Lockdown hasn't spread to these parts
There's no liquor at the lake either
No restaurant seating or stores and supplies
              small business too small for all this

But that hasn't stopped the stimulus package
The aid of bygone knowledge delivered

So, from the flat highway
      step into accessible relief
        the scraggly edge and mottled scrub
          not wishing too much to obstruct
There's no such thing as stumbling

The mind is a minority opinion
      looking for an argument
        with simple precaution

While The Pure Land
      having added new real estate
      has set to revising Buddhist topo maps
An expansion to go with unlimited grace

The rocks have smooth, safe edges
              if you let them be
And the birds don't mind you happened by
Though they are made to be moved to fly
Maybe it's those tiny shrimp
      keeps them standing there
        not minding the intrusion
I'll just keep giving lessons to my legs
      in the moss and scattered detritus

Only yards from the KIA
      I'd entered a grey and green zone
          of alien sensations
Searching for the surest ground
And managing curiosity's steps
      having a membership
        in Abert's mostly dry aquarium

        shallow as it is

This evening   this daylight   will replay
Like history
      just to be sure we get it
Just as caution's needed to advance
So the landscape prepares a welcome
      with reciprocal care
          in the scorching afternoon

There ought to be horses
      enrolled in these marginal lands
          on scholarships of horse timeouts

For good beginnings
What Auntie Mame was saying
We'll have a show in the desert!
There could be espresso served!
              caffeine to accentuate the positive

Coming through it all
      like a prophet in the wilderness
      who hasn't settled on a religion
      and so has no reason to say,
          "Behold!" or "Arise!" or
                "Go ye unto the multitudes!"

It would not make sense
      to go tell it on the mountain
        spread the word
        announce the news
          for the good news is bad

I want Abert all to myself
The lake to stay a secret in plain sight
A gentle acupressure on the mind
      to imagine fresh water past
      where now only a briny present obtains

Please, a dictionary of every word
The extra word for extra land
      and the paintings it makes of photographs
Pictures with   or without   killdeer
              and the northern shoveler

Bright as clouds
  the top of the morning
    leaves well-enough alone
And lets the afternoon commence unmuted

"Nice" is a word
  that will have a place
    among the words for the winds
Any story of their travels
I keep arriving as they do

Beyond that I'm nearly collapsed
A lowly dictator ready for reform
The program to foster our inquisitive side
I'll be recombinative
  all DNA to be a part of it

The fires have been to Lake Abert too
The lake's west side consumed
    and aged to ashes
They seeded something foreign
In the aftermath they planted anew
  and started again
  a Mame beginning

This is how I'd sell a thing if I would sell at all
This blue-and-white this ink
  for you'd have to read it slowly then
Slowly you'd acquire the shore as now
When the gods should be paid
  for the beauty they've made

Since January last I prepared for late summer
The tour of the Outback
  to include the gallery of Abert
All its art saying, "Come hither! it's free!"

There ought to be camels and bison
The wild things finding their way
  with a megathere's idea of open range
    as if their hooves were a plan
    to survive the Holocene

I am listening for their hoofbeats

Their big-hearted pounding
       in otherwise silence
              that's died down to vacancy

"Pick up the phone and call someone…"

I said it   whispering
       what wasn't possible without a satellite phone

Wanted to say a Spanish name
              to go with the lake's
              the interloping English
                  offset some
The latecoming Fremont exploring everywhere
Wishing to know the full extent
       of Monroe's presumptions
           filing claims on all the atoms of the continent

I wished to count the hours
       we should rather create at the start
It's a fortune just to see it all
A good beginning   a confidence bestowed

What I quit smoking for
       so long ago the nicotine's lonely
       disintegrated
           the pack that held the smokes
It was done to be more oneself
Without a substance to define the ending

Let it be a well-kept secret   like the night
The wilderness as rescue medicine
More than a mother's deliberations
              or gift of a piano, even
                with music's misdirection

I want to ask Columbo
Just a few questions of my own
       concerning the unsolved crime
           of Personality
              the mystery of why it should matter
When it came to "Principles before Personality"
       Principles opted out
          said there was nothing to see

                pled "no contest"

But right now a rehearsal's in progress
A finale is staged
       and props prepared
              for an afterlife of right here
              the scene to continue
Like a set for Fred Astaire
Always astounding down Infinity's staircase
       down streets and alleys
       dancing till others finally learn the steps

Imagination satisfied
Full attention to detail
Every color of the shore
Those dark greens and ashen sands
The black-and-brown
       of what has tumbled down
                  to gravity's one-note symphony

And   surreptitiously   the collector pauses
Safe from a docent's ghostly prose
      the expository pen   blue-on-white

I thought for awhile
"Letting the thoughts come any way they hit"
       as Doctor Ostrow had done
           in Philip MacDonald's book
           the one with Robby the Robot

Thought the whole truth
       of a planet forbidden as Altair 4
           the whole story
As much as industry could access

I remembered other voices
Other rooms of outdoor places
Other times
       and what was strewn so artfully
           at the edge of briny Lake Abert

That fire   this present reconnaissance
       and book-length essay
       of which this blue-on-white is preamble

Something written before you get lost

Return to reverie and waken Rousseau
Just long enough to catch his drift
                     have him as a piece of me if possible

Strewn also is remnant language
The parts of all speeches
      scattered past cohesion
       so that visitors and guests
           can back up to first dates
                  and first meanings

Even murder may be understood
A sort of BCE necessity
        intentional foolery
            and the mammoths fell
The fruits and the vegetables were not enough

A better movie than DeMille
The comedy and tragedy fused
      in a wraparound trending every which way
And soulfully   as if a premeditation

You turn attention to the birds
And where they roost
      almost geometrically
         where the waterline's a straight edge

You notice
      the accessible lake is a study in silver
                that leads to conjecture

There's no one to service the quicksand
No one else to make sense of the sage
      while the liquor flows
      or drugs are taken
But the surroundings take note
        with autocratic sternness

The flat highway from Valley Falls
        still a tether to the town hall there
        its minimalist structure
           a virtual governance

And past tense as all the rest
                              imagined lakeside of nevertheless

That minority opinion becoming a certainty

The map is out and consulted
      for a prayer's refinement
As well the tracings done of random stone
                        crooked with Egypt's carvings
                                needing touch to be understood

They are lessons as much as sinew's protests
Melancholy wants a place to stay
      with an eastern wall of going, going, gone
Magnificent Yester
          when the Earth was fluid

This evening   this daylight
                  will indeed be reprised
The rock house the lava became
Immense   and floor-by-floor to shadow
The saline/alkali lowlands
                  a graben at rest and needing more

Scholarship
And love to make it useful to others
      the DNA of remembrance
      the things that are discovered
Slowly   with those counted hours one creates

And sensible shoes
For what's so beautifully strewn
                  there's only primal curiosity

22. WAGONTIRE

Five out of five stars twinkling
Wagontire   named for a mountain

A town purchased
    a year before the end
        of the terrible twentieth century

Cafe, motel and RV park to be restored

And the little airport readied
    for landings and refuelings
        when the planes will once more roll
            across 395 to the filling station
                its two pumps too long abandoned

Wagontire   an exclusive little town
Though I did manage to enter the cafe once
There were two citizens   the sum total
             and they talked about a revival

Perhaps through hypnosis
    their story
        exactly what they said
           how they lived
                who they were
                    all of this
                    might be relearned

I had not imagined it
They'd talked   they were real
But many letters it would take
    to tell the Christmas possible
        gift the whole of it
        that was so nearly deserted

They say a wagon tire was found
That a mountain was named for the tire
And a town for the mountain
            all 6,464 feet of it

Having entered the cafe

        one might have heard the name
        the woman that bought the town
              every acre of it
A lady empowered by her past
When she'd run a bar
              and would not abide bad behavior

She would stay in the moment in Wagontire
      and nevermore have to mind the ruffians

The five stars stand for strange passions
      made familial loving
When you need to see some distance to destiny
The better to change it   like a tire
Having pulled up and into wayside
           singing "My Baby Loves" open space

It's said the burgers were juicy
      and the Warners delightful
         (ah, finally a proper name!)

And they'd be waving hello *and* goodbye
While the airplanes landed and departed
      from the international airport
               hell, why *not* international?!

When *they* bought the place
      they learned that "Willie" came with it
      a spoiled burro they kept on spoiling
        till they sold the town themselves
        so they could see the rest of the West
What was still unknown

Once   the New York Times came bicycling by
But could their story be trusted?
City folk with filtered lenses
      who see with crowd-mind
        the mysteries of solitude

Attempting life in a low-cost setting
Pleased the speed of east coast hours
                may be slowed
Yet baffled by the Nothingness involved
Such that any intelligence report

>   will lack meaningful detail

Think 1960 for a minute
Think there may have been more than desertion

A two-storey motel
And a certain Mrs. Carr running the store
Wagontire had a City Hall, too
>   that superseded the buying and selling

Then there's that invention
The wheel
>   lost somewhere on the mountain
>   wheel   tire   where is it?
Where in this foolish world is the artifact?
The *objet trouvé*?

Well, straight ahead
>   like pioneer news recited with a flat affect
>   imminent discovery

Not to choose favorites
>   but "What's wrong with right here?"
>   (Bogart's invitation to a fist fight)
Why *not* Wagontire?

And what can be done in the sun
>   to a final resting place for mercy?

Perhaps say a few words
About making ends meet
>   and wearing old clothes

Faraway Salem had pictures
The library there   the archives
>   black-and-white and giving pause
It was once a bigger town but not by much

Still unincorporated
But what is seen I will assimilate
Be part of
>   as a dream is a part of waking
>   and may come to govern the conscious
>   escort it through its every trial

So find out everything

Find out if there are actually streets
And if Shirley Temple ever strolled them
No drugs are needed
        for the scented air is sufficient prompting

I knew I'd come back
       once the signage said to do it
           the briefest of instructions
                     a "Poetry of Place" in capitals

One need not go hungry on returning
Though the cafe's closed
       and all structures latched
           for a break-in's expected direct action
Mister Anton Arensky will find entry
And his first symphony
       entertain the last townspeople

But there's only one left
       living in a do-it-yourself nursing home
They'll send me cards around the holidays
While I'm out there in Wagontire

"Who wants a hamburger?   one that's expert?"

The one the road is always looking for
       hoping it's there at the next stop
       the cafe open
           and the cook clean and sober
The Wheel undented
And the Circle   *all* the Circles
                       unbroken

Like a crazy sixties certainty
       entertainment's not enough
           and will bring you down
           a bad trip one soon regrets

I knew that Wagontire's ghostly committee
                the one with cultural expectations
                well, they would be no different
Knew that Elsewhere was after all the model

Still I made it a target dot   a map's temptation
Because of sweetness and near invisibility
It had appeal   it was awful resisting
So I'd just stay relaxed
     and continue like a haunting
          one brand-new to the town

Imagine opera here!
Or *wherever* we are feeling secure
     and don't forget a green room
          with ultimate attention paid

This straight stretch of Highway 395
Like a knowledge
     a dear Savior's birth
         but they all keep going
       to stay ahead of the weather

But I'd said, "Excuse me, you open?"

They weren't sure
As if they hadn't made up their minds
         and needed a stranger to settle the issue
Say what's up and what's wanted
          even if it's toast

With hypnosis   perhaps their last words
Maybe all of them
     in a windy afternoon of remembrance
Turn the door handle slowly on behalf of history
Not hungry for anything else
     so the order's an easy one

How I really feel served on a bun

And Wagontire's halcyon enough
       to say it will continue
     a Joy to the World
  of the high desert
  found two months prior to Yule

"Collecting dust" is a cliché
       enabled by indifference

                and Wi-Fi obsessions
A phrase without roses
Forgettable as extra words
                when the ones you needed
                              disappeared altogether

An exclusive   five stars "at eleven"
A town has a mountain sometime   somehow
A town that may be bought
                the way others' made machines are sold
And a wheel's lost to haste, perhaps

Make it your business
Like a recurring dream that's still a surprise
        with an airport
           and minimalist poetry
                in place of stop signs

And you think
        they forgot to mention
                so very many things
Those welcomes and goodbyes

Five stars   two citizens   or even one
How they lived and lived on
                to be relearned as friends of the Outback

I'd like a room, too
You may disturb any hour
        as long as checkout's just a theory
One of many
Surely the Salem library
              will keep the archives safe
              debt-free
                    all expenses paid   forever

23. VALLEY FALLS JUNCTION

Unbroken

What we shared
      had come to be shared
           had been directed to those
                who seek a perfect ending
                who would be experts
        at finales

As there is a junction here
And travel is directed
           a beautiful union is understood in passing

It's not so much a valley as a plain
      where you ask,
           "Is anyone home?"
           "Any chance of a map?"

We'd play together   inland
The neglected works of certain masters
      and their talented mistresses
Trying to see   in the dark and the light
         what loneliness may recount
              without saying it too loudly

I'll try to talk to her at the junction
For I want to have better knowledge
      of her whereabouts
           though she sits right there beside me

All the dear children are watching
      and listening for the sound of engines
        they know not danger
           all is parotic   near to the ear
              aural
                the music of the Falls

A thousand thank-you's!
For knowing the way
For joining the scavenger hunt
          catch-and-release

There are plenty of others
      who might have chosen to come along
            but I'd have refused them
For it's an esoteric journey
One with passion
Yelling till laryngitis
A concert boisterous
      growing up and growing into
                further cacophony!

A lovely event
Stir up some feelings
      west   north   south
      but no east
         with climbing shoes
         what the Abert Rim demands

It's a day for some 5/4
The off-kilter time
      Arensky's pet prescription for happiness

He came *along*, you know
He   and all the Russias
          to see if the West was suitable steppe
            with room for czar-guarding Cossacks

And Valley Falls will have the privilege
The formal welcome
The little town has said,
    "Are you sure?"
        and we'll say,
           "Of course!"

There'll be storytelling too
The Klamath and Modoc have tales
There will be new petroglyphs carved

The Hudson Bay Company to be reimagined
I'll be John Work himself
            on recon again so far from home
             who makes use of the livery stables
               and mails a postcard to Canada
               in the dying light

The cabins are found
Like the hidden meanings
     of very complicated poems
          that are nevertheless charming

But I want a mystery to have its way
                    each day of the weeks of travel
Tea taken though the heat holds sway
And winter will be damned near impossible

Unbroken   unexpected
Having no postmark
     what the Falls have fallen for

24.   THE BURNS SWING

They never moved

They were a sculpture once made
                in the Eastern Oregon sun
The work intended for a Burns front yard
A patch of playground
         perfect for art

Installed to favor children
And "the green grass grew all around"
As it did in the song by the Countdown Kids

A sculptor's connivance   or sculptress's
     fathering or mothering
          a swing convinced by suggestion
        Nothingness hanging high-end

And the children
     belonging to halfway parents
     in half-baked cities
They are very happy but motionless
I've stopped living

        to be with them   mid-air
        leading a different life than California

A willing chance-taker
Like in a medical society
                bereft of sponges and band-aids

And the swing that swings the girl
        and the boy who helps with pushes
                are at home in the town of Burns
So young they're a second dual Noel

With no visible support
        the swing is a partial thing
        a pendulum's imaginary oscillations

A spirit of giving that chooses sculpture
Chooses someone famous
        to go to Burns in the loudness of traffic
                entering or leaving the hotel
                on a budget of limited attention

Still the swing means timeout
For shooting the Moon in a land without fear
The whole country reflagged as foreign
                but in a good way

The swing has the strength of a jackstay
Frozen for sailing Infinity's reefs without danger

See!   How the metal's enlivened
                      with boyish assistance
Captured is the arc of gravity's summons
And the grass that grows all around
        belies the summer's drought of dry old hay

All the clocks   as if in solidarity   pause
With amazement do they synchronize
        their grey art of centuries planned
            before the girl is done with flying
                      and the boy with helping

25. RILEY, OREGON

Two postcards only
Cards about elsewhere

In the shade
in Riley write
      where a very real post office waits
        collects itself each day to collect the mail
                        a concerted posting

And it's hot enough to start fires in the brain
Write *cards* about that

Just a couple of rest-easy accounts
Something accomplished
              gassed and ready for the miles to Burns

Riley

There's ice and archery and towing, too
And a garage that says,
    "We can keep you going   if you want"

"There are apartments if you don't want"

A card for alfalfa and one for the hay
And sign them "Amos"

A ten-minute channeling
              of all things Riley and pertaining to farms

26. NO SMOKE

No smoke!

When you couldn't watch anymore
And time was running out

And all holidays were canceled
                           it cleared
                             the sky cleared
                                            and it was blue up there

Not all over
You can wait for that

But certainly a clearing
        and sudden transparency
                and finding true distance again
                        the highways' grades
                                the mountains to come

You won't want to miss it
A new nursery prepared for reincarnation!

There's something more substantial now
        than pale dreams
            recorded with Impressionist expanse
                                        without *sigla* to assist

And one felt non-responsive then
Or perhaps broken
        like after the last act of "The Red Shoes"

Let me tell you all about it
As if it were a marriage
        when we are without protection

Gods and goddesses of all the prairies guide
Sight itself dependent
Life without symptoms of anything else

There is no smoke
        drifting   wafting   lingering
The enemy sun that made an oven of Outback
This tyrant's relented
        and burns far away
                for only a few minutes or hours

Technicolor's back and crisply informs
It's a holiday journey

                        where the holidays are extra
                unknown to any calendar
Each one of them named
                        for something you've done
                        to endear yourself to myself

Think I knew you as far back as the Ordovician
Or it may be I just like saying "Ordovician"

The structure of the planet is known too
Inferred from all this new-found clarity
Between Then and Now
        the sky congratulated itself
            for meeting a higher standard than haze
                built a palace in the light of it
                grew a theory of education
Even the ancestors might have learned from it!

Evidence of upright walking
That coming together
        then deciding to spread out

It will be fun to sleep in fresh air!
Bring our family and friends!
Be off-trail with gurus
                    undeterred by any cancer!

Blue is the color
Blue is the horizon
        all its ceremonies of strangeness
                            after the many prisons of ash
                in the waterless plains

No smoke

And during the reprieve
        there is a heap of luggage found
            for word had gotten out
Everyone has fled to ironic Burns to breathe
As if on a mission they'd brought stew pans
All the accoutrements of camping
                    wanting to celebrate!

There'd be poetry   and plays written

Relief that had seemed a piliform strand
        was now an abundance of certainty

I wanted meteorology to say things
Claim the absence of smoke was not a fluke
        but some good beginning
                recovery
                entitlement
                better habits
                mind reading!

The arsonists found before they can act

Now more than ever
        there must be such intensity
                as rescued Spain from the caliphate!
Now more than ever
        new stages of life entered into
                where security depends on foresight

The bottom is known and we'll be all right
I would have taken a bullet to breathe again!
Ten minutes so far and the blue continues
Like a dream not subject to waking
        one of millions, but the gods seem to care about this one

What am I talking about?

I'd like to help you out
But sometimes the words   they get stuck
        no matter how much coaxing
There can be no specifics
                beyond the sound of solo vowels

It was saturation   the term applied to colors
The look of things after so many veils
One knows nothing of before
        but a house   a car   and a livelihood
        and that, *barely*!

Nature had seemed almost military
Had worn a capote
Was a fashion statement   a sickness
        atmospherics recommended by the devil

        when the latitude
        and longitude
            of fear
            is refreshed

The eye of the firestorm
    just when you couldn't watch anymore
        and there was no time *to* watch
Blue like an innovation!

Let's enscroll the spectacle
Praise the sudden paradise its colors attest to!
Powell and Pressburger's very first spectrum
    their accomplishment   interactive
        their audience enthralled
            and lingering well past the credits!

A faraway feeling shy of Burns, Oregon
A vision heretofore unknown
A planet only deduced till now

I've known you as long as the Earth has spun
Many lifetimes and palaces
All the promises made by upstart rulers

What is your ambition
    if not these scented spaces?
Where is waiting
    if not right here
        when patience might be grasped?

Off-trail   tinted   resplendent

Why should we not fall in love again
            like the song wants to know?
Why should we not come to represent?

For it's an optimal calm
    that was thought to be impossible
And it feels like an appointment kept
        with well-wishing angels   who
        surprised the forests were burning
        acted to dampen the conflagration

And this light that illumines
                         seems a faucet of pristine
                         the sky of ice ages to come
The final push of fierce photons

No one thought to demand it
Still   would it have been too much to ask
       given everything else
       that's been so devoutly wished-for?

Oregon's exaggerated
Standing corrected
A second dawn
       as if the first had complained
             that it wasn't beautiful enough
             and insisted on a Land of Oz
                   albeit one sparsely populated

There'd not been a stop at Alkali Lake
No time for invisibility
       or blindness comprised of nothing at all
And the pearl of all that obfuscation
                    could not be accepted as art
                    or parsed as anything else

The no-smoke vista had the clarity of the moon
When they walked on it
That moon   colorized
       to include all the shades of Harney County
The acid flashback you never had till now
         complete with a Sixties waterbed
        that happiness   floating warmly
Remember?

Of course you do!
There's no reason to put more miles on the KIA

Here might we homestead the weather
In plain sight
       of the Silvies River
       and the Columbia Plateau
The Great Sandy Desert's never looked so good

The black-tailed jackrabbit

The mule deer and sage grouse
All have noticed the difference a day makes!

Dare to be a Paiute   a northern one
Take it steps further
       and find yourself in ancient sandals
           before   during   and after
                      the Christ
                      and all his doings

No fires
No danger

Just the moderate alarm felt
       at the approach of the American Lion
       panthera leo atrox
           with its pantherene stride
              a thing of wonder   of amazement!

Just sticks aflame
       in the joyous hovels of the Paisley Caves

Reason has improved
The mind made certain the cirrus stays clean
The upper air to remain a graceful authority
       what sobriety confers or at least intends

There's a court convened
       wherein humanity's charged in absentia
           the gravamen the crime of arson
           that comes and goes
Secret ignitions no larruping discovers

As in a wilderness of pianos
       where virtuosi await the fine-tuning
           works of Liszt and Chopin require
So in a Land of Painting
       travelers abide glaucoma
           until the gift of an operation
                     performed on a budget
                     of supernatural skills

Greatness has come to ironical Burns
To reward its innocence despite the ski masks

Ownership's passed to us ancestors
Who   out of gratitude
                  opened the sky to all its blues

Said okay
For the while we transit   you and I
        The Great Sandy
            with plans for Malheur
            the Round Barn of Mister French

And the Diamond Craters   deserted as all else
        whose red cinders we'll see
        with heightened senses

The perfect crimes of the hominid delayed
Placed in abeyance
      that your touch
            may receive all my attention!

27.   THE SUNDOWNER

Some motel!
The Sundowner Motel
      the best in Burns
        and Burns the best of all happy endings

There was memory foam
You can do it   lie down
                and let the foam be recollection

What a motel should be and not be costly

And the young man was kind
Kind enough to troubleshoot the set
So that "Sundown" the movie might be seen
            to go with the west of Harney County

I thought I could live through anything

>   if later this bed may be found!

There are so many ways to crash in a car
Think this *other* crash
>   is a need the Sundowner satisfied

The crowd noise fades
>   and a gentle dog wriggles
>   At the door to room 10

28. THE MISSED CONCERT DREAM

It started in a bar
>   with no preliminaries
>   beyond a scotch-and-soda

And soon enough I was asked out
As if it were 1973
>   and she thought I was handsome enough
>   to take a chance on

A romantic evening was planned
>   before I realized
>   I was due at the Opera House
>   due to play a piano part on stage
An integral keyboard assignment!
The work demanded keys!

What to do?
Would she tag along?

I didn't have the music I needed
I had to go get it and quickly!
Some college students in a van said they'd help
>   for a price   I paid

I would check the chapel of a church
But they got lost and we lost time getting there
Frantically I searched

> but the score could not be found

Seven o'clock came   I was a no-show
I'd failed to appear at the Opera House!

What a strange feeling it was
And the conductor was someone I knew
                someone close   a *friend*, even!

In time   after the canceled concert
        he arrived at the house of a woman
        she's throwing a party
        I try to hear his conversation with her
Eavesdropping to learn if I'd ever been missed

Things had cooled between me and my date
I tried to explain but she wanted to leave
                                and she did

29.   THE REPUBLICANS

They were overheard to say things
They were finishing their Breakfast Specials
And their words were assumptions made
                measured speech   spoken evenly

The truth they thought of
        over eggs-over-hard
        with maybe biscuits and gravy

A morning menu meant for the country
And the coffee came and went
        between politics
                and voices' expectations

Before long they'd summarized
                the times as they saw them
                the scandals and missed chances
It was a kind of court

      comprised of two farming couples

They presented evidence of foreign notions
And they tried together a case of intrigue

They calmly reasoned the goodness possible
      say, a high school reunion
          despite a certain ambient treachery

Between bites
      Conservatism strove to embrace the Other
      what the decades had birthed
          and wildly raised with tantrums

Still the witnesses propose a middle
Some moderation
Some sign
      the old days may at least allow a patina
A newer shine

They had an appetite for this   and more
Extra jam and a V-8 cocktail
Accidental encores of extra helpings
      to help the defense decide
         if progress was worth
            the chasm begun and starting to widen

It was a breakfast
      where mutual support was a starter
And tipping the waitress
         was unstoppable gratitude
           that at least for today's good morning
               no one must sit in judgment

30. THE ROUND BARN WITH XENA

Before the Barn
Before the pictures
      that were abstracts

    yearning for better geometry

Before I learned his name
  the man who built the Barn
  and who was later killed by a homesteader neighbor

There was Xena in the gift shop
And a real piano to play!
Xena who welcomed
  with a back-to-basics charm

"Glad you stopped by!" and she *was*

I wanted everything for sale to be my own gifts
One could make it so
  but a warehouse would be needed

"Keep it all!"
She didn't say it I pretended she did

It was all too good to be remotely seen
I used free speech and told her so
  and in a private language
   one learned a long time ago
When family
  was thought to be too familiar a tongue

The words she used I had to look up
The time it took was preamble acquaintance
A look at ownership expressed as hospitality

Yet there was understatement told
A modesty beyond display
As if she protected the business that way
  and made souvenirs more than memories
      life-changing talismans, even

The piano was out of tune
Some of the keys were stuck
  but with a judicious touch
    they might be made to sing nocturnes
    in the middle of the day

Someone's hands and a recess of doubt

The inability of talk
       to convey the mystery of feeling
Xena's improv become a short sonata
          concerning horses
         and how to train them
               in the winter months

What the Round Barn was for

And every key struck
     having something to say of T-shirts
     and trinkets
         prepared to enchant the present day
            when exploration may be random

Ersatz discovery
The unplanned itinerary
         resembling frontiers

31. THE OWL

You had to get close to hear the "hoo!"
     but it was real

And perhaps the toy itself was that
A bird from the woods
     with the power to dissemble
        as gift of the outdoors
           to be taken home and squeezed
               by someone who's stay-at-home
              or *can't*-get-out

No matter it's made-in-China
With every hoot
     the owl is convinced
        he's truly international
        and answers to no one

The subtlest dinosaur

With a gentle voice
          whose double vowel
              almost secretly transmits a flight plan
Slight predation for the sake of the young'uns

The entire story a little mysterious
Of the forest
Belonging to the night

Even holding it and pressing
       where it says, "Press here"
             a nocturne unfolds with a foreign feel
Nature held in your hand
       you want to answer its soft sounds
          with your own best voice
                   perhaps reassuring as its own

What the owl is talking about
                when pressed to do so

How it speaks so adorably!
With that tufted crown
        and all that staring   unblinking
                          yellow-eyed

What a flashlight may discover
This polyester of the forest
Almost a baby's attempt at "da-da"
                     absurdly haunting the daytime

What identity's to be believed?
The excellent art of a captive populace
       or perfect evolution somehow toyed with
                yet realistic as it wants to be
The woodlands and barnyard
            intensely apprehended

Just squeeze   and babysit the creature
Long after its maturity
       still yearning for nourishment

Nothing in the night is like it
When feathers say their thank-you's
       and starfields are assessed

       for direction
Commerce whispering present moments
                            in a time-stream of trillions

This solitary owl to settle down
As a dual being
Both a toy
       and the truth concerning lineage

Everyone knocking on the door of it
And coming to depend
            on merest hints and minimal hoots

The owl is a believer
A believer in many things
But does make excuses for others less hopeful

Or the owl is more generous
And this is what you feel
      hands-on
      squeezing
           quick and easy
           as the drafts and gliding

Watch it anytime
And it watches you back
      with the power of suggestion
Just listen!

Learn tolerance with touch
A modest survival
          entrusted to Xena of the Round Barn
                then allowed to be lovingly removed

A capture intended for the dot com city
Where subtlety wants example
      and crowds could use a solitary bird
           the possibility of intimate silence
                the exception of "hoo-hoo!"

Said twice   like its cousin, the dove

32. THE SCENT OF WEED

Diamond Craters

It wasn't so long ago, really
There's even a consensus
          this great solitude once resounded
              with steam explosions and more

Craters as therapy as soon as one arrives
An austerity to each hour   seeing everything
The flora wakening
    gifting the senses with ground cover

Getting to the basalt
The cinders
     and the maar with the lake
        distant cousin
            to Alaska's mile-wide basins
                    that sleep in the tundra

Getting to it all
     before the shadows tell a different story
        than full sunlight
           something new had been added

There was the unmistakable scent of weed!

Was it even possible?!
A crop of cannabis growing *here*?!
What?   who?   when?
              in the crumbly circle of cinders

With free will   consider life without it
When paranoia waits to pounce on the user
     initiate a "bummer" such
        you follow the dealer around
              hoping for some better product

Since no one else has come to the Craters
and   since other plants
          can mimic
          like incense

        the pungence of hemp
Don't worry!
The "high" is innocent as Bible study

Let fancy have its way
Improve the visit
      make it a "contact" trip
      and nurtured remembrance

Couldn't ask for a nicer place
                  for a little marijuana nostalgia
This monogenetic volcanic field!
My goodness!   there's still all day

To see The Central Crater Complex
The Oval Crater
The Keyhole, Big Bomb and Cloverleaf
The Dry Maar   The Lava Pit
    with weed in your head
           and weed in the wind!

You don't settle for less
But continue into reveries of paleobotany
     and what's been around
         since the explosions

Survey the Graben Dome
And walk the sunken middle
               where the lava settled
               and found places to go
                        beyond the swollen ground

So what is the herb
     if not the alluring leaves of *Cannabaceae*?
What aromatic double
     far from Humboldt forests
         and the schemes of cartels?

Whatever the source   it is catnip for people
Like the late-summer tarweed
     that hazes the pastures and meadows
         of the Coast Ranges in California
A masterpiece of flora!
The sticky resin savored

        for as long as the season lasts

And here it is   or it might as well be
Almost the same
Close enough for jazz
     and having the power
        to heighten exploration

A scent to motivate
Something to die for
Enhancing the *pahoehoe* and the *aa*
     yesterday's stop-frame conclusion
        to the flow
           unnoticing the centuries

What happened not to stay hidden

And just when I need to be paying attention
Just *breathe*!
Senses to attest to the rewards
               embarrassed   though alone

Where's NA?
Does the Program have something to say?
What's its reach this far from meetings?

Think it's still something of a choice here
In the Diamond Craters
     that got their name from a ranch
     it was a brand   a diamond

A thought
That this "relapse"
     may not mean a new sobriety date
In this Somewhere
     weed is a memory
         that hangs around the future
           only to tease   and
                    it must be admitted
                    delightfully so!

And once more returning
     through the red marbles of cinder
        collecting evidence of a spurious "slip"

Once more a deep draft of Diamond air
Imagination's rodeo rewritten
                        to be more inclusive

Make a promise to reappear as well
On the Lava Beds Road
                on its way to 205
                and the haven of Frenchglen

To return the same time of year
      when aromas
             will serve a newcomer's needs
                        for reconnaissance

Innocent   in spite of a heady perfume
Like the essence of a Hippie paradigm

33.   THE ROUND INTERIOR

The Round Barn   and Peter French

In the heat of the day
       after Xena's greeting
       and superb hospitality
           you enter a structure so strange
                      its uses seem a cover story

There it was
Like a wooden UFO
      that's landed in broad daylight
              to prove the aliens were real
              if dependent on timber   to fly

It stood beyond the parking   pragmatic
Yet having outlived the ranching that raised it

If I am eager to see
      the Barn is happy to have me all to itself
And I am more than pleased   a solo transient

Reading the explanatory large print posted

Mind-melding   like Spock   with the boards
Smooth with the custom of touch
     letting hands-on lead on
          to comprehension

The sunlight begging to enter
     through cracks and knots
          trying to discover the interior
The idea's a good one
But the Barn will stay unfound by the rays
          a more interesting story somehow

Be a horse and be trained
Going round
     and round
         the Round Barn   in winter
All you need   to have a purpose in life

For the second time is the building seen
Like a refresher course concerning ingenuity
         taught by the ghost of Peter French
And I want to ask him,
     "It's really a temple, right?"

The conical attic with all that wooden bracing
Somehow there's a resemblance
Somehow it's Sunday's playa
The last day
     and a last look at the rafters
     prior to the final fire

The poles have a polish
        long-standing
           hard to explain to any city-slicker

Today is yesterday for as long as I want
Believing lumber belongs
     to who's willing to remember
And returning added time to time before

Wonder what Karl would have made of all this
The Austrian master equestrian

          who would travel the country instructing
A one-man riding school
Bet he could have trained those horses
                              to do anything!

Perhaps the Round Barn
          Peter French's enclosure
                    will make us well-rounded
                              make us slats and stone
But a softer version of that protection
With its juniper center
          and dimensional supports

How wild were the horses?
Did they like the inner stable?
And were they warm enough?

To experience the Barn is to be proven innocent
And we keep it going
          this location to the heights of Steens
               with the amazing grace of ghosts
                    intent on telling stories
                         of ranch hands
                              and monopoly's overreach

One hundred and forty years
          separates construction's dawn
                    and the noon of its renown
I'm sharing the Barn to get you to go there
Though the hour's late and there's more to see

Could be it's a hallowed place   a dream
A wraparound prescribed
                    by peer counseling millennials
                         determined to help their elders

Where's the creek?
Shouldn't there be water?
Could I train myself to find it?
Do something truly different than usual?
Be in a circle round and round till I get it?

It isn't necessary to wait till winter
Start now   when it's easy get going

What's lost means
    something new will be found
        in the Barn that's round

It's just a matter of curiosity
What a theater of absurdity may accomplish
  with a set like this
  the stage enclosed
  and seeming to revolve
    while only stillness has been proven

Please study the paradox
The production waits upon your scholarship

With every circuit old Oregon is better known
Like a free revelation
  by pioneers willing to return
  who talk cowboy
    and revise the language accordingly

Let the afternoon settle into closing
  when Xena shall wish to know things
    like how I liked the Round Barn
And I'll only say I wondered about a bird
What bird had built a nest in the beams

Nothing more because
  though she knows the rest of the answer
        knowing French
        Peter French

All of her confidence
  showing the way to horsemanship
  and its metaphysical twin
    an equivalent mastery
    made possible by that central juniper

34. RED CINDERS

Whether it makes any sense or not   listen
You'll be left with the red cinders of what was

Embers   entire lives

You're alerted to downfall
The Craters of the Diamond
    their red marbles strewn
      where spent eruptions
        are shallow dimples seen

The Earth slightly recycled
    like a mortgage of the interior
And now   in the uncertain years since
And with the pressure eased
    a simpler landscape's evolved
        the heat gone out of it
        all energy lost

The pale valentine left to wish for otherwise
Different stories
    of the same cessation of heartfelt

And strange plants thrive in the rubble
A botany informed by discount conviction
      as if there were a price for survival

Across the austerity
    of ropy *pahoehoe* and impassable *aa*
      a past tense happens
      an altogether meager resolve
        to explode again

Be a fireworks there in the night
    as if there were a geologic rally
Be a principled heat   bursting with relevance!
Gaia the perfect girl for this

Right now the aftermath's mindfulness
One turns to planetary remembrance
The *sine qua non*

   since humans are inconstant
   telling sometime truths
     to suit circumstance

It is said the Diamond Craters fired just once
As if a single example might serve
A red for all time
  shattering!
    purposeful!

Assuming their multiple blasts
       were certain teaching by example

A volcanic tutoring
Everyone rapt with sensible comprehension
   who was witness
Prepared to enflame others
    with some red cinders of their own

The impassioned parts of speech
  as embers long enough lasting
    to stay discovered
Like a good doctor's advice taken
     despite the hoarse cries of shamans

One's attention is divided
Until a better faith is found than charisma

Take copious notes
While the peace of cinders
  details their heyday of outburst
How the craters would murder the miles around
   with nothing but inner truth
   and knowing the ways of magma
     that writes letters to the surface
     meant for the docile

Meant to be studied by the complacent
Redly tinged instruction
The longer wavelength messaged with sanity

Wherever we are
  the Earth's vibrations
  those tremors

        may paradoxically summon the timid

Perhaps we sense a better way
      than indolence and its cousins
            of inaction
            and doubt   and

While the lavas fountain fragments
              of themselves
You watch yourself grow up
Right there
      in the presence of red cinders emplaced

But do not think there is a legacy
      beyond the ruination
Do not think there's any help
           that's ready to go when you are
The moment's passed
When iron
      or whatever it is has rusted the rocks
              may impart a therapy
              and empower

The volcanoes quit
They were ahead of the time
      when their eruptions
      would have mattered most

Now they improve one's sleep
At the longitude and latitude
      of a land prepared
          for the pastime of forensics
          the most tiresome of sciences

Now   with distant Steens observing
The ghosts of bygone geologists pry
              into your research

There's been another death
Nature's like that   wants you to understand
But the bowl of the red cinders
      makes me prefer to assign tragedy
        to bad timing
I want to cancel acceptance

And pray   irrationally   for rumblings

Pray in furtherance of future diamonds
The hardest substance a metaphor
Hard carbon to cradle the volcanic field

I'm sorry l cannot tell you more
                 but the cinema's running
                 that explains everything
And before *you* know
        I will need to see it through

What day it is the answer's found
     will be the start of a scandal so profound
           geology will need adjusting

It was democracy that sought the surface
Offering its depth and boisterous minerals
Driving the price of freedom down
     so that it's opportunity
    a last shot
       before the silence of centuries after
            promotes a false sense of awe

I would pay well for that color
Those cinders' red

As an elected official make a first donation
Acquire at auction the very same shade
Just to be a mentored by a *mafic igneous*
Hear its real name recited
      if only by chance

Make a run at history   make it all-new
The monogenetic craters to blast out!
   lose the adjective
    do what they should in the sun or shadow
Babies of the Basin and Range
      with snap-on diapers
         reliving birth by clever guesswork

It only feels deadly for a moment
The cinders arcing artistic glitter!

We are standing in need of Hawaii
In need of its prayers
      well inland from the Pacific
The words for iron applied to the chemistry
Saying it should not be doing that
      if it doesn't mean that

Be a surprise if you can manage
Didn't I tell you I'd be down for that
          whether it makes any sense
                    to redly re-erupt?

I'd listen for the noise deep down
With those who want a better province
      one that's active-volcanic
          like a breakthrough
Entire lives lived for the embers alone

The science says it's over
Though a voice-over echoes,
    "who's going to stop us?"
        till the wind rises
             and disquiet's recycled

35. THE OTLEY BROTHERS

Your symptoms
      require the ranch to make it right

You mustn't order just *any* prescription
If the malady's perfect
         the remedy must be also   perfect

A wagon was positioned roadside
With a sign proclaiming "The Otley Brothers"
    that might have read
      "This way to red angus
          and the Cucamunga!"

Their square miles many
And the short and grassy
        a connected rangeland

There's a picture
The family and a pickup posed
        a four generations look

Right away you know the work is good
Sure to relieve the symptoms
That which started in L.A.
    and worsened till this Diamond ranch
        its irrigated meadows
        almost empty of juniper
The burns controlled as tradition

Just by looking
    I'd say the dogs are happy
    the pups especially
        playing in the distant quaking aspens

Everything's a therapy of sound
Then a management uncanny

The trail has ended
    in sight of mother cows and calves
The green hay a little late   but scentful
An unpaid-for ad for recovery

For the contemplation of Mary Geraldine
    and all she put in
        to the success of the place
        the schools she coached
            the plans she made

She'd been one of the WAVES in the War
Eloping after that to live on Steens
    with just a few amenities
The prelude
    that's now a postlude understanding
        my illness relaxed   maybe over

And the Otley Brothers' tag-team

Those physicians of Diamond Valley
    bringing their know-how with bulls
    and so much more
        to bear on a romantic

So I'm an outpatient ending dependence
Wanting so much to see so much
    of wells and lava walls
            like the parts of a massive nursery

36. WITH HAY AND LAVA

There were questions of course
And around the edges of the valley
        the stone is antithesis
The laws of settlement obeyed by the basalt

The exact same money in your pocket
        as elsewhere ranching

And the golden hay
    is scattered all over the green
    a splotchy two-toned and level land

You keep your heart healthy
    with this supplement of ranch world
A very shiny sun making it perfectly clear
    for as long as needed for revival
        albeit one of a secular nature
          for now

Questions starting to be answered
    just listen to what *they* listen to
    with the motor cut like too busy a life

Just have a little chocolate   seeing all of it
The sweets impressed on the palate
    like a valentine's view
Ever and again supposing

        mystery must be a part
            of anything so grand

Getting home late
    one's sleep is well-prepared
Rehearsed, even   with this serious resting

No mistakes have been made
Though there's plenty of room for error
              the room as large as all of outdoors

Nor has domestic terror taken root
    where such fearless farms are
There's nothing wrong
       that the diamond hasn't scratched
       and caused to yield to what's right

So a one-sided comfort's known
And extra days added to the week
The only danger   long-passed
     when the Miocene came alive
     with streaming basalt
        its searing news from the mantle

Flooding sensationally
    the headline lava screamed, "Extra!"
    all over the place
      and, "If you aren't perfect
          you haven't a chance!"

And the lava was foundation
Earth's freedom of information
Borrowed medicine
    that may not be returned

Perhaps Nick Zentner's due for a story
The Northwest guy
One who's dedicated to all his geology
    how he always makes it interesting
           something to be saved for later

Whose hay?
And whose fields
    underlying its tan crescendo?

Trust the musical term to highlight
The beauty become an audible harvest

Someone's playing chess with aesthetics
A win assured   if the weather holds

The French language a part of this
Only the nuance of its words
            may tell the shading
Life between the lava
        bookending the volumes
        of splendid solitaire

Minerva!   oh, pioneer!
If you're still a goddess of art somehow
        hear my voice!
            advise the length of Swamp Creek
                protect its sculpted trees!
Take liberties!

Familiar as you are l'Il call you "Dolly"
Have you name more than "Kiger Gorge"
                        and "Cucamunga"

Let you be stage managing the valley
Finding peace again
                where Steens Mountain
                has poured its pristine waters down

Dear history!   Dear Dolly!
Do the present the favor it requires
        and so desperately
For the present
        wants to know what to call itself
                    besides fine-looking!

The basalt's a bodyguarding stone
Dilapidated
        as befits age-old protection
Saying things:

"I've done this for you"

Hotel Diamond will take you in

And take you back to Dolly's day
If you want to start over
Be in pursuit of all your murder suspects
                who've had sufficient time to escape
                but didn't think you'd come after them

The hay and the lava
Like a patency depending
    on a good enough ground game
        to forego football

Make the reservation for spring
But be crazy enough
    to return off-season
        to rehearse habitation
Reliving the symptoms
So that you neatly accomplish distress
        when you wanted only to live in peace
        one without fever

That is why the winter will do
So much seen in September
    it won't matter the season

Antithesis
The opposite of all mere autobiography
    answering every question with "I do"
As if it were marriage
    with an attainable future

Be careful of the chocolate
For the wedding cake's too busy with sugar
            to bother with your health
No mistakes this near to the truth

37.   SEVERITY, AUSTERITY

There's every reason to ride
A road   two-laned   a little dangerous

A pampered traveler
      with a few extra dollars

A reason to drive
Into a refuge linked to Malheur
      and the mostly level lands between

The colors of the hour
      attest to austerity
           and last-minute flight
Birds to-and-from
Like variations on a theme
           of getting somewhere

And what reincarnation is so determined?

The radio's faint
      and the cell phone fainter
        belonging to a theory of calling
          all the strangers you know
            to get an idea discussed:
Has austerity   or severity   turned up?
Has either bedeviled you
      elsewhere as you are?

Not that wildlife should care or seem upset
      but the animals seem empathic
Shoestring survival being the norm
And creatures used to countless privations
      their stoicism catching

I'm always asking,
      "Who could have done this?
          set it all in motion?"

Who, indeed?!
It's all right
Harney County
      like a movie mystery
          sustains all the life there is
          its rights and wrongs overseen
So the police will have no questions

The swampland painted

        for its shades of bladed green
        that improve the heart's ability
        to beat in total isolation
Or when you're door-to-door
                with importunings
Trying to fix a problem
Making it up as you go along

Is this really what I want?
A pink slip from sanity?

I didn't eat much
Something other than food had nourished
What I'm thinking of and saying
                that's barren as the hills

Evil like a nightmare that's chosen the day
And looking for day dreams to haunt
It isn't right
The best we can hope for's amnesia
    but going home
        will be impossible afterwards

It's a kind of homestead begun
A reincarnation
        and having proof enough
               to make it a hit song
              sung to the avifauna
                      every day of a new life
                                that is ironic survival

In all this tilted jail of basalt
A meantime place
For as long as anxiety's
                a free-range explorer

What gold there is cannot be seen
The creek just runs along
        a silted identity
A different direction is quite impossible

Diamond's
        a higher-than-recommended dose
                          of freedom

A town so spread out it isn't a town at all
And must be called a library of lava
Where you learn more about deep-down
                           with colored reading glasses

A place to be abandoned

There are reasons the landscape oppresses
Tomorrow
     maybe tonight
          it may be different   but
                   there must be a key found first

There's been an attack of nerves
Keep moving like the creek till it's over

There's everything you need in the gears
And they are smooth
          as the machinations of the unfaithful

For this valley there wasn't a plan
     being shallow
     being bordered by the rock
         and so informally

The hairless babe is not more dependent
More wanted by the Void
     from which it sprang with conception

There's not a storm in sight
         but the rocks are a kind of weather
              weathering
The party   if there *was* one   is over
And all the figurative trains have left

I want to talk in a black-and-white way
     to express the *noir* that's happened
The police line's crossed
         whose yellow tape is now bright white

Accidents at this speed?   not likely
The severity of the austerity's
     rhymed down
         to a mere fifteen miles-per-hour

Made demands on the attention span
                               there was no other way

Any accidents that happen
       will happen to the spirit
            the pictures of ourselves
                 what's left of one's family

There's always a reason
      to ride the roads of eastern Oregon
Their long stories of Basin and Range
Their exquisite two-laned narratives!

The dollars don't matter
Like the coins lost to slots

There's a faintness that intrigues
And a sense of belonging
       that's local
       as you are
           for the duration

Tending to a wrong
       overseen by psychic bullies
         who paint the swampland
            with dread   with uncertainty
And make it up as they go along

They who ignored all pink slips
                       and settled for the color of fear
And it isn't right the demons roam
Looking for innocent daydreamers

Shall I tell you also freedom's not a hit-song
      and barely qualifies for the charts?

Don't ask   and don't tell what you've heard
                    so far

Or put your shoes on and walk to the door
As if you'd take the car
       and find what I've found

We'll keep It   confidential for now

There are so many reasons
                    why it must be so!

38.   FRENCHGLEN'S MERCANTILE STORE

"I'll be non-invasive," I said
The store seems to say
      "off-limits to looting"
            which any purchase
         by *moi* would be

Forget it!
The fruits and vegetables bought in Burns
     they   are enough supplies

It's to just to get a *look* at a business I enter
Frenchglen Mercantile
Take its picture

Mercantile!
The word with a ring to it!
Quiet commerce
      with the summer
           heading for a cold conclusion
           and living on the tree-lined edge

Not even a Mounds candy bar?

Naw! just admiration for a sign
      saying "social distancing since 1872!"
And a white bench   empty

Oh, it's open all right
Ice and gas and so much more
What the third condition of hospitality adds
                           to remoteness
                           and uncertainty

39. THE ALKALI LAKE DISASTER

Was it just in time the fault was found?
Or a killing from the start?

Too bad!
Too bad the barrels came
      were crushed and buried!
Too bad the chemicals blushed
          and bloomed beneath the soil!
Too bad the leak was certain
Was alien
      nothing natural
      nothing known

The periodic table's malicious daydreams
            taking safety to new lows

It was something so simple they missed it
"Containment"
      three syllables of caution
          lost in a shortcut short-sighted
If you don't have the long version of vision
          your desert's destroyed
            and it's Alkali Lake
              made more lonely

Let's not raise our voices yet
Sun Tzu   "The Art"
Only deception   being helpless in the night
Follow the book to future light
      master the lingo for later

"The Department of Environmental Quality"
Follow arguments back
      to Beaverton where it started
Think of Agent Orange
      the Sixties   the Seventies

They shut their mouths
      and the military sprayed
          wasting the forests

"Chemical Waste Storage and Disposition"

Give me a bottle and let me sample some!
I'm immortal!

When pronouncing
    the accent's important
Which syllables of the chlorophenols
                  are to be stressed?
Get "polymeric" right!
And "dichloro phenoxy"

Say all of it
    as if you had an appointment
        with Lake County Commissioners
And would also be seeing
        The Oregon Natural Desert Association

I'm thinking Vietnam is transferred
The defoliants brought   the dioxins

And there's paint thinner too in the ground
And pesticides crammed
Count to twenty-five thousand   (drums)
        then that times fifty   (gallons)

We'll never get rich, though
It's not a treasure   but parts-per-trillion
Behind barbed wire
    where you're dead to the world!

And the Hutton Springs *tui chub*
    has been following the story
        for a long time, actually
How the ground water's seeping
The aquifer in peril
The scientific advisors
        with *film noir* cred   going:

"No!   don't do it!
    don't crush!
        don't bury!
           what about liners?!
           we need liners!

                     what about *containment*?!"

"Methanohalophilus oregonense"   say it!
Whoop!   there it is!   salt-loving
       under alkaline expanses
                  it's what's happened

Before you say, "That's wonderful!"
       remember the out-of-town buyers
           and that what they say is okay
The company's defunct
      that let the leaks begin

"Tetrachlorofibenzo-p-dioxin"   pronounce!
Right this way!
Spend cheerfully the millions required
               to make right the mess underground!

When no trace of the war is buried
But brought above
       no matter how distant the jungle!
The ground's worn out
The Lake's had it too
     and worried ranchers
         are dancing as fast as they can
                  past wells and monitors

The plume of poison's stopped
     "It has?"
     "Oh, yes…"
Though it east-to-west traveled   seeping

Call Emergency!   cry out for silence!
The while Oregon Metallurgic
       catches its breath
             and talks pillow talk in the dark
           with the Chipman Division of Rhodia

I never want to be so far away again
                and think of nothing else

40. JOHN, HOTELIER

It was a brief encounter
He was busy
It didn't matter
        we didn't talk   it was all okay

I would have loved to have heard his story
I only said "Hello"   as in shorthand
There'll be a next time for longhand
For staying again in the Frenchglen Hotel
              where dinner's served
              and there's no TV

There won't be any questions
     because there isn't any time this time
I'll wonder   but security's enough
I won't die and the town's still here

I would bring her back
Make a home right here
     where the leaves are falling
     easy on   easy off
        in color   in love
              pastel's *résumé*

Something very simple   like open arms
The sun porch
     the immanent domain
        of the present tense
           and no death to follow

John and Kelly care
And the staff ensures a weightlessness

There's an historical breeze
     with thank yous for coming
        for remembering the mountain
              its wind-chill challenges

Traveler as performer
The landscape a piano you play
John is busy   it's August 30th   a Sunday

and curiosity is renting rooms
                with perspectives

There are no criminal conspiracies
Just the jazz of enterprise
    and people in motion here
               in a very small town

Do not make its inventory known all at once
    lest silence too quickly follow
I'm just glad
    to see him going back to the movies
        the Westerns
           pouring across the prairie
                with random stories
                with plans for Oscars

Small business calling the wilderness daily
    to keep in touch
    keep it personal

The Inner Circle's expanded
    as far
        as unaccompanied singers
           may be heard
           and never more beautifully

The hotelier says
    not everyone wanted the same thing
                till now
These fenceless dreams of Malheur wildlife
And every day a Sunday of visible freedom

How sweet!
Hotelier once   and then always
    and without a worry
    like a perfect vaccination

Critical times   loss of innocence
Write the list that's longer every day

The heritage site brought to you by John!
Let him show you the amenities
                when you will tell a story of your own

                without rehearsal
Helpless yet certain
       that Singapore governs from afar
       assuring safety will go
               with a good night's sleep!

Exhibit "A" and "B" for bucolic
August in the must-see Harney
            the County of Marriage
Where you go   right now   if you're sure

If you've decided
The decision like a breakthrough
                   the way everything's simple after that!

As guests begin your lives
With John
      seeing to Chapter One
      the accommodations of course
              and all-season-long

Is it ballet?
Is it planning another City of Atlantis?
Or speaking in Greek   your native language
             misremembering how the island sank?
We're going to have to talk about that

I'm just doing my job
       which means I'm at your service
             John and I, actually
Both of us detectives
      to find out exactly what you want
                that you never mentioned before
                because you wanted us to guess

And when we get it right you might say:
          "Pretty-please-with-sugar-on-top
        could you make it so, Jean-Luc?"

The hotel like a ship
      that's fastened to the sea
Yet knows the fresh taste of inland Oregon

The hotel is John's

            and living clear of confusion
               never having to say he's sorry he's late
And guess what?
The colors are coordinated
                  memorial hues
                              colors the Indians knew

Colors they saw in vision quests
When "keeping it real"
            was the work of artists

The solar brain alights on Frenchglen
With animal rights
        and three hundred and sixty degrees
            of both company
            and melancholy's miles around

With a rage to succeed in driving the Loop
        to all its inclined destinations
And do things differently   afterwards

John I trust
        to be that magician
             who knows the right tricks
                    to accomplish hospitality
At no additional cost all is forgotten
Just warm boards and warm beds

And we are only   weakly   not content
As in surrender
As in the syllables of "helpless"
                          in a *good* way

Paradise   that was always a theory
Until you are gently ushered
        into the outdoors' very best indoors!
A protection program for inquiring minds

Yours, dear!
        whose every thought
                is family wherever it's found
And let me quote you often
That others get the message at last!

I was rescued
They found me   delirious
        and wandering with Donner and Blitzen
             keeping the company of wild animals

That's all changed
There was no notice but deliverance
        and you had a hand in it
                I hadn't noticed I'd been separated

The hotel took me in
John   and Kelly of course   were asked
            to make all the arrangements

And the ghosts of camels and horses
      all the megatheres
          that roamed anciently
Every phantom approved the capture

As you yourself had
        and long before any other's okay

41. SPIRIT

Spirit!   of imagination
Of open passage through
Of past lives lived
      and remembered into the next

Spirit of dance!
Of hours added to every minute
Of heaven's introductory remarks
Of morning's enlightenment
            and evening's crosswords

Spirit of uplands courtship
Of psychic disturbance and trusted chaos

Spirit of journals

Of interstate travel
Of final wishes
Of best friends' whispers!

The spirits of children advising
Secure in their knowledge
 of small creatures
 with large ambitions

42. COMPANIONS ON THE PRECIPICE OF KIGER

There are others at the edge
They join me or we join them
 a little at a time this time of day

Their dogs seem very happy
Can they be our dogs, too?
It takes a mountain to make it so
 and our companions have paused
 there's no doubt of this

They've fully stopped to consider the Gorge
Let's introduce ourselves
 we who are far from the cities
 who are broken down to be remade
 with heightened pastoral sensibilities

The danger past
 that narrowed trust in strangers
 while a bright sun
 traveled to the zenith
Things have changed since first sight
And we'll say hello

This close to the drop-off
 there is nothing to fear
We're instant neighbors   for now
This is where we live   for now
In a neighborhood of rocks uplifted

                on a budget of earthquakes

The terriers seem eager to be acquainted
We're all assembled by chance
                but there's a theory
                some kind of plan was part of it

We're safe at home
Though we drove the Loop to 9,000 feet

Go ahead with the first *plié*
Your ballet never-ending
        by way of introduction

Perhaps it's the look of the land
        some angle of light
But Steens turned Persian while you danced

There may have been a santir heard
One that was tuned to your key
A soft accompaniment
        to this meeting
        and meeting place
               when the words of greeting
                      are small poems recited
                            with space between the lines

The gladsome silence afterwards a clue
Even the dogs know better than barking
There being so much room
        they needn't stand their ground
        or defend any part of it

Again there are others
        delighted to see you
                as if you'd always been known to them
Delighted as I am always pleased
            to see you   here
            or any place any day
                you've ever been part of!

Whatever transpires now   remember:
Having once happened
        it always is happening

      like family
A time frame of Eveready remembrance
The battery of Steens   its vault of power
        prepared to repeat all encounters!

Beauty being told to come out of hiding
And rightly   for a fair trial

We are the lucky ones   for now
Being interglacial
      the story of the ice a U-shaped tale

The terriers just ahead of us
    know the way
        to a long-term alertness
        and belonging

The K-word, "Kiger"
    sounding like an invocation

43.   A BRAND NEW BRINK

If you say too much you'll jinx it
    but here goes
Shake your head if you've been there before
Yeah   or just nod

Follow the signs to the edge
The ultimate metaphor
The Edge   at 9,000 feet
        above the distant sea

Late in the evening   or right at dawn
    discover it again
    that thorough letting-go
As if New Age actually had potential

Picture it
Exploration like a part-time job

    of just one day
      on the edge of Steens Mountain
Unfamiliar ground but go ahead

Walking the uneven slant
    the angle unsteady
Watching old black-and-white movies
   in your head
     that turn to technicolor
       midway to empty space
Chasing imaginary waterfalls
       of will overthrown

When you know you're welcome
   the Void is a pleasure
     and not so very you know dreadful

Think hours of embers
A fireplace after this sunny cold
   being up and almost over
     somewhere
        the Hot Spot found some fissures
         and expressed itself
Always the exhibitionist!

I'm looking
   for the line of sight you taught me
A tutoring the valley proposed
Like engagement
    everything you wanted for me
      in the aftermath of politics

This would be yet another looking-down
Staring into Alvord's inland playa
     again the viewpoint displaced
     having been ever so slightly shifted
       from what has gone before

And dreaming only of mountain mahogany
And meadow knotweed
Thinking only of what lives here
       a distant pronghorn leaps
        without knowledge of doubt

And so you will continue
        ascending the broken rocks
                until you're convinced of a crest
Being brief
And brand new
        as bring-only-what-you-can-carry

There's the hardware
        over there on the summit
The highest place
Technology's turning point

But from now on it's retro
The fault block returning to the level
This edge will be different
        a different drop
                from the factory of stone

Spending time
        as if eternity intended
                the entire mountain to be known
                        as well as one's apartment

Has someone spoken to you already?
Because   if so
        you'll recall the precipice encountered
                ceased to be dangerous
                      and stayed a scenic interlude only
Did not too much entice into accident

Nor commit any robbery
Since all that could be taken is already gone
                        and can never be replaced

Survive the ledges
No more slips
        you can help if you want   it is easy
Inevitable as life
        when you try to imagine nothingness

What brought us here
With obsessions stirring   risk-free
        like a playground devoid of bullies
                the monkey bars shiny

        waiting on first usage

And being aloft
      with errant gusts playing tag

Go a new way up for a biblical "Behold!"
With gestures to Alvord's great Beyond
As lonely as Reason
      in the decades of Gomorrah

I'd been feeling a lot of pain
So I found the key
      that started the ignition
           with such excruciating promise
                  and drove

Something safe to do at the peak of empire
Something that seemed a remedy

And here
      in Oregon's Outback again
         the ancient ways are tried
At least that looking
        from great heights
           at great depths

Without guides to deceive the seeing

From a new vantage
      a resolve
        to say Steens Mountain is home
Though the "house" is known
              for one hour of a single day

Where you are is where you live
      with construction moot shelter
         where beauty sleep is possible
            and all genders are at peace

A few square feet at a time
Or all at once   as now

Stepping up and thinking over
         just to be free of gravity

While the grass is whirlwind-stirred
                              in late afternoon

44. A CERTAIN BEAUTIFUL BONOBO

It had worked before
It would be tried again
In regions unaccustomed
                to any speech at all

I tried in the dark
      because of a theory
           a thought it might be easier
                getting through and getting heard

If radios sound better in the night
So your voice may not have static's tinge
      but be heard with admissible clarity
              the hearer intent as always

It's only three days of stumbling
        and changing landscapes
Three days since your last serenade
Your long and slender discourse
            a form of freedom

I am that grouch
      with no power to treat the condition
          until the words you say
          with such sweet assurance
              at last change my outlook
Your blessing a turning point

This far removed
      speed-dialing the city
          seems an absurdist's delight
Running a theater long-distance

Or it's some kind of funny business

Standing on the ceremony of non-profit
                              except for the gold of your soprano

Turn Italian   "*Ricordanza*"
Remembrance
      something for later
            when you say, "I didn't say that!"
But you did   completely

It worked before
The trick was played
       the cell tower fooled
            and a connection made
And I was talking you out of
               and *into*   twilight mansions
Asking what side of the mountain you prefer
What fortunate clefts
      and swift-running radiance

Mercy and its synonyms finally understood

But it's a party-line of spirits
         in a vastness locked from the inside
             where we read the mystery
                   of how our voices
                          somehow travel

And we're told it's just waves
         coached by the electromagnetic

I'm always ready to receive
Is now a good time?
You're going to sleep?
You're staying up like me
       to see a moonrise going public
            with a brand new phase?

The pronghorn antelope are jealous
Our own instincts are recovered
And we communal go into further evolution
                      you'd think they'd be happy for us

It is enchantment to consider what's next
You want to give it a name

       but I'll say your name to the tower
           trusting that tower
             wherever it stands

The open road included Steens
Two days before
      it didn't seem possible
          the mountain was accessible

Would the Loop be impossible?
I'd arrived with provisions
      supplies for as long
          as enlightenment could take

The kitchen was the car
And the table a boulder
Definitive cuisine
      when appetite
          is a gourmet's desire
          for discovery's sustenance

Could we be as lucky as before
And get through
      as if we were accustomed to it?

Here   surrounded as usual
              by sympathetic angels
Nothing in the night may lead to a crisis

You said not to go away
That it has the appearance of desertion
But the truth is
      togetherness is needed
              to go anywhere at *all*

And Steens
      that would make melancholy
          the most determined soloist
              rewards who hears your voice
                    with fearless meditations

Trying to call you I mortgaged expectation
Avidly thumbed the keypad with hope
      just to be somehow complete

Working from home, now home is the hills
All ready   been ready

You tell me what you're doing
Take the lead
      while the woods in lower places
              pile up the moonbeams possible

You start without me
As promised once in a tryst at the Crater
      the one with the lake
           where the art of explosion is taught

We've been separated
Nature did it and Nature can remedy

Hiding in the dark
         every moment
           has the power to protect
Every risk is affordable

In regions unaccustomed to surety
      the radio sounds better
           and your broadcast too

You going to let me get away with this?
Between us the questions subside
We've made it all better   like an "owie!"

The destruction of Academia
              is nearly complete
So very soon I will bring you here
To the "moral high ground" of Steens
And hear it preach
      a better way than books altogether

Beloved!
Even the amorous bonobos
         are not more committed!
You're today's news
      that waited for sundown
As if the world were truly an ordered place
And peace of mind
      proceeds at a fixed rate of recovery

I wish everything were as easy
                              as talking to you
Your voice crying out in the wilderness

We've buried the demagogues
But I hear they'll be back
                if we are not ever-vigilant
One of the things we could talk about
We can talk about anything, right?
That's right!

You're loud and clear
And the caretaker skies
                love you almost as much as I do!

That bed is brought
        as soon as you say "I'm tired!"
                so that we're tired together

My specialty: teleportation
It's the DNA
The genes of rescue
        when "Please help!" is heard
Or even "Pretty-please-with-sugar-on-top!"

Don't get up   I'm on it
We're going to be gone
        like investments in caution

The inside's outside   now and later
All-governing dualism allowed its purview
        unfought
Resistance in abeyance

To learn more
        we'll let black-and-white have its way
For the quality of our education
                        depends on surrender

Right now
        the moon's dimensions are complete
And its outline a silhouette of canyon rims
The horizon's graph

      whose relief
           is my own jagged acceptance
                    and *ricordanza*

A prolonged twilight
An association of mysteries
      dispelled by love's certainty
       and final report on miracles
Like going to sleep
      still tethered to waking

Here   in the midst of
      the Alvord milkvetch
      the northwestern grapefern
      dwarf cryptanth
      holly ferns
      alpine spikemoss
      Cusick's horsemint
      downingia
        and Modoc hawksbeard

Should we mention discoid goldenweed?
Sure!   and I would love to list it all
The flora found where I found you
               and was provisioned

Luckily   freely
Enough success
    to make further fortune a moot pursuit

Tchaikovsky's offered sugar
              his operatic instinct summoned
Though we're doing just fine
      an audience of two
      with Russian chamber music

Familiar works with no appreciable breaks
Or breaking up
      so hard to do we didn't bother
            and stayed on pitch

I was talking out of season
Remembering how the wind
      one autumn

        disgraced itself
        and fell coldly over the ramparts
        giving loud notice of departure
                past midnight buffeting

But returned to this calm mountain
        and your calm voice
Reentering freedom
With a ceremony of blessing you
        for your powers
                to treat the very foolish
                        with doses of wisdom

For the worst times alone
When you still put down roots
        and gifted safety
                for the victims of despair

But I'll credit you with more
And see to it the mountain finds out
This far up
        you can hear for miles
        unaccompanied!

The pandemic stayed below
Never came this way, even
Was paying its debt
        to the evil that spawned it
In all the turned-downside world
                        normalcy needed the heights

You and I are a youth organization
        whose membership's so strict
                only ourselves are admitted

Geography in charge of all distance
All those hyphenated digits
        and parentheses
Say anything!   the cell is waiting
And I am waiting on the next word
                the next theory
                that may be the last
                            but spoken sweetly!

Did you know I take you very seriously?
Oh, yes!
      as if you held the secret of immortality
      and you'll tell me tonight
           with our single satellite shining
                    as if it wants to know too

And would thereafter fill its empty craters
            with a better moon philosophy

I'm more alert to the light this way
The light you bring
And bring out
      of home-free topography

Change inhabits all your speech
A here-and-now dimension
      that inflames the present
        with the very perfume
           of all the other tenses

I called you
From the great fault in Oregon dialed
From the most northern wall
            of the great Great Basin
The outdoors indoors and heavenly

And can you also hear the many angels
      swirling and texting
        wishing to stay on your good side?
Mass communication
         hand-held
           in alpine sanctuary

45. THE MANY MOONS TILL NOW

I am the moon's secretary
      and I control her appointments

We'll Always Have Stockton

Steve Arntson

We meet often   we're friendly
I tell the moon she has no rivals
     and we work together
          in supreme serene

There are many moons
     because the moon is moody
          by nature   with all those phases

And now she's here again   the highlight!
I saw her rise   reddened a little
     over the Alvord's eastern desert space
Rise with a message
With criticism too of lesser lights

The moons keep strange hours
An unpredictable caring   almost motherly

The early morning moon
Those moons in bright blue skies
     that want discovery
          in the scattered light of the day
And that rarest moon that silvers the rain!

What she's made of is far-off unknowable
But she's a bad week's beautiful ending!

I'm waiting on her next installment
Always sorry there's so little time
          those billions of years notwithstanding

Maybe she's a "know-what-you-mean" moon
She's certainly appreciative
I experience her shine
     ready in seconds to consider her love
     her amazing stories told
         as many ways
         as lunacy's rays decide!

Sometimes she calls me from Space
With special requests
         at a fixed rate of enchantment

And it's pillow talk

As new as the new moon
                that thinly sets with the setting sun

You may call her "Selene"   it's better
The pale fire of her countenance
        refreshing the existences
                of all who meet her gaze
                        and respond to chaotic seduction

It is Moon Meadow's theater of strange
                        and wonderful

I'm never without a home
Whenever the moon's multiple charms
                      commence
Even worlds in collision will pause to admire
Selene!
As much as the heart can say
                and astronomy tell   till now

The eight-year eightfold child
            says, "I didn't do it!"
Like the many moons
      the many times a war began
           and never ever ended

When I signed on to manage things
        that Selene might shine
            without a care
            without distractions
I never imagined she'd see more clearly
Question those many moons of hers

The so-called Indian measure of time

Selene's returned the "m" to neutral
And "many moons" can be said
                    without the summary of suffering
                      that westward expansion found

The enemy inside's the usage now
Where the planet
      lives   plots
      and walks in the moonlight

        having werewolf thoughts!

No doctor may be trusted
And they surrender to medicine's gods
Awful Latin
      that is so very far from Cicero's garden

Beauty came and went
The spirit takes notice   invokes welcome!
The moon's secretary's energized!
His hopelessness assuaged!
His resilience widened
          like a beach at ebb tide

And joy extends its walkabout

Look up!
The prime mover
      is shifting places in the sky
          and trains the ocean
            to rise and fall
Its own spooky tether a fastening secure

Things are round that gravity loves
And floats
      as many moons
        other forms of knowledge
            drifting over Oregon

Things we had to lose
That they may be seen this way
And witnessed
        as something always personified

You are called to do nothing
Say nothing at all
Be reciprocal   abeyant

Stunned silence in the realms of "thank you"
Pale learning
      with clouds
          till now
              connected

46. A WINDBREAK WITH STONES

It would help   but not entirely
This far up
      with Ice Age cold
            you wonder
            for how long
                you'd want to stay

They were still working
The wall was not complete
      the way it should be
Was still to be decided
      but there was hope
           they'd be cozy on the ridge

The sight was seen in passing
            passing much else besides
It was something briefly glimpsed
As if the rest of a frontline
      had still to be checked
      and rumors had lent an urgency
                to the inspection

And we were not to feel too comfortable
Not while there was light left

So it seemed part of the Great War
An entrenchment
      with soldiers telling stories
           of how they'd stayed alive
I wanted to stay alive myself
And beat the devil   like Humphrey Bogart

I may return to see their work

Geology had unrolled and gone haywire
            the Earth still barely known
Made a case for tundra
You recognize it now
      a piece of the arctic
           come to rest in the temperate zone

The windbreak was archaeology newborn
When all the questions will be answered
Who did it and when
        no actual archeologist required

You just breathe at nine thousand feet
        thinking Halloween
           shouldn't be one day only
                        in the orbit
That Halloween should orangely appear
Anytime   as sudden as instinct

And provide spears
        to pierce with awareness
           out of season
The hour of just enough fear
        to get smart
           in the midst of indolence

Like a sudden "click"
When you implore the mountain
        to continue as machine
               just to see what its motor requires

I'm pretending the boys are building a town
Their work so far
        is the first shallow basement
           the first home begun
No unions yet

And the chinks in the wall of the windbreak
        the wind will find
           and be robust with drafting
I would not leave it ever   so constructed

They're busy
Even a brief surveil tells the dedication
                    a dream taking its time   lifelong
A master class in stone told

The architects hiked
Coming slowly up the Blitzen Gorge
              reading slowly the canyon
              feeling out of place somehow

They made no other home
        except this alien platform
                the last stop
Patience preferring to be in a hurry

I could have interrupted
Yeah, could have chatted them up
                for a second chance
                      of closing distance
But the encounter fluttered past
A longitude and latitude left alone

I would share their bivouac remotely
The same clock the same night
Steens Mountain like a ramp
        uplifting itself and the westerlies
        so that a hurricane was known
                      that spilled the atmosphere over
                                    with chaotic cold

As if to say,

"Do you need help with anything?
Let me   the west wind
        chill your foolish ambition
        to be all you were never meant to be!
Return your hominid gaze
        to the Serengeti plain!"

Like an overnight's sudden reprise of origins
When the continent's jail is opened
        and what lay beyond
                turns out to be a lie

Is it pre-planned construction?
Is it a last stand
        in some forgotten revolution?
Who will it be who overruns?

It felt good to be involved   however briefly
I'm thinking I'm wanting a fort for myself
One for the two of us
        when you'll tell me a story
         your gold standard met for the truth

In faraway Washington State
      Nick Zentner will hear of this geology
          and the "cozy fort" of windbreak
          waiting on his lecture
While camped on the narrowest land
                above it all

Enjoy the exposure
Withdraw to a summit
      for the pleasure of good company
              in bad weather

It's hard to find this combination
This long night of listening to the wind
              mother of all memories
Earning comfort with prayers for strangers
Putting fears to rest with an aerie

And the cold is lively   updrafting
A family of winds
      around and through
          telling of their origins
              and black sheep possibilities

They set an example
Don't stop   this is where we build
You'll love it here
      everything on the house
You can't stop smiling
          so we'll make it official
            be kind to ourselves
            the way we were
            in Tehachapi that time

Right now we're north enough
      the future won't mind
      and will keep running
          all the way to eternity

The boys were good
It could have been Mars
            or the Moon
            that they'd fortified

They'd learned to control their tempers too

By dawn they'll see the day
                             a little worn down
                                              but they'll see it rightly
A trophy sun up there for beautiful hours!

These are the side effects:
Eye contact with the inexplicable
                           and affordable wonder

At the top of the Loop   land's end
Quicksilver Messenger Service
                               begins with a windbreak
I can hear the sixties singing again
Breathe more freely   airflow assured

A better game than video played
                                 and less sugar

Just couldn't wait for Earth Week
The demand for altitude was way too great
The onset of sadness
        like the first stroke of an engine
               that runs on melancholy regular
This too compelled ascent

The ghosts of our grandparents
                                   are wearing warm clothes
Talk to us!   help us to build!
As of this minute pretend we need showing
It will do us all good   what do you think?

The windbreak's better   nearly complete
The boys will have an appetite

I started singing in Spanish
        but the words were a mystery
       their meanings blocked
             by a helpless monomania
                   for English
A hallmark of a xenophobia
                 I was determined to quash

If we get up high
        maybe the big picture of Oregon
                would jog other perspectives
Pain doesn't care and will visit any age

Hadrian had an outpost wall in England
                              part of some frontier
Occasional stones put together with clarity
As if it were a backyard fort extended
                completed in time for supper

Brave volunteers
        with lifespans of single digits
I saw a dog   a poodle
Not the least concerned about hurricanes
                      for its comfort zone was boundless

I'm telling you a story devoid of politics
What politics on Mars would look like
                the first day of landing   unaware
A way of life that's yet to be

I thought of Ayan Hirsi Ali
The courage it took to exit the Faith
She is a country of one
        a powerful heaven
           Somalia right here
                in the aboriginal tundra

The windbreak   cozy
            a patch of metaphor
Where the whispers all night
          are "How you doing?"
                    and "Having fun?"
And the answer's a simple:
    "We're learning to fly!"

So far and so good
                we see the whole mountain at once
We've parked at the windbreak after all
Hoping the stones stay in place
        that made it cozy all night long

It's even a sport!
A sport without a name
      and known only to wizards
            using swear words
                  when they mess up

Hopefully you will enjoy geology enough
      to find your way
      from the south and the north
Freelancing the omens

Letting history play a part
Like an all-purpose pharmacy
      of remedies for short-term memory
Count a thousand years
            in the time allowed this sequestering

And when we're finally back
      in better homes than rough ruins
            still a change of vision is yours
You will protect what you love
As long as Love gives the okay

The wind auditions
And all I know is
      it's sure to get the part of elemental

It would help to summarize
                    but not entirely
For this far up the Ice Age ramp
      leave approximate be
            and stay awake   as audience

47. SUICIDE BY WIND

Close enough to do it
Have it done by the wind
            by the time it takes to decide

Even sober
       you find yourself   at times
             an *objet trouvé*
             an art gallery's presumption

Or creature with certain merits perhaps
       but still one
       with significant behavioral issues

I'm close enough to the edge
       to let the wind
             the buoyant wind
                   take over
                     as if by accident

No one deciding
          or thinking the wind is dangerous
No one afraid of a fall
       or that there's accidental intention
       or unpleasant consequences
That *Scrabble* plural
       that never gets played

There were never any threats
Just a feeling it wouldn't be right
       to let a powerful gust
                you know   push you over
So that you're a pushover
           when it comes to End Time singular

It's like dating it
      not knowing what to say   sort of
Or shopping all day for the right way
                maybe shifting from foot to foot
                                with shyness

No matter what time it is
          it may be time to die
Just kidding   but my age is perfect
The gambling's a luxury!

Perhaps an affluent spoiled brat
                      seeks thrills
       and it's the same thing as despair

A wedding march to the Church of Outdoors
                              that halts uncertainly short of oblivion
Downtown's ledge relocated just for fun

Do you see anything wrong?
Sudden problems with balance
              then enjoyable surprise
              and relief it isn't fatal?
A series of odd encouragements
                         and fantasies?

I care enough to say it
But not entice others
      to do this dance
           they may be sorry for

Oh!   just then!
A two-step and a roar
        and small rocks blown about!
How many knots?
           for it's a sea on solid ground!

Place to lose your best friend   or yourself
Scares the hell out of birds, even
But just for a moment
        I'm lifted and shifted close to the edge
            one's whole life nearly starting again
                    just as they say it does
                            those times

What was not understood in that life
            is now a whole production
Might have been hurt   still may be
Whose will's involved??

It's a ballet
A willingness
      to follow the wishes
           of the choreographer
Saying "Yes!"   like never before

Thinking to imbue the basalt
      with your very own blood
           in case of your accidental suicide

A conscious thought of reunion
Every day to be returned
     your bonny come to rescue
     be of help

Something in our minds   the first wounds
Don't settle for answers
Stand here   stand there
     according to the winds
        depending on the pressure

If the weather were different
If I heard you say "My treasure!"
           once more   and
           heard you say the rest of remission

When sorrow's gone camping it's out there
We're more than meat   say it again
Step back just a little
     just enough
Not fighting the whirlwinds so much

Make it deliberate
     a different posture
        no longer accidental
A qualified risk arranged by your memory
              if only to like what you do

How many times
     will the wind be suggesting
        you just   let it   happen?
Suddenly and with permission
As if the westerlies
        were assigned the summit of Steens
           where you had to be to have it done

If it *was* to be done
     by the time it takes to decide
         entirely sober at that!

48. LORANGER LONG DISTANCE

With twists and turns of a narrative
      that was as dangerous
           as the loop road on Steens Mountain
He tries to describe it
How he fought   and with what weapons

How he got in the act and *stayed* in the act
And remained in its electronic embrace
Its maze a part of the body of God
           whose theology includes a little warfare
      call it "gaming"

Even among second century Christians
      there was squabbling and bickering
           fisticuffs too   at least
           and they used Rome's computers
           got good at that
           good enough to testify

I wondered if any bluff was involved
                          as in cards

The video drama is heard   like early radio
The deaths and rebirths
He is distracted
      because of the game
           for it had reached a critical phase!

There are dead ducks everywhere
And digital thunder   he says
      because I don't know
      and *cannot* know

There is lightning, too
The kind that sends down the forks
      and sticks them into well-done landscapes
                     with all-at-once singeing

He fought   *is* fighting   hard
           ferociously, even
As if a victory meant the end to cyber crime

And the beginning of his total security and mine
He is an expert
       but so is the designer
              who'd conceived the thing

Was it possible the battle wasn't fair?
Or that it wasn't ever over
       and Richard knew that
              still tried   and prevailed anyway?
Helping himself to booty?
Bringing it all back home
       as facsimile's plunder?

Our phone call is a last transmission
        prior to next day's travels
He's helping me with valor   the concept
As if his blow-by-blow
               were a kind of contact high of combat

The fighting made easy   made shareable
With no side effects or wounds

So I'm urging him on
        to a series of last resorts
              with lasers and blasters
He says the battlefields are full-color
The corpses are clean and the pixels many

Some of his opponents   well
They have to be killed more than once!
I'd be frazzled but he takes it in stride
       gets speeding tickets in hyperspace

Though it's a crazy world   Richard is winning!
Each step of the way
       the entire assault accomplished
            with flawless posture
                unseen   but strongly inferred

I think he must see in the dark
It's the infrared that says so:

"Right this way, Mister Loranger
                      the enemy isn't the wiser!"

So with twists and turns he attacks
With antique cunning derived from the Mongols
That the act of overtaking
      may inform other projects
         letting Someday's sense of hereabouts
            matter

Fifth, sixth and seventh heavens found
Something he'd been expecting
                      and searching for awhile
Deaths and rebirths in a maze of theology

He still has work to do
And the power of suggestion
      is playing him hard
         like a Christian persistence
            that wants him to lay down his arms

But   nothing doing!
He's raided the arsenal
                barking orders   taking prisoners
It's a natural talent he'd surely deny

It was kind of hard to have a conversation

And not yet had he heard about Steens
Hadn't caught the drift of it
      the mountain just prior to bedtime's moon
Not yet can he concentrate
              on more than the maze
              and strategy
                    but he will be able

I said I'd driven safe to the mountain
For the fun of listening to lowland voices
For the novelty of staying in touch
                though the wilds surround
For the vicarious thrills of warfare
      bought and paid for in private

"Richard, you there?"
"Just a second
      the alien lizards started using artillery!"

"Gotcha'!"

The Earth's moon shifts
                while Richard struggles
                        to secure a *second* moon of Saturn

He doesn't say if he's been captured or killed
I've heard it doesn't matter
      you keep coming back to life
He doesn't reveal the points   the tally
                        the war so far

He wants to stop
He wants to talk
He thinks my therapy useful
                if words are ever truly that
I had so much on my mind
      it seemed a video maze as well
      the *advanced* version!   one with Pluto!

But the home world was enough
I would not be on my way anywhere
Having found the world of Basin and Range
                        you destroy the rocket

He asks what I think he should do
Shelter in place?
       or try to sneak up on the Obsidian Fortress
                      dispatch the guardian snakes
                      and gain entry?

"I would hope you're ready
      for the consequences
         of too much ambition
While you're mulling your options
     I'm remembering other phone calls
                  other answers than human"

Caring goes a long way then   long distance
He is as young as I want to be
With a dog and toy soldiers
        in a Fifties backyard
        before ones and zeros
           and a certain detachment

A few years ago has become a gulf
A widening Atlantic   proud of its Rift

The courts have ordered him
      to take a break
      obey a ceasefire
But he's looking for new excitement
And I   for one   will respect his search
                keep up with the battle ongoing

There are more and more interruptions
More silences
      though at times   with distant explosions
      and reports of gunfire   faint
            even without the ear buds

I've been above the clouds for hours
It is a desultory chat
      with incomplete phrases
           and plenty of dangling participles
A slip-and-fall conversation

Two glasses   one empty   one full
I am a movie star my own self
While Richard kills a giant Saturnian scorpion
      the feature film of life in alpine places
           races through a nighttime's projector
The state of the world is enacted
Right here in a mountain meadow

Where, the day having ended
      the good stuff started
      with the moon and all
Moon of *this* world
Moon of the sixth planet
         spinning with all those rings
           those trillions of ice chunks
                and mayhem!

Asking for what I want, I say I'm a lunatic, too

"Do you think I could tutor your skills
                though no monsters threaten?"

We are Starsky and Hutch
       on separate assignments
Two versions of emergency escape
A summer's bifurcation
Social distancing taken to absurdity
                          where it plans to stay

His game is played on Ruby Street in Oakland
Mine while making an appraisal
            of south-central Oregon
Making it sound brand-new
                 in spite of the ancient tipping
                 the basalt angled with uplift

Top stories both
And we are helping ourselves
            to cell tower power
Managing the narratives well

"Still there?"
"*Oh*, yeah!   just a second   incoming!"
"Check!"

That I huddle in the darkness
            essentially homeless
This is proof of a latest round of unrest
Personal   overwhelming
But with limited aims

Hoping to merely refresh
While Richard seeks to resume his campaign
                     nevermind the blurred vision
                     from incessant rocket attacks!

We're both feeling local in a weird way
It has something to do with the adage:
         "Where you are is where you live"

Openly   if at times defensively

He's listening, I know it
So he learns all about Frenchglen
      the four-wheel loop road and the gorges

He learns intermittently
A multitasking warrior
      whose senses are informed
           by a bunny rabbit's caution as needed

"Hey, you won't believe this
      but I just scored a thousand for prudence!"
"Wonderful!   now as I was saying…"
"Hold on!   one second!"
"What?"
"There's this force field!
      I'll have to use auxiliary power!   ah!
          okay! I'm in!   and you were saying…"
"I don't remember   oh, yes   I'm sleepy"

Roadside   the night is strange and silvery
The moon is unleashed and wandering
It is revolution's muted recess

"Bang! bang!   take that!   and that!!"

Loranger offers up a cartoon moment
      that tells me he's acquired timeout too
And he yearns for a voice-over
      and getting to sleep as well

There is a sequence to it
Like yawning and trying to resist it till you can't

Fractured talk
That aches for the language poetry of dreamscapes
That may or may not include multiple moons
           and more than one very dark planet!

49.   THE LOST CAR KEY

Never had a lost car key mattered more
Mel C. Thompson was remembering
Let's break it down though

Never had he transitioned more swiftly
      from the hubbub of a bar
         to a getaway
And never had a girl
         seemed more willing to go

From the first little tease
        to wholehearted surrender
                had been a very short crescendo
              of   yes   seduction

It was a lucid dream's best sequence
And so easily accomplished
     they seemed a righteous team
     everything a preview
             of the fun to come!

She wiggled and giggled
She was lithe
They reached his car.   he said
     and kissed like sex maniacs

Until he realized his car key was missing

There'd been the dance floor
And just the two of them   dancing at first
So familiar with each other
     five minutes after meeting
        the rest of the bar watched
        getting ideas of their own

She'd whispered
"Let's go!   let's get outta' here!
               my place!"

It was perfect and unfolding
Unlawfully   wickedly
    and then
        and   then

"Uh, I can't seem to find the car key"

 And she said
     with a dismissive air

>   "You blew it!"
>   and went back into the bar
>   bewildered   and remonstrating

50. THAT FRENCHGLEN GREEN

It was seeing things
A green-more-than-emerald lawn
              where all else was tan

The all-around ranges
       like a thanks expressed
         for bright green's exception
                   surrounding the hotel
Making it easy for a picnic
       with toasts to manicure
            enclosed by white bark

Any time of day
       conflict comes here
              to settle down with sarsaparilla

Green is the color
What Oz has sent to calm the country
       so that the ordinary's beautiful
Frenchglen waits all afternoon
                  for blankets and salads

It's the movie's intermission
Where the plot's watered down
         to manageable botany
           fences loosely geometric
Monoculture's masterpiece
              whose blades each
              are soft assurance
              that green has a place set aside

Maybe apple cider and *Scrabble*
With proper names allowed

    perhaps your own triple word score

You know what this is?

The way of the world on pause
    for the rainbow's best part
A green exposure
    for as long as a camera may last
        with reasonable care

51. THE GREY HOUSE WITH THE RED ROOF

Yes, there is a house
    most likely with dinners and desserts

Frenchglen's inhabited
The almost fictitious town is non-ghost
Except for the spirits you choose yourself
    being on your own
      and earnestly recounting

There will not be any overcrowding here
    even for a fee
Whatever it is
    the grey house
      with the red roof
        is almost a neighborhood
            of just one dwelling

The archaic word kind of floating in the air
Like pollen from a bygone springtime

And the lumber that made it
    firmly insists on a future
      despite a borrowed optimism
      its slice of uncertainty

The house has a neutral look
There's piano music to be heard

Perhaps an old upright
      being tested for antique possibilities

I'm ruling out invasion
Whatever evil's out there
      it's after the cities   not this

The grey house with the red roof
      will slow and contain
        letting the seasons decide everything
Beliefs and ideals
      assigned counterparts
        in the countryside

A political system to be a rock
Or some creature that scurried
      like essential amendments

Something going on
      that fixes the edges
      sees to it the weave is by consensus
And what is out-of-whack
      at least takes turns with stability

Let's do get physical
That the hominid mind
      may fasten onto animist simplicity
      ascribe some power to Frenchglen
        with its ordinary appointments

Listen to me!
Forget what's the matter!

We'll find mementos made
      with exclusive skills
        a long time mastered
Have another wedding day
There in the house
      with the red roof and the grey shingles
      with firewood stashed
        and a sun porch for strategic tea

Its two storeys waiting on more non-fiction

As if it would publish in stages
  as much as may be easy
Like the Koran or Laura Ingalls
        once she got going
        and relaxed into prairie lands

So we'll let ourselves go
Down highway 205
  to knock on the door
  see if anyone's home
Never running out of reasons to visit

"Can we see your cat?
Couldn't bring ours on the road trip
  thought maybe you might have one!
Please! It would only take five minutes

"But don't bother if it doesn't purr or drool!"

52. A COW IN COMMAND OF THE OTHERS

Goes beyond just pasture
Faster than you can think
  a cow has gone metaphor
   gone symbolic
     and will not stay bovine merely

Ascribing command to one of them was easy
It had the stomachs for leadership
      and was not too sickened by sin

It was a big moment seeing this cow
The black-and-white exception
   to earth tones
Yet seeming to belong
    being bossy and all

It's like an extended family of one cow only
Taking no sides in any cow quarrels

                    the whole package now standing there
                    imposing her will
                              on the rest of the herd

They are thinking,
"Finally a leader!
          nevermind
                    the leader may be untrustworthy!
                                        we're good
                                        we'll take her!"

In the windy field   order at last
Not that the other cows
          had been especially unruly
                              far from it
There was always plenty of grass

But there was plenty of boredom too
The Cow in Command
                    was there to alleviate that

It said,
"Stop kidding yourselves!
        there's more to life
                    than chewing your cud
You're isolated   each of you absurd
But we'll work it all out
                    like Rock 'n Roll said to do!

"And you won't ever have to be milked
Unless you *want* that
You'll live years-at-a-time
        yet find yourself a calf
                for as long as you want *that*

"Now how can I control you?
Even for a short time?
Charisma!   twenty-four hours a day
        doing my part
                so you can do your part!

"Even when I'm silent you'll be learning
And I'll say all your prayers
          for there isn't any god, you understand"

The herd was stirring

The herd said, "Moo!"
       so many meanings
              minding their business
              in a single solitary syllable!
Call it a vowel
A super-vowel resounding
The cow bodies a-tremble with vibration

The gamut from ho-to-hum
       contained in that magnificent yawn
       that seemed without a purpose
Until the Cow in Command of the Others
                                spoke   four-footed and sure

She was saying there was more
       than the outdoors bathroom
             in which they found themselves
              unaware   albeit stoic
A habit of togetherness wanting purpose

Passive-aggressive's masterpiece of "Moo!"
Their bad temper
       such as it was
              restricted to curses
              upon the flies in their eyes

For the first time ever
       there would not be flies in their future
There'd be life without them!

The Cow in Command
       was happy to have the work
An almost human cradling

Later the herd would learn abstract art
              with their hooves
Take music appreciation
Make up for lost time
Be given cell phones
       and told not to sleep with them
                                too close to their brains

They would channel the will of the leader
      who would be prancing to-and-fro
         deceptively   leisurely

A "Last Year at Marienbad" of cows
Enjoying their colonnades and pools
                    and pasture garden

And no problems
They'll ask each other, "Remember me?"
And the answers will come:
      "Can't say that I do"
      "Nope"
      "Maybe"
      "Yes, but l forgot"
          and, "Kind of…"

They'll be working on cognition
Making long lists and memorizing them
Enjoying novel stimuli
              their right eyes and left eyes in concert

The Cow in Command then said:
"I will see to it
      only nice people
         come around to pet you
I will shield you from industry
              it is my duty

"Your freedom takes shape most truly
Lack of ideas is cowardly   so think!
Imbrue yourselves
      with a rainbow's coloration

"*Bos taurus*!
Resorts have I planned for you
            with tennis, even!"

"When will you make an end?"
                  cried the herd

"When your agony's changed to ecstasy!!

I've spoken with Charlton Heston
      and he wants to paint you
      as he painted the figures
             on the ceiling of the Sistine Chapel
This time without a nagging Rex Harrison

"You are merchant stock no longer
They made things seem true that weren't
And the cancers listed are nightmares only
             thrashing illusions!   heed not!

"Go to Cow Church with me now
And sing your hymn of a single syllable!
Hear the 'Good News!'
      you have no choice!"

These were images
      that chased perspective around
The herbivore in all of us longs for authority
Waits for it to show up
      however imperative

And like cows ourselves
      we're lonely alone
          even five minutes
          I'm sad enough to die

So if by some miracle commands are given
If the level terrain
      should see a summit raised
      and a commander ascend
    it is welcome preaching!

Any way these cows could be sacred?
Nah!   they'd be turned down   unholy
What hurts the most is
      no new knowledge seems to matter

The big story's conformity
Without it you're alone
I mean the cows, of course
      and they're waiting

When the Cow in Command of the Others   said:

"Wait a minute   I'll be right back…"
                                           the herd was uncertain
                                           the herd was depressed
                              immediately
Reviving only when the leader reappeared

She who made all contentment possible
If I told you what joy you should be jealous!

Intriguingly
            the "vowel" had dissolved into Latin
                        for the leader was a pope of milk cows
And there were ceremonies
And mumbling *of* that Latin that said,
                                    "Don't die until surrender!"

 A relief factor
The brand   the program
Weak in the legs until orders are given
              every cow a student of instruction
It's all there in black-and-white

The herd is hungry but lessons come first
A cloven curriculum
          all parts of Entirety studied
Should anything happen to the Super Cow...
But they mustn't think of that
          only pay for the protection
                    for she's the only hope they have

Of course this something better be good
Let an orchestra play   together as these
Conducted and rehearsed
          as violins and trumpets are

They know one thing as many things
                too hot or too cold
                for polite discussion
The Cow in Command of the Others
          is not amused by riddles
           or flat-footed paradox
                              and hurries them along

              to simpler pastures

53.   THE DISTANT "GUNSIGHT"

Funny   it wasn't a gunsight
                until the literature said so
Then   like a Scientology's engram
                                it stuck

And Steens Mountain's notch
                        had a nickname
Was a bite out of the ridge taken
        affirming weaponry
        ascribing "aim" to the Ice Age
                when glaciers overflowed
                and carried rock away

Created a dip in the straight line of the ridge
Created myopia
        for the gap was ginormous
                and just a gunsight from afar

A smaller conception
        concerning how to shoot straight
                hunting for sport
                        or doing in your neighbor

From the west
        where the wetlands border Frenchglen
                is a barrel imagined
                    and what it takes
                    to take a bead
Remembering to squeeze I suppose
Out of control but steady when it counts

Kill a mountain off with gun powder too
The great gash at Kiger Gorge made
                        a tunnel's vision

If only it might be ignored
                like a made-up story
The mountain's outline safe from scrutiny
The way wildlife is to-and-fro
                        with indifference

Unless there is the "crack!" of a loud report
      that haunts Forever
    with recent metal invention

54. SLANTED TREES

The birches leaned
As though Nature
    knew a preference at times

And the trees tipped away
    from vertical
        to other angles

Or it's a religious service
    begun with birch leaves aflutter
    like so many colored coins
Millions at least!
My savings that are free of earnings

Except for coming here
Blank walls abandoned
    for the adult medicine of birch trees
        their detailed little forest
        there for emergencies
The eyes shuttering
    with grateful comprehension

This is where you go   if you go
In the wind
Seeing the West
    without history to cushion its fall

Access   is a liberty taken with maps
Wearing rings and things
Fashion brought to the forest
            out of respect for tribal wishes
The road maintained by superstition

At the sight of leaning trees
       their white bark a textured dream
            a version of "Vocalise" is heard
Mister Rachmaninoff's wordless song
Especially arranged for this day off

They say the trees are joined   underground
The roots all linked
       so it's a single plant aslant
        incentivized by togetherness

Make it a Sunday-gone-to-meeting grove
With hammocks stretched
The nearby lake beheld from the horizontal
     all-natural
        like a commercial's truth for once

The water lightly ruffled
And crisscrossed with avifauna
      from secret nests flown
        to ensure the survival of their young
Something no longer of interest
         to the hominid
          tending his anti-garden
                of grief

This is a rare chance to think differently

In the House of Birch Trees
     summon the patience
        to hear the whole answer

Have the pleasure   late afternoon
     of an address found for lavage
       playing close attention the while
The grouty universe forced to look away

In all fairness   for all innocence
Let the Void be considered
Let nothingness be suggested
        by these shifting branches
And "What's happening?"
     be your barely audible prayer
      though freedom of speech still

I brought *crostatas*   just two
For fasting in the forest
        two *crostatas* to go with simplicity

The fruit tarts tasty   just right
    as the hammock moves
        ever so slightly
          north-south-north-south
Like the oscillations of moderate doubt

It's treatment
There's traveling to do
    but I can pretend
        the lake and its slanted trees
          were the destination all along

Immediately on setting out
      the journey was transformed
      from runabout   to birches
And still pretending
The calming heat
      is a home world's question
      "What is to come?"

Once, when the red sun rose
      made pale the mountain
        and tortured sight
          with fire's dust and soot
We waited and checked into Frenchglen
The hotel's peaceful room
        that had no television

Waited until the smoke changed direction
Then kissed our way to Kiger Gorge

The trees that bent were undiscovered then
It was before we learned
      anywhere on the mountain's a summit
      even glades far removed
        and quite deserted
        whose wayside charms
              would detain

A woods
>that makes a free offer of campground
>and shelter

And now more pretending
>that we found them after all
>>tilting as they do
>>>from ninety degrees
>>>>of upright symbolic

The mobile animal of humankind
>allowed a metaphor
Dancing to it
Lithe as the branches
>splotchy with shadows and dappling

The light touch of twisting trees
>>>filling in the foreground

More pretending
>that from now on
>we know a grace
>>unexpected on a ravenous planet
Knowing justice is always momentary

But I'm happy for you and happy for me
And maybe
>it's time the younger grades
>and our single digit selves
>>are reclaimed for ballet
>>when we are standing straight
>>>>and taking deep breaths

Before the downland's found
The treeless slopes   barren perhaps

This little lake and minimal mirror
While the white trees are entrusted to us
>who are right now beyond all costing

I think the crackie would have liked all this
>but not the leash
>so he had to stay home
We could not have stood his disappearance

We however
        are entitled to this vanishing
                this eclogue
                these seconds allowed

And ourselves   new patients
For a limited time
        that's been expanded
                to hear your songs   also wordless
                                    that Rachmaninoff would love

Culture of two in the temperate trees
Public figures, even
With freedom of speech
        to eschew the bitcoin
                and facepalming
                all the endless emojis

We're listening to other voices
                in other rooms than rented

Entirely lawless
Except for the rule
      that dreams may be as precise
                            as cubics

55.   BRIGHT TREES

We stopped our sugar cravings
                            in the presence of the bright trees

Their bark was like a sobriety
                based on texture and feel

The bright trees
        had caught the light just right
        had sought a city
That they might share their achievement

But they were turned back at the gates
For the city was of stone
                      and showed no interest beyond its limits

We stopped our drinking, too
There was something about the branches
A more agreeable complexity
                      than drunkenness

The way they respond to the slightest draft
      proved a sensibility
            beyond alcohol's resentments

In the presence of the bright trees
        we said our amends
             to matters inexplicable
And to the birds which nevermind
                      by the shore of the nameless lake

And the light was like
                a special offer of clarity
As when you decide
      to walk out on oppression
      and find a way to do that
            so you are not missed at all

Now, there's no one left
In the emperors' palaces
      no one truly caring
So the world
            will set its own thermostat
                          accordingly

And Gaia   the forgotten   will be sad

Yet the bright trees and their birds
              confound the clocks there are
Those second hands
      that would measure the moments
      and presume to acquire
            with rapid spinning
           some semblance
                of enlightenment

Slowing for nothing
Revolving past "Aha!"
     to pester the future with impatience

The bright trees' roots
          have taken care of everything
                    we know!

For this is our home
     that's made a home planet possible
         long lasting
            as the gods
            and goddesses
                may show an interest

Look carefully!
There's a recovery possible
A theory
     that takes the bright trees
          as a starting point

That moment
     when language begins all over again
A perfect syntax prior to dissembling
And perhaps
     if those same words turn into song
          then language stays respected
          and not subject to any subpoena

The computers
     have ceased their publications
         and await disconnection
         and the peace of shallow lakes
It had been wrong of electricity
         to lead them on

Just so have we stopped our cravings
         for absolutely anything at all

56. LAGO TRANQUILO

Call it "Lago Tranquilo"

Lake on the way
A reverie

It was to study the level
     and be on it
         thinking of the flatness

Call upon a lake
     to improve the EKGs
         their worrisome oscillations
Calm the spikes
Diminish the graph

Even the Spanish have settled down
And do not risk any heart attacks
            with further conquests

That is why we'll call it "Lago Tranquilo"
Even if no one else does
     passing by so very *agitato*
     they miss the *quietoso*

I say it's an ocean of less than an acre
And going in   it stays still   mostly
Even splashing fails to ruffle the *wa*
     which is like a gift
         from zen-modified Japan
         that keeps on gleaming

Not everyone's lucky enough
But I remember
Like an act of defiance is recall
     and romantic even
         though one's partner is solitude
And getting back to the hotel
         thinking of phone calls made
         to doctors the day I was born

Lago Tranquilo was a variety of mirror

    made for the sky
      that captured the clouds
Like a preternatural theory of reflection
A pool that's fairy tale

One that starts small
      then spills into everything
     everywhere you go
A baptism in search of a celebrant faith
Ready as the water is exquisitely still

Old letters rewritten for brand new reasons

The one-year-old's mind
The amniotic realm remaining fresh
  the baby knowing how good he has it
  and will float in the *crib*
    as long as possible

Delaying speech
So that mothers and fathers are surprised
      by sudden complete sentences!

 It's a professional lake
A precious body's last act
  that allows you to take a dip
    in what the truth has been hiding

The things that can be fixed in half an hour
Mistakes which resemble such fixing
You just wade in
  it's rocky but oozy
    like the bottom of the sea
     where a fivefold oblivion waits
       music
       patience
       kindness
    love
    and drowning

You are Narcissus
  unaware there's only one of you
   the transition to perfection vicarious
A best-tasting alternative

An afterwards before an anything
Clear-complexioned
      as the day youth came courting
           and schools
              were its theater of strange

Not even a kiss was required
The way a lake is evenly balanced
                          between its shores

I began speaking Spanish
A tailored glossolalia
      far beyond mere "Lago Tranquilo"

It was an historical Spanish
What Coronado might have said
      if he'd have made it to the lake
         come this far north to swim

It could happen again
           with horses and Indians
The search for The Seven Cities of Cibola
      renewed!
That looking for love in all the wrong places

With lovely "L" the 12th letter
And two "I's" sounding

It was to study the glass
The watershed of level light
Thoroughly cognitive
           shy of the parkway's washboard gravel

Pray the car stays started while it's tested

Sadly   the EKG will resume
The lake earthquakes pulsing
Sadly   The Science
      will climb back on its throne
         of certainty
         and anonymous conclusions

And the places you don't go
                are sorry you leave

With no help
      was Lago Tranquilo "discovered"
And no teacher taught the language
                    of Coronado
No team of experts counseled awareness

Steens Mountain was motive enough
The cracked-open sky has truly fallen down
      to be a symbolic pond
         whose miniature shore
            is for baby steps and first dates
When you're on-the-level
And disbelieving
      there could ever be another

That time before
      when a hometown was safety

That reverie of single digits
Before they double
      and make strange demands of children

If war was like the lake
      it could not be fought

And now ghostly inner tubes drift
      in a grade school breeze
      while the study concludes
A little *agitato* despite barely a ripple
              for all of half an hour

The first moments of beginner zen
An amusing version
      that seeks the earliest *wa*
         one that boys and girls would take to
            being so recently of the Void

This will be a Spanish moment
The West and the East in a glade of Steens
Their union finally afforded and sparkling
                      balanced between its beaches

Lago Tranquilo

A lake on the way to unseen heights
Completing the slant from the wetlands
      unafraid of the curves
          and coming around
                  at last

57.   LAKE STONES AND TAN HILLS DESERTED

Deserted   this neighboring shore
These boulders made a margin of error
      that edges placid   multicolored
Its years and years ago brought up to date

All our friends would agree
And do so without using big words

How does it work?
The landscape's self-expression
      like a form of anticipation
          answers prior to questions

The lake's an emergency service
      provided in a Land of Numbers
A colonial mind may rest from the fever
These stones an agreeable respite
                and cooling-off

Set foot in these waters
The megahit of fame postponed
      for the sake of one's health

Tan is the color

And just for fun
          shows all its *shades* of tan
      in all that space forthwith
A quality of light
      parsed for its pioneer thought
      knowing we understand

        once stopped
             and *allowed* understanding

Southeast Oregon
     presenting a better life than stardom

The producers and directors are out of script
I ran off and ran out of gas
There'd been an oath to continue anyway
     until a caliper's measure
          told a story of correctness

There's a secret recipe that followed
Displays of emotion not qualified by witness
One might be executed privately and
     accept the ending
         as if with a bystander's calm

History was happening
Just starting
     with a bouldered lake
        and those tan surroundings
        memory's reality

The past has conjured a mountain
     whose lower slopes
        dismiss the present
          with Ice Age gestures
          while providing brochures
Another world's exactitude

I behave accordingly
Boulder to boulder   a confession of faith
The middle distance raised up ochre
     and inviting angels of an afternoon
     that attend to wide-open
Their marathon protection
          extended to every guest

The lake is a watery court
          conceived for cinema's sake
The movie's epic understated
When out-of-this-world runs back in
     to be accessible enchantment

One's classy pajamas
                              worn in broad daylight
The End has never seemed such a holiday!
A new book opened to the best part
      and never minding the rest of the plot

Spying on the wilderness
      with Nature's permission
      with whispered encouragement

The stones are a sunken pavement
Wanting bare feet
      for a stationary rodeo with ripples

The Space Race ended
                              from the look of things
I'll say nothing else till you get here
In your Fifties rocket
      with fins and organ music

And don't tell anyone!   not yet
That same Wurlitzer is warning against it
I put the dots together
      with the help of sage
           and scenes supernatural

Sought the edge and finish
Two heads and no tails
When duality's bested
      by just a minute of monomania

Here   soaking
      other music than what you've made
           is rehearsed and played
                for an audience of ancestors
                      beloved of mythmakers

I hardly know them
How long have the good witches waited
      to captivate
         dispel the sobbing   and wailing
                              of all the world?

When you think about it
Somehow airless   helpless

Just see how the lake and its stones oblige!
How settled!   like a country of Indians
                           the first months and years since Asia
The first intelligence and native surmising
First swim begun
     wading from a stony shore

As a tribal ensemble come to fresh water
     and so much more amidst the birches
The anthem of the megafauna still heard
Their injuries suffered
                   with awful premonition

58. ORDINATION AT KIGER

You'll be made a minister, my love
A Minister of Kiger
Your full-time cathedral
        a groove of the glacier
A full-time position with nearby piano keys

You'll have the run of the place
You will say,
     "I made it back to ballet
         even here
         in the pure chill of the westerlies!"

A woman you are
         who will much become the honor
And I've brought you Super Beets
              for the occasion
We've returned to the place
           where you once stood
     so very expectant
  at the great void of Kiger   scary

And you'd shied away
Not entirely trusting the viewpoint
Like an accomplished musician
                        wary of the conductor
                        the wand   a delicate transparency

"Made it back…"
It was always a refrain
                  one that encouraged   like scripture

Your robes have arrived
Think you're going to love the getup!
It's festive   and colors you lovelily
      like the best of purple
               its darkest shade

A dye applied
        to balance the Old West's earth tones
We've talked about them   remember?
               the bequest

You'll be primsie thus attired
A pupil and a preacher both!
A foreign feeling   qualified by magic

I am your acolyte
        here   and elsewhere   always
I'll take back your smile to the lowlands
A way to supplement the good times
The *also* benefit of knowing you
                   young as you are

A new day promised by your ministry

We have gone beyond Beyond
                     to get you here
To be on high   ordained
Orthodox as a nod to Constantinople
      the incense of sage added
      that "one more thing"
                     of Columbo's searching
A part of the mystery *you're* a part of
With icons and Russians
            meddling and elusive

Kindness   *your* kindness
                              has come to Kiger
    that only expected rough winds
        and bad weather
          the length of its canyon

The green must now intensify
The watercourse accentuate itself
      the last of the snowfields brighten
Even shadows will doubt themselves
      and do not too much darken the walls

My thoughts are of you
Beginning with "Petrushka"
When Stravinski became the best
                         of Ballet Russes
    and so was seen again and again!

It was the treasures of a displaced culture
One may become an *aficionado*
      wishing *all* of it were known
We are neighbors in time
And easily go next door to pre-war Europe

Of course we can!
Creatures of a future suspected by Picasso
      we see how this ceremony
           honors Nijinsky
           and all his company

Artists in Oregon
      witness your ordination
        well-wishing   time traveling
Asking what secular concerns
            have come 'round to ritual

That will be over and over
As Diaghilev's proscriptions
        and peremptory commands
           what he always had in mind

But the door is unlocked
        that is "entrance" only

Nearly invisible   with stepping stones, too
The cathedral a terrain
        that nobody knows
            until obsession is known
The grownup version of "let's pretend"

Costumes sewn with holy intentions
Testing the fabric for belief
You'll be a minister of music
        played by the absent glacier
            that "made it back"
                to cool the fevers there are

While there's a lull in the proceedings
While everything waits
            to rush over the brink
We'll be wonderful
        happy with this tomorrow
                this state of mind
International before there were nations!

Your first words awaited like an education
As guests of the mountain
                for its final hours as tourist attraction

We've come from the abandoned rooms
        of the Juniper Lodge
We're here to spread an existential gospel
At Kiger   cathedral and gorge
Its emptiness an invitation accepted

I will believe what you say
        enrobed and windily enhanced
Will say it's a solution
The truth of a text
        that is bland without your recital

Introductions made
        it was your turn
            to say what you see
            from the brink of Kiger
What ministry is possible
What ceremonies

We're here for the answers
For when a new job's a holiday from crime
And noticing
       every crevice
            ridge and tower   of Steens

The leftover snow
      like a verified ideal
           prays for more of the same
           and the winter storms
                      to make it so

Where you are, my love, is a reference point
      the first consideration
And the cassock and stole
           draped about you
     purple as can be
         is a fashion's vacation

Last year you'd promised
And earlier than planned
      were your vestments found
      and worn as preview
          of the day down which
              your ordination should proceed

I have trouble trusting anyone but you
If that's a faith
      then Now will know its formal start
With yourself in the aisle of blessed stone
Always appealing

The only place
         geology's second fiddle is played

How can we lose?
I'm only thinking
      the answers come before the questions
That's how certain I am of your loyalty
To a truth transcending curiosity

The perfect crime of the hominid
         was learning to love the lie
It has taken this many years

                              to discover the mistake
Nothing quicker was possible
And not much more of the mystery
                                        is known
         though the road to knowledge
                     was always toll-free

The hologram church is now attended
                              by transparency
Spirits   creatures of pure logic
The sum of learning sung
         kneeling or standing ghostly

And there's no rush
For it's understood
         the ordination
            your induction
                  will never be over
But proceed with uncanny precision
         to summer's last portal
                  and know its clarity

A marathon of thought
Like the winds' abundance

Any requests?
You can't be turned down
If you ask for Rachmaninoff
         his "Vespers"
                  then a choir's found forthwith
And its background entered into

Full-time is the chorus, then!
As your ministry is also that
Out on your own
         the better to bring it all back home
                  in some sixties sense
                  and having the run of the place

A place for us with a discount peace
                  that was always priceless
The great void amenable
         to accomplished musicians

A different kind of hospital constructed
                    one for those who are well

You were always a refrain
      that applied balance
            to light-and-dark earth tones
Young as you are
      yet a newer day is not impossible

The watercourse
            spreads its green downstream
Picasso's been notified
And all his acolytes swim to his palette

Obsession is known   gives relief
Wants no payment but continuation
Your first words remembered
                  like the mountain

Or a beautiful plot with robes mostly purple
A verified ideal
      when I am trusting no one but yourself
      that this will lead
            to acceptance of others

It was to discover mistakes
                  I brought you to Kiger
I can live with knowing
      there was no ulterior motive but love

Let's talk about this
We can talk about *anything*, right?

This road before us?
A time period
      that's only the moment it takes
      to say "Yes!" to a U-shaped immensity
                  and the ordination it longs for!

59. WHY YOU WENT

I could say it was why
That the "gunsight" was why
Why the long drive on the washboard loop

Could mention the bite taken
                         out of the horizon

The interrupted ridge
The feature with the nickname
             derived from weaponry

What's going on is   "gunsight"   is
                                       not to be
"Gunsight" is canceled
The tag   the label   the conformity   removed

Something left to no imagination
If it's pure geology
        one will not travel it
             to enter into hunting
               the very land an aid to aiming

If the sun shines the name will go missing
The arcuate go missing a bead
The "cut" mean something else
Bringing you closer little by little
        the skyline enlarging
          until it's a hugely-known notch
              that language will resist
                        with keening

Why you went is spared the culture
                        of violence

The jagged draw
      which the ice has made
          will conjure a wordless reset

The senses are the lesson   winding
The goal in and out of view
      and out of reach entirely

"Gunsight" is coercion
So this advice to the world:
        shut up for awhile
            leave the landscapes alone
                      until further notice

The overlook at Kiger attests to silence
Why you came   no gunshots
For once history's told without battles
                            and plots

Before the full extent of our injuries are
                            known
Please!   nirvana bursting with just-as-is
I'm the empire's pillows   satin-comfy
I'm bedding down without inventions
And behold the heights above
                      with indifferent calm

Pleased to fall out of favor
Explanations why anything matters?
We'll just tell the muse, "Good girl!"
She's made it perfectly clear
               she doesn't need us

Maybe it's a good thing "gunsight" isn't said
Isn't recited or jotted down
Around a corner of birches
               the epic gap is unwritten

One may be surprised by its grandeur
All over again freed of description
                    that seeks to artificially preserve

It's better this way
Magnificent as it wants to be
     without myself
    or anyone at all
            having a say

The price of a label unaffordable, too
Understanding one another not at all

It's better   and Nature wants it that way
        however shocking that may seem
Even "Kiger Gorge" is just pieing
                        a jumble of letters

60. MOON PERFECT

The moon was perfect arising
Perfectly round   perfectly bright

And the rocks beneath its theater
        took no notice
                owing to their own perfection

They simply didn't like the moon's ideas
                                and looked away

61. THOSE MILLIONS OF YEARS

Those millions of years
So long unattended
                the prehistory quit altogether

It could have been many countries
                        in all that time
The basics of life barely known
A goalless time
When the lavas were stacked and layered
        and called a geologic success
                        of the Miocene

The nearly forgotten rocks
Their astounding dimensions
        like a framework for giants

        who have their say and get their way

So long adamantine
        the planet's a fortress of itself
Such real estate
        the price is a fantastic fiction

You leave your house
And leave it to the whims
            of a deep-seated mantle
Its millions of years exposed
        as push-back surface

It's possible to see things so unknown
        the very crust of the Earth's impeached

What's done in the dark
        is today a rapture of the sunlight
        and leverage
            exposing irresistible energies
The next Sundays adjoined
        for one long service of stone
            that tells no human lies
            and credits heat alone
                with wisdom

A just-nevermind mountain
Blameless   forgiving
The last universe we will ever need

You said something
        about a better way to worship
        than being constantly surprised by evil
Something about a search
        for a low-cost monastery

The suspense of having patience
        in the prison of a dream
            that seemed destined to recur
            as cruel reality
            whose warden is conscience
                saying, "Please be fair!"

The razored centuries are sharpened further

They ask the questions raised by karma
What was done right
      that allowed this look into immensity
      and its phases
           paying volcanic dues
           to friendly ghosts
                from the Hot Spot
                      that started it all

We've come to see the ages
They'll talk to us
      but it will be a private conversation

The first day of Eternity was sunny
We'll be married as if it's the Thirties
      make it the Forties
      when people said
           "Swell!" and "Sure!"
                followed by "Now beat it!"
In the culture's *own* millions of years

We'll never give up
But make good sense of it all
Another chance
      like basalt's second chance
           beneath the worrisome Earth

In a moment you'll be asleep   splendidly
With the Pleistocene returned

I'll be fierce as all those years compressed
The right demeanor
      for the first decades
           of the incoherent 21st century
           its horizon not trustworthy
Its excuses
      a chain of countless murmurings

I don't understand unless you tell me
And   most recently
    your summary seemed a blessing
    unlikely to expire
        though Steens
        and all its millions of years

>   fully fall down

A lasting sentiment to confound geology's
Its crumbling future like a futile aside

62. FAST-FORWARD

Worse shape?
Worst shape?

The original world
>   though coaxed by Rachmaninoff
>   yet insisted on popularity merely
>   and paper-thin morality

Favorite things become dreadful things

Who will keep it all from uncontrolled
>   tumbling
>   like an asteroid's journey
>   to nothing at all but proton decay?

Technically it's early spring and that's swell
But we want December
>   no matter the gifts that appear

Delight alone will be enough
When the future says we're still together
>   still have rings and things of our own
And with this momentum it won't be long

You have to have the right poem in hand
One with the right wording and syntax
All the lost ones as well
>   together with the crooks
>   who stole them to pay for People Magazine

The original world is the worst
With its icy oughts and shoulds

and cruisin' for a bruisin'

A short time from now
      the last minute of the universe
          will tick its seconds off
When we're still together
      and we figure out the night and the day

If you prefer other opposites   that's fine
Or something extra added to finale
A gamble it won't get worse than oblivion
      the start of the original world
              not so different

We'll keep it all in mind gazing at the Alvord
      that's sinking further
         and perhaps fast-forward
Keep perspective entrained in a technical
                      spring
Our favorite things to outlast dreadful

I don't know what to do
I don't know how I met you
And wonder always
      why I was so gifted by your voice

And right now
          your crimson scarf
            evokes an acceptable conclusion
 The final pages of all else
      being turned by cosmic shut-ins
     who wish to dance
         to your rings and things
            that jingle dangerously
                    as befits finale

Rushing forward in the dark
    it is easy to die
        without appreciation *of* dy*ing*
So I pray the gifts of tumbling clocks
                may not distract

The East Rim of it all
    is left to a cello   in recital

        of Rachmaninoff's off-center sonata
            that insists
                on coaxing the Immortals
                                to uncertainty

All the while speeding   uncontrolled
Our own companion spirits
        that enable and promote
                the mystery of Distance

63.   CALL BACK

You know what I mean   and always do
And yet you won't call back

Call back
You know what survival means
        and said we might manage that
             yet you haven't called

Call back
We do not all believe the same
        or think too much of living space

But we can talk   talk about anything
Call back

You know that taffy's bad for you
And the bag of it
        you brought from Mount Rushmore
                     well, it's almost gone

Can't you call?
Call back
        my own call not deserving of this silence
It's so much quicker than a letter
The phone's what the future was for
Get my drift?   do you?

Sure!   always you know

It's not as if I lecture newly
The rest of my life is calling   call back
      whatever the dimes it takes
          and warnings given not to

I'll stand by
The ending is amends
A call-back
      knowing all you know
          and want to find out

I'm serious   today and tomorrow
Reciting the familiar words
      as if first introduced to them
      and time is a novelty
          just a hunch
              as in detective stories

Your confession is wanted
Our weather's
      an inversion layer
          that meteorology has arranged

You know survival depends on getting air
Your controlled study
        your patient suspicion
             that all is not well

Please answer

Put together your hands
        and more seriously
          than the last time you prayed
And I will answer   quietly
            with reassurance

I'll ask,
    "Is it really you
      or a spirit's convenient deception?"

I'm telling you only what I've been told
        in the wilds of Steens Mountain
And if you'll only call
      we'll believe the same things

>   if only for a little while
>   watching and listening

64. NOT SOMEONE WHO MAKES A LIVING

I'm not someone who makes a living
Living here is not a job well-done
                    but that's expected

The landscape listens   learns your identity
Protects its gold and silver

Best I stay unemployed
        when any stitch of work
                must stop my own learning

This is the next stop made the last
A good night's sleep that taps the Void
I'll not be someone set on leaving
        or how to go on   life under control
        my voice so many recommendations

Remove the mountain
Or let it lie flat
        as it did before the basalt raised itself

There isn't a theory   a future   a court
And random Nature
        will make its living and dying
            as if it's a job
                what's expected
                    however suddenly
                    or infinitely later

Out here
        I only wish you'd stayed a little longer
Your voice to calm the chasm
            that this assessment is
Your hands to shape the stone

Your wisdom to outwit unfeeling destiny
The certain medicine you bring to healing

And just heading down a highway
      patient   as always   I'll be
        that certain science fiction might be told
           in the semi-arid fastness

65.   ALVORD, BELOW THE AIRPLANE OF LAND

Look down

Alvord   the remnant   the seasonal lake
What the Holocene left out to dry
     as if in a hurry
        to make arid its pluvial masterpiece

And sky-high   the view's complete
All of its very square miles
     in tandem with agriculture's circles
      the sign
         that something more than desert
           strives

I stayed healthy only for this
Acceded to nutrition's austerity
Kept strong
     so that a farewell said
        should capture the crux
           of that devotion

Hoping I'd still see something of you
     seeing over this   edge
       to the Alvord's imaginary waters

There's coffee at the top
     where the airplane of altitude boils the brew

A solitary cup

Like secrets sipped
The wilderness is learned
Something may be safely told

Depth is a mother being
      brought to philosophy
Delivered alone as her offspring is found
                                      in perspective

The awful height has made us aware
And lightning thought
      for the moment touches doubt
      with rumbling consequence
Getting after the dreamer
      with sudden waking
          when the dreamer was entitled
                                    to more

Let Steens Mountain be my claim
And Alvord down there
      a better friend than the cities
Its small intermittent ocean of inches
      seen from a fifties plane
                    with propellers

Think about thousands of years
      as thousands of feet
So many   your own dozens of steps
              seem as seconds of life

A brevity above in the airplane of land
The hardware's lovely
Even the needlework
      that stitches the summit
      as if it aspired
          to a greatness it knows of
              but will not share entirely

Let the remnants   all the pieces placed
      return to the time
          of their separation from the whole

I heard you singing

        just when I was falling asleep

The altitude had lulled
Indiana came to mind
        though Alvord's level ground was all
I was back-and-forth
Thinking the midwest might be dry
        if I were sky-high eastwards
                over uncircled green

Let health announce new connections
And let your voice say
        they're made as soon
             as your song's sustaining tones

The first time we came to Kiger
The first instance of Big Indian Gorge
All of it was saved for later   every view
                  this had to be done

Though temporary pauses
        the briefest stops on the loop road
Yet the strange joys that commenced
The make-believe of it stuck around
        and became a beloved perspective

Something you saw
        that let me see better afterwards
Seeming aloft   as now
Alvord and a bride-to-be of the uplands
        looking forward
           to a full night's sleep
                in Holocene Nevada

I will never be set on leaving
The mountain can be a theory all alone
        whose proof is like a mind made up
A sudden waking to the same singer
        that offered intermittent lullabies

And brevity's
        granted a more substantive meaning

This is a study done before landing

       in lightning
          in thousands of feet of empty air
The dreamer is entitled
The dreamer knows everything

How grandly I wished
     for the Truth to land
          from out of Shelley's skiey places

Now the mystery is made a novel
     spinning subplots of itself
          till the story's open-ended
The Alvord to receive us
With its hot springs waiting   precisely

No one knowing the extent of our injuries
And no new developments
     in the realm of misfortune

Wide as Oregon our vision
Long as a dead sea can be
Tall as bird skyscrapers
        lost to migration

Our farewells postponed by wishful thinking

I stayed healthy
     that you might be reassured
         science
           and democracy
              are much the same
A politics of two persons only
Being a minimum jeopardy

Where trust is devotion   cross-country
Seeing something of you
     in the landscape's lightning

Who would have thought
     the seconds of life
        might be these steps taken with you
The remnants of all else abandoned

It's worked out well

>   despite ecstasy mistaken
>   for a fear of flying

66. IT'S A MILE

One mile
It's a mile
      that meant so much
A term
      an English measurement
        in conflict with Napoleon's kilometers

It *could* have stayed relevant
          the desert's distance down
          that mile made an exclamation
One's attention drawn to extremes
Topography's shout-out

But you'd have to be here for that
You'd have to be that someone to ask
      if the mile down was not a drama

So the Alvord's just depression
         where the meters and feet
          no longer compete
And the scenery's a model
             that keeps to itself

67. THE BLUE EAST

The car had a rattle
But enough of it worked to make it here

High up   divorced with a view
The blue east a comfort zone of light
        one's back to the west
              the more *obvious* attraction
              what the camera likes
                      and even prompts

It is not a land of sports
No competition
        stuns the silence with haste
              and frantic shouting
Thus the clock's enlarged
        that keeps Steens time

The blue east
        to last as long as you can stand it
The blue east baffled
The modest shade
        forcing philosophy past its doorstep
                      and far into the real world

What the coyote sees so well
A Cinerama that takes its own time
        everywhere seeking to be included

Blue has brought its better self to sundown
        dancing opposite the glare
              a mode of permission to impress
              that relies on less

It is a pale preserve
Wanting "Only the Lonely's" country western
                            thought

Mao's little red book reimagined
Reworded for solo capitalist appeal
Cagney's "Top of the world, Ma!" proclaimed
        in an improbable afterlife on Steens Mountain
What was the blue east planning?

What was I trying to say
        when the sky betrayed intentions?
And why does it matter you *know*?

It's astounding
      how the blue east fairly trembles
      with insistence it be found
Fleetingly perhaps
Like the last day
      before an asteroid's plummet
            spoils the view

This blue needs a placard
One that says it's a privilege
      an exceptional hue not easily afforded

And wheelbarrows filled with manuscripts
      are brought to rustic appointments
        with protest
        against a digital world

I'm staying faithful
To something I cannot describe
Something far   connected to the near
Empowered distance
      that fills in the foreground
        with thanksgiving's light
A blue recognition of common sense
            extending eastward as far as possible

Like an answer unexpected
      that came before the question
As many miles
      as the engine may imagine

The blue east makes music
Its very own soundtrack
24/7   the sounds of governance
      neither Left nor Right
      a symphony   a percentage of nirvana

There was a need
There was always a need
      to hear your main theme of marriage
A union entrusted to chance horizons
Where I   a favored customer
      end the program presented by fear

Never going to be the same
Yet I photograph your kind color for later
                          as if it were not true
And volunteer my artwork
        as the blue east volunteers eternity

A done deal that's gifted
        for the sake of some justice that lurks
                all ready to worry some villains

And the blue east
        is a little bit like going off to college
The way leaving home involves vistas
One celebrates the setting out
                proud before any achievement

The Hallmark card cannot be made
And Steens has stayed out of the blank rack even

Wait, though!
There might yet be a greeting possible
        one that says I'd do anything for you
                without rhyming
Words to make you wonder
        what's up so far from home
            you *make* it home
                for there's no going back

This same day
        the center of the world
        took advantage of peripheral error
The blue become companion sky
                            with no separation

The art unsold   and therefore safe

Is it too much to ask
        that the clocks be more comprehensive
That they stop for certain insights
            to show real character
                as ministers of time?

Perhaps there's time

For youthful grandparents' plans
        to see your *own* self ageless
All the things you talked about
        are topics that echo
                off sudden basalts discovered

Let roses tumble into the shadows
        to be nothing in the night to come
        but perfect love
                a scentful absurdity
All the square feet of Alvorto receive their petals

The better instincts of prayer rely on twilight
The names of ancient playmates
        yourself included
Very well!   the laws of childhood taught

Make it a comfort zone
        with the winds
                to soften the slightest prompt
                        of its lofty eddies

The sport of watching
        for as long as the east stays blue
The silence unhurried
        almost a holiday *present* of insight
Like those dreams among gifts
        that must wait till morning
The special privilege
        of sleep beneath the Christmas branches
                and their colored lights

But for how long?

A World War concluded
        there's a loss of electricity   strangely
The memory arriving last minute
Right here   almost modestly
                in a land without decorations
                where none are needed
                        besides the sun and moon
                            and sparse beacons
                                of nighttime's desert

Nothing can stop blue's journey to grey
"I've never seen you so beautiful!"
      talking aloud
I was about to say more
But the soliloquy must be all-at-once thought

Save something for later
For the real world   the ears of coyotes
If the Cinerama's true-to-life
      you'll dance to it
What was I trying to say to see you through?
Steens trembles with insistence
      to know all things
      that may not be described
The questions and answers
            like a dualism undesired

Only a symphony's free reign now
      that's never going to be the same twice
          yet gifts for the sake of justice
Music that is tethered to the Center
              till new notes suggest themselves

Is it too much to ask?
Blue to come true and continue
Last minute
      into the first hours
          of brand new mountains

68.   ALPINE PLACES TO COME

There are times in the future
      when you have to act it out
      when the future's blank spots need something

The landscapes are screenshots' kindly filler

These alpine places   are
      the future's retirement

                           gently exposed
The important moments
        that insanely expand
        to be hours and days
                of red-hot concern

You're pictured approximate
In a technicolor context

There are times to come
        that require
                the rogue strands of DNA be replaced
At least you have to act as if it's all all right

The bright future
        is slimmed down amid awkward segues
The tundra will do
With Rachmaninoff's "Vocalise"
                to smooth things over

Maybe you thought transitioning easy
If you just went along   just sayin'
The Universe is cracked
        its most foolish dimension
                the fourth
                is time stuck in doubt

This only happens in the future
But method acting and props help
Such a background as Steens' highest places
                        and your fearless soprano to sound!

You didn't know you were needed this badly
These alpine scenes
        comprise a no-nonsense setting
                for repairing an imperfect epic

God's movie
With a cast of billions busy in the sprockets

That's when the stand-ins step up
Their most tentative substitutions
        enough to stitch the future back together

So the angels can make all their appointments

It will be fun to see how it all turns out
I mean   past the present future
     with entropy wanting to end it all

Think I'll keep this background awhile
     the millennia furious to unravel
Any reservations to be serviced on high
     like the gaps that lie ahead
     the continuum's potholes
     asphalted with deceptions

My acting's earned an Academy-level award
Being in place
     for when the script runs out
     and the words wind down
A little jealous of the perfect past
So shapely and detailed
     and becoming more so
     with retrospective scrutiny

I'm envious
Of Certainty knowing
     exactly when
     the gladiators fell in early C.E.

Oh!   call it A.D. again!
     just to make trouble
     just to be in the In Crowd
Showing black-and-white-and-grainy
The home movies of Caligula

Sometimes   in the future
     there aren't even stills
     and you have to take selfies
     or ask onlookers to snap
Not just yourself
But all the others in the quicksand of timeout

The flora and fauna
     that outlast the cold
     are the future's stopgap
The *many* futures foretold as final bedtime stories

The ones that try to keep you awake
    as long as possible
Look, it's cheery here in Nostradamus Land
The thinnest slice of Antarctica trending
               like a theory of completion

The only way I'll complain
    is if you try to strike the set
Don't you know that being grateful's becoming?
Aren't you glad
    you found out what to expect
    when you go fishing in the future, too?

Is it not reassuring
    the life you'll live
        will be a director's cut
            with coaching, even?
The Stanislowski Method
An all-encompassing cosmology of takes

The guy with scene numbers
    fulltime snapping and folding his slats
And the extras to-and-fro with rehearsals
Ready to say something   anything
              if the set falls silent

In the future
    the stars will hunt for mountain goats
    bemoaning the lesser role of fame

"You won't drink so much," I tell them
"When you can't even afford a spear
    in your faulty retirement from stage and screen
"But learn well these tidings!
Even technicolor's returning
       to cocoon your afterlife!"

69. SHIPS

Revealed   the prow
Or is it the stern?

                an exotic construction
            in a region of hulls aslant
                    ancient ships
                            jammed in the mountain
                            their destinations forgotten

A public understanding
        of private enterprise run aground
And all in one place
It was the ship of uplift
        like a mother's imposing questions asked

Revealed   the deck is a wreck
                            its priceless cargo strewn

What pilgrim vessels are these
        uncovered by imaginary seas withdrawn!
Their stone timbers
                like crushed experiments
                        cartooning the terrain

The rich and famous wild-scheming
        where the sky's limits
                were found   catastrophically
Born balloonist vessels snagged
                                        and gone beyond

The blue east
        silhouettes the ship's rough decking
Lofty ports now impractical dreams
For   permanent is the dry dock

And sorry the seas that miss their boats
        now petrified entirely
            their boards
                    made a rampart's profile

70. DISTANCE

With even bionic vision
    the maximum's unseen
    unknown
    unusable beauty

Like a *destiny*
    is distance seen without eyesight's consent
What's not understood is blindly sought
But somebody had to try
And now   anywhere
    fans out to be somewhere   removed
        used before and safely

No telescope remembers
Out of nowhere
    the pleasing apprehension of here to there
        dangerous as it may be to go

Though far away is hard to see
    the mind acquires a sense of dancing
        in the *streets* of distance
And towns   if there are any
        are just like a home

What pioneer months it might take!

Your arrival's
    going to look like this closeup constant
Any signal sent in your name
    is received
        as if a gentle voice
        had whispered something
And you turn over the concept of separation

I'm out of everything but untrustworthy visions
Of the thousand other peaks and valleys
    I'd like to think there was a last time
            for them all

Why is it
    those lands far removed are preferred?

The indefensible foreground perhaps
Standing on the ceremony of helplessness
Standing right here without bionic abilities
                            bullies make their beds in plain sight

And   their wickedness identified
        a place is imagined
                or maybe glimpsed in the haze

A maximum unknown   slightly revealed
Enough it seems a paradise or even heaven
"Over there" without a war to go to
Just a formal uncertainty
        and possible promise
An appealing suggestion
        that Christmas may be year-round
                      should distance be found

Like a destiny future soldiers look for
        in all those formations
               with banners and slogans
That better life
        whispered by tyrants
        when the shouting's over

Strange how what is known's become a trap
The familiar become a kind of oppression
        fostered by a limited vision

I'll go for the warfare of fog
        that shines invitingly far
                an injunction pronounced
                        to stay put
I'll follow the silhouette of hills barely seen
        their vague horizon
        like a mandate for wandering

It's going to be interesting   all this freedom
The symptoms of *ennui*
        returned to their box

Right now the moon itself has plans
                to travel its own space
                eager for the next orbit

                and brighter for the chance

It isn't world fame that's sought from afar
Rather a decent percentage of privacy
      for the sake of continued study
      and its viable fantasias

The control these summit surroundings exert
        with their crisp rocks and plants
            and scurrilous demands
            they be a measured environment
                and not scolding the daydreamer

I'm applying for a scholarship in effortless art
The subconscious playground
      that's not unlike this beautiful distance

Shall I offer you the flight?
      the visa?
           the time you'll need?
And if there are others like yourself
           might they be persuaded?
Their arrival there   and yours
                a celebration!

Make a wish that involves distance
That better life
      those questions remaining
           that a telescope sights
Nowhere's superior credentials
Its scrambled pixels devoutly to be wished for

Let the sweep of music's *lontana* direction
                summon the will to fully escape

71.   TUFTS

I couldn't do it
There was a schedule but I couldn't come down

Not right away leave that white sun summit
        the late day bleaching the inclined grass
It would be harder
        to follow the washboard later down
                far down
                where it winds
                      by the edge of Big Indian Gorge
But see it *now*
The sublime benign neglect
        that leaves the mountain alone
                and lets a larger past than human
                      take over

No loudspeakers
And no mindless vowel of collective awe
The patient axons atop the rise of Steens
The alpine tufts so slightly aquiver!
How easily they held captive the stranger
        who would stay a stranger here
            for no matter how long
                descent was delayed

So I couldn't budge
The paper that named the plants
        concentrating on the land high up
            and bursting with tundra
Concerning a different tundra
                from the Rockies
                      from elsewhere

All of this mountain's zones
Sufficient islands
        their botany's solo presentation

A distant planet embedded in our own
        and wanting my discovery
            and a heads-up in Houston
And lingering   like astronomy

Oh, I'll get to the science
        if you'll only stay awake a little longer
The Latin recital
        a performance poem
                of thank-yous

       for the prompt of tawny tufts
            their elevated perfection

The information given to runaway children
Knowing they'd come here first
     to play marbles
     or just sit quietly   forever elusive

I can see well enough
       to know it's hay that trembles
           that will never be a harvest
           that eschews machines

Now, since I couldn't retreat
And saw only a destination achieved
Nothing in the night of lower down attracts
This is how a tourist turns to ash or stone
       and is windswept-enlightened, even
                     though it isn't required

The clock that's ceased its project
      of minutes   and seconds
           yet tells enough time
               you fall short of *za-zen*

It's safety that's surprise
       when you consider the geology
And the grass is secure
        albeit roughly anchored
           with roots in the rocks

Rocks that seek a miracle
     promised by the Ice Age

I have strength and dexterity
      though there is no task to perform
The late day understands
Pauses for the newcomer
Willing even
       to be part of an alternate universe
          to do so

Mine's a following gaze   uninterrupted
I follow the sweep of this Space pasture

      follow the edges
      follow the space of add-on worlds
How they join with our own
              when no one's looking

Follow Steens
The ridge where *you* may be
              in some sense of being!

Yes another reason I remain
And remain your most devoted admirer
Here you could ride
Here in Horse Heaven go bareback
              effortless again   as always

And I'm waiting the way you do
    between the measures of Bach
            to make sure
And the larger past than our own
    takes bets with the future
    on just how long we'll hang around

We're sunlit   strangely unchilled
    in Steens' pantry
Its final assembly and commission
                most northerly
The fault block of God's Great Basin
        composed in F Minor

Things may have moved around too much
But the birds are happy
    and float at will
        in the waterfall of air over

I couldn't leave the education
      of the tufted heights
      with imaginary drum solos
      wanting commencement's exercise
                  and pushing back

Wanting the road and its washboard
      to wind even higher
          through patient eons

        enticing strangers
                to study the ground cover

Slowly pronouncing the Latin lightly
        that treats us to uncommon syllables
So that you linger past information
Seeing well enough to know
        perfection's possible landing places

If you fall asleep it's over
Those stabilizing tufts
        to lose consciousness as well
                and be times remembered
                as Bill Evans is remembered

The fable can accommodate tufts
There may be a fable such
        the botany of bunch grass is central
It might be just a page-and-a-half
But poetry's the explanation
        how a fable might be brief

Who has ever known betrayal can relate

Think I'll leave out
        the list of tufts
        not trusting their scientific canon

This is a chapter of staying
                in place
                in time
In the middle of the mountain's lengthy ridge

Here it is possible
        to understand one thing
        the way a gardener
                concentrates on roses
The white sun's regime
        to sense the need for intermission

An almost Persian remoteness
The slightest memory of Xerxes
Some day
        when his ambition exceeded his borders

I could not have escaped
And remain
      out of certainty this day
      that the eons are waiting
           on just this gamble
A game to become a vigil
Something not planned
      but once begun
      must run its course
           in a single late afternoon

Like a foreign language that becomes your own
Or a fate narrowed to specifics
Your destiny
      written down in small notebooks for later

If ever the winding road is resumed
Past the drop-off of Big Indian Gorge
      and thence to those wild horses
                gathered below

72.   GREY AND GREEN

The air itself has color
The air is happy to be painted
      and that way connected to the land

On a slow ride   departing
      grey and green
           are a contest for attention
           one that gets inside you
                and startles the artist-self

And I'd investigate
Delve into those shades
      see what's new in the sense of sight
Let grey and green
      be as important as they want to be

        and beyond the rubber stamp
                of black-and-white

Picasso's inner circle's been consulted
They say he's still number one
Say he'd agree
        that grey and green
          should run together
             down the mountain
In such a way
        that colors and listening conjoin

Having come back
        to Steens   to the outback
            the going away is tough
               but doable
The next destinations reached
       to be a road trip's product
         perhaps decided upon
               with mathematical precision

The life beyond
        with horses to come
           will be a new way
          to manage the old
             without a doctor, even

Who was your father
        that he never gave warning?
Or said what it would take to see in color
        though your identity were stolen?

This is no next-best thing
Rather a palette's perfection
I don't know what I'm doing
        but I'm almost done doing it
Twisting on the washboard road
        where the ghosts of Big Indian Gorge
                 grab the wheel
               attempting total control

But I'm down safely
And shopping for light in the gloaming
For a special grey-green edition of country

      where families strove to farm
      and first faced the winters of the West

A grey and green interior fresh
The snows a happening
      without interference
The greater comfort of adversity
      informing all else

Until I met you
    warehoused I was
    in a city of *noir*
    not knowing
      I wanted
        so very much more
          after so very little

73. DREAM OF AN ARGUMENT

I'm wondering
    what the bullet will do that finds me
    determined as myself
      to be discordant emissary

I'll look but will not see
The Christians have given up
      grown hateful even

There's a fire built that burns beyond quenching

And   barely alive
    a journey's resumed
      without a champion spirit to guide
        or impart a lifegiving truth

It was an argument
There isn't a lot of detail
    since all the dreaming
Long enough later

a letter of introduction
      would be needed
         to gain admittance to the memory

I know she cared for another
Who could it be?
Her husband?
      but I am that!

And she said she wished
      to work a job I myself had done
I'm sure I couldn't say
      why she wished to work in storage
But I said some nice things in between outbursts

I argued two days a week
      were two too many for a ballet girl
And the manager was not to be trusted
There seemed to be mail
      and he seemed to be throwing away
            the unclassified mail

I said to say Mass
That she must see to it the children attend
      though we believed in other things
            than catholic gods

Then the dream and its arguments vanished
Except for my questions left over
      that bridged into waking

"Who are you?
      and why must we fight in confusion?
Are two husbands not enough?
Or will you choose only one at last?
My better nature revived by your industry?"

There was a bullet
      but the bullet then slowed
      fires found a better fuel
         and travel was restricted to gratitude

74. VENUS CASTS A SHADOW

It could be insanity to wander alone
       and let the night lead you away astray
        to where longitude and latitude
           are unknowable crosshairs
           and you wind up dead ahead

Having the right stuff's a useless honor
For a patron of the arts adrift in *de facto*
       delusion may only worsen one's chances

And having strength you wander further
Ended   ending
       the way Rachmaninoff's symphonies do
       in a wilderness of theaters and major keys

It should be madness
       to be walking away
           into a strange meadow and thicket
           not knowing the exit
Indulging an obsession to lose direction
A search for Judy Garland
       all the Gumm Sisters
           overriding common sense

You find *reasons* to be lost
No one taking notice
It could mean the end
       but one stretching out all-inclusive

The early evening's heat
       perfect for reconnaissance
In the summer woods   a warning
                   though danger itself is sought

What does it matter you've no way home
       when Venus herself has cast her shadow?
There is no doubt the planet's done it
She's close enough
       and it's dark enough for this

Venus is Susan Hayward

   young and willing
      to shine as brightly as needed
      to accomplish her magic
As if she were trying out for the part

If there's a metaphor in all this
If shadows always signal sadness
If the darker outline
    darker than the land that Venus loves
      should feel left out of the light
            no matter

It's a muted spectacle
The strangeness of undoubted contrast
      the slightest
      albeit sharply seen!

The nearby planet proving its affection
Having something on its mind
    myself a wandering detective
    attempting telepathy with Susan
      beautiful and *happy* to shine

You don't sit in a chair
    but roam a wilderness accompanied
      not caring to return
Go for the reassurance of constancy
The hours to come attended un-alone

I'll find my way back
    if Venus is impressed with my devotion
If she fails to see why I should return
    it was enough
      to see that faint-definite cutout self
        that tracked the excursion
        her shadow   mine

But there's really no ownership
Wanting to know what's out there
    became a refrain of astronomy

"You ain't seen nothin' yet!"

Finding the right words

        is like detecting the umbra
You have to keep moving
        the blacker black to discern

And the pen stays in motion
        outlining its own shadows
            easier to see
                with that forward and ongoing rush

No passport was required
        in the land that Susan's Venus lighted
No passport whispered
        to a whispering goddess

A consultant might have cautioned,
"Don't do it!   don't go there!"
        in the New Age sense of "going there"
            when "there" is much more than a destination

Perhaps the risks involved
                might well have been argued
But ruin had never been a worry
        knowing utter destruction
            was already well on its way
            and further surrender
                    was an ironic extra

The pursuit of the second planet's shadow cast
        so far beyond a need for security
            I'm reckless on purpose

When last such a shadow was seen
        it was the ghost town of Garlock
            that provided the stage
An otherwise mean-spirited Mojave desert allowed it
With twilight's ending barely over
        the sky turned searchlight for the lonely

But I stood my ground   defiant, even
The rest of the Roman pantheon bemused

This time   oblivious
Now, in the night with Susan
        and returning to the forties

>   I concede the single Venus left
>   is determined on utter destruction

All playing
      in the big backyard
            of Steens Mountain concluded

75. THREE HOURS WITH THE WILD HORSES

The New World's just an island
A very large island but an island just the same

And the wild horses have it all to themselves
They could run from
      Alaska to Magellan's Strait
      under northern stars and southern
Unbroken distance   unbroken steeds

In the middle of that distance there they are
Gathered where the river
      called "Donner and Blitzen"
          smoothes out after the Gorge
          with no obligation to spill

The horses are surprised to see me
      so apparently tame
      with civilized ways
But I'm not what I seem

I'm ready to ride them   bareback
      the length and breadth of the island
Live happily ever after
        with hoofbeats' authentic tally
Developing veterinary instincts
      for endless equine holidays

A gallop that's simply jobs and kids
Three hours with equus

Wondering again
       how they get so big and strong
                      just by grazing

It's only a prairie
How is it possible
       I'd come to say goodbye so wildly?

The wild horses are ensembles
       under skies
             whose greys
             combine with blue
So appealingly I'll study them for understanding

The great island awaits
Its tremendous mass proposing I see it all
       a night watchman
              to watch the day from horseback
Perhaps the black beauty before me
             or the grey one

They are peacefully wild and deceptively celebrate
Do like I said and get some carrots
I'll make it worth your while
       maybe some sugar, too
       the mercantile store   Frenchglen

I'll practice being fearless
This is church
This is Colorado all over again
       Pueblo   when we rode the mesa
             the dry land
             cold in a February lull

I can't wait for that same state
It came calling with the first sight of the steeds
And a dream was recalled
       of the plains
       a beach before the Rockies
Like an inland coast range

We knew this littoral together
While the Spanish Peaks
       distant and evocative

    were saved for a future reconnaissance

I hated to say goodbye to them

But now there's a sudden reprise
What it means for all time
  to surrender to T.S.
  and be a quartet of tenses
Past, present and future
   to have a new companion:
   the stopped clock of emotion

How we outlive the lesser gods
    of routine measure

The wild horses are a lottery won
I was listening to music I remembered
That happens
  you hear it like a performance
A concert in Pueblo
   that tours the New World island
The cello players prominent
Smoothing the score
   its rough edges elided

A course is set
The great island
   undiscovered
    even by the First Peoples

A new start forever in ageless Hollywood
The "Western"
  an eastern northern and southern
Lands before thermostats
Lands that were lifted

For three hours manes
Evolution making sure
  that beauty makes a fortune
   all the shows since Hopalong rode

Am I still awake?
Or is it dreaming so new
   it only seems that way?

A high-pitched neighing
A whinny
    like an ancient voice
      calling in all directions
Unbroken distance inviting
        when the moment's right

You surprise the horses and yourself

Altogether comfortable
    and feeling strangely civilized
In concert with migration
    those millions of years
      since the eohippus roamed
        grew big
          and took the land bridge to Asia

Some lowered sea of the Ice Age
The great island become a *world* island
      and wild as it would ever be

These three hours waiting
    happily-ever-after's pause
    imagination's corral
      studied for an exit strategy
        with pounding hooves!

76. LITTLE BLITZEN TO PAGE SPRINGS

What were the German soldiers doing?
Why had they crossed that river
    in the county known as Harney?
And in all that stormy weather, too!

Were they a sometime army far from home
Afraid of thunder and lightning
Shipped overseas from the Russian wars
    sounding like Arnold

and whistling Beethoven?

Perhaps a little dueling
    when you pace because you *have* to
Or fencing with the sharp and shiny
Maybe none of that

Were they Americans
    serving in a far western brigade
Where Donner and Blitzen   the river
        twists
        from the mountain to Malheur
            with extreme caution
            before ending in the marshes
                    still far from the ocean?

"Let's cross the river," they'd said

But the storm was a war's soundtrack
    played to prove
        that nothingness mattered
The sky wishing to bring to a halt their wagons

But there's so much more
The legal residents of Page Springs insist in
    their equal housing
        long after
        and long before
            the German crossing

The only thing to do is give thanks
    a campground was spread
    in the prettiest part
The river calm
        with a cargo of redband trout
        to catch and release

The Page is turned like a book
    where each chapter's
        a different day of the Spring
Or the waters are as many awakenings as daybreaks

It is accessible soaking
A flashback cleansing

   that educates body and soul

I'm thinking the Germans would have called it
      by another name
The word is "bad"
The etymology uncertain "bath?"
It's not fair the words are not forever
  but I'm clear
    in the questioning that must be done

Was there a nineteenth century
   prepared to show kindness
   in the cold of winter?
Would the Donner and Blitzen have frozen over?
Were the Springs ever warm
   or simply freshwater's addition?

There *is* a trail
Perhaps the one the Germans found
  in thunder
     when the lightning lit their way
         in the full-time wilderness

Men who'd left their fathers and mothers
Their supreme assurance
    each minute-at-a-time
    that tests your schooling

Here may the cynics
   defer their acerbic pronouncements
   as they rethink harshness
     exploring ways of working
        likely to erase it altogether

Making personal plans
   in accordance with spiritual safety
Latching onto a special edition of simplicity
Growing up in such surroundings as these
   with plenty of room for error
       you have something to talk about

Those Germans
And their scary crossing
   while the water swirled

Mostly silent pioneers
       the labels torn
              from the box of their enterprise

Your ballet's choreography
       to use all available canyon
              and be publicly viewed
Like a painting told to move
And teach art to young people
       their toy soldiers set aside

Another day that seems this day's hours
So that the future needn't bother us
          so very much
      its veil lifted on the Donner and Blitzen

Roll up those trousers!
Get wet in Deutschland!
So much alive
      you don't know what to say
            that isn't shouting

Let me tell you a story
One that starts and ends in the Outback
Where the weather says, "Get lost!"
           no matter where you're from

Here in the summer   think of winter
      and what you'd do
      a soldier citizen of ice and snow

"*Auf wiedersehen!*"

Wear some *lederhosen*
Go ethnic to honor the naming
If this is a narrative there'll be no conclusion

All that thunder and lightning
      ready for new footfalls on the trail
Having once happened it always is happening
        inside of you
           as if it were nature's way
              of keeping you here
             when all else is lost

A beneficent gifting

Goethe was here
And Schumann's orchestra among the trees
And heaven-sent second chances
    to avoid the twentieth century
      The Holy Roman Empire barely over with

What were they doing in Harney County to come?
What history had they heard
    that so transfixed
      only the West would do?

And so they would tolerate
    "Donner und Blitzen! save your life!"
In the wild horse sage
Something extra known
    that makes you think more clearly
      being out-of-bounds

The middle of the mind to assess one's chances
The next thing never more obvious
Page Springs
    like a guideline fountain
      from the interior authorities
The complex Earth administers ablution

On the verge of eastern thought
    a West preserves its wells and rivers
From different directions
    the same desire flows

This is about doing nothing
Though not in a *za-zen* sense of trance
    you're just being unilateral

The thunder and the lightning
    like someone's secret weapon employed
      to frighten the lazy
One more minute I'll be ready   honorable
Able to remember those I hold dear

A string Theory of Everything around my finger

The day is unknown
       that Nature will resume its warnings
The gravel shifts   and predictable silts
Hydrology's dream child
       in liberty descending
              with German sensibility

You feel used by a vision
The water gleaming with explanation

On probation from the crime of belief
Only pretty pictures matter
       a recumbent career
       it should matter but it doesn't
I'll do what's best
          but that will take a time machine

For a better life in the century of Bismarck
       the journey is made to Harney
            to the wellspring's riches

Ask no favors of the locals
       only that they ignore license plates
Say it's disinformation
I'd stand the cold, cold winters same as they

A detective asked,
       "You could help us all
          if you could just remember
                even one of their names"

"Gunther! yes it was Gunther
          Gunther Schmidt
But what do you want with him?
He's done nothing
Only named a river one dark-and-stormy
              with his troop

"Or was it Karl
       who laughed
           and said 'Donner und Blitzen!'"

"You must reenter the dream and learn more
It is important we find them!"

I answered, "But it's only a dream!"

And was told, "Not anymore...
                                   The Springs, the path and the campground
    may be a loss of consciousness
But it's where the truth lies sleeping
Like the Long Ago
    having found its comfort zone"

And so   tireless   I turned the pages
Careful not to run away
    when German thunder and lightning
        spend their savings on the river

What I wanted all along

Captain George Byron Currey: First Oregon Cavalry 1864
Discovering it was otherwise than we thought;
the Captain had learned German just enough
to name a river fancifully and impress

77.　THE RIDDLE BROTHERS

Hot and dry and quite okay
This is what's left
    and left all alone
        to be wooden history
           come 'round to pester the present
Reason built it

No firebugs came
    from the crumbling American experiment
      whose daily word is "Burn"
        as in "Burn, baby, burn!"
A soothing balm become kerosene
              in a century's twinkle

Make the ranch a riddle beyond any naming

We'll have to figure it out
       so that the place is a question
       an old one
             with 360 degrees of answers

A way of life with a willow branch corral
The generations left a blacksmith shed
       and a tool shop
           there's the barn
The approximate ranch house mansion

All of it a recreation
       that once was hard labor
           and cattle drives to Winnemucca
           so far away even now I won't go

The Little Blitzen
       still waters whatever season you choose
It's just a shame Peter French had to die
                      elsewhere in this West

There were neighbors
       and arrowheads scattered
Here one may imagine
       what roots were kept in the cellar
       who slept in the bunkhouse
               dreaming like Indians

The volunteers have gone native
And speak language they don't understand
       as if they'd riddle for the visitors
           with their pioneer minds
           and pens in their pockets
               ready for notetaking

A positive approach   with equity
The ranch still telling stories
               past writer's cramp
Like a psychic reading performed by ghosts
       the paper held up to the light

On the South Steens road
I was lost in a tiredness
Wishing for the pride of flamenco

        and being treated as human
        finding a way
                to this open-air museum
Even if only to deliver supplies to the caretaker

Feeling normal would be nice
Being sponsored even better
        when the AA involved
        would be more than the devil could handle

You can find it all in Riddle's realm
But you'd have to be ready
        to see what's possible
        what you need all the time
The generations known
        like an echo in the hot and dry valley

What's left is a wooden fantasia
It's easy to conjure
Control the narrative deep brown's begun
        most memorably
A different kind of cabin fever
            where structure's your eyesight
            your entry and scrutiny

Being thus enclosed you want to stay
            see the interiors later
When you're not there but want to be
Wishing for that confinement
        likely to improve your chances
            of persisting past all expectations

Would the Riddle Brothers bring us together?
As if true victory looked like that
            without gunfire either!
            wild parties started!

If you look at me
        the way you sometimes do
            that will make all the difference
Hemingway or Mozart

The Little Blitzen   just over there
The only metaphor

   after a hard and dangerous journey

All the ideas in the world
  are begging for consideration
And sights that hope to catch your eye
      out of all this beauty
The ladies and gentlemen there
  to do a little dancing and raise a barn

What's in my will as of this summer day
  with its key to the homestead
If there's any justice
    the Riddle stays a family secret
    in debt to honesty

78. CATLOW'S CREEKS AND FARMS

205 found the bottomland

And the instant belied the crater of Catlow
  its imaginary lake a soulmate expanse
  an invitational body
A lake that lost its contest with evaporation

So long ago that love could not assist
And its moisture was surrendered
  that might have been an exciting game
      the climate played

Arthur Rubenstein is here
Reincarnated
  and searching for a sweetheart
    as I am looking
     for someone to make easy
      the tricky Chopin passages

Things are going to be different
As different as Catlow is
  from the warrens of urbania

Baby evil nurtured for the sake of later on

With Beaty's Butte to the south
And Hart Mountain rising westward
And the cliff of Steens barricading the east
    only the north knows a city
    or maybe it's a town

When certain facts keep you company
And peaceful Hines is built into the plains
    as if it would do something cities never do

I could almost swear
    you said to go to Catlow
Thank you for yesterday   think we will
Such an interesting book you were reading!
                the story so   mysterious

The real problems of the world solved
Directly   without subterfuge
Something we should all afford
Finding each creek
    that winds down to the plain
        and remembers to pause in its marshes
           before sinking   like instinct
              down
                to what we cannot see

Close your eyes it is the same
Even here
    where the canyons
        like halls
           seem to ask,
                "Now that you know
                what will you do?"

If we are to bear witness
    Catlow must oblige
    and be more than a valley

But so far
    its acts are too slowly played
            for human patience
No performance that may be discerned

To call it public land's not good enough
Because the public's out of business
                        and bothered by tyrants

All bird-watching in abeyance
All hunting and fishing just a rumor

It's because of the caves the truth has come
It flies about the entrance to Roaring Springs
                        and the cave called Catlow

And truth wings the valley entire
Its high desert's alluvial basin
The truth that always keeps you waiting
                        and may take hours

In the sage steppe
      and dry juniper forests
           along Home Creek
           Three-Mile and Skull
On Faraway Rock Creek and Guano
              from the northwest
          and southwest

As creatures of direction it's important
Like someone you know well

The scent of Big Sage and Low
     a kind of catnip for people
       looking for the wayward
          who would run all the way
                to be in that outdoors

Oh! the wild horses also run
Beneath the American kestrel
       and red-tailed hawk

I want the alertness of the antelope squirrel
The further awareness of the myotis bats
Just a moment!
The pronghorn are even now traversing!
     their idle gossip
       a body-language that's inter-species

A *film noir* feel tries to waste time
        and slick Catlow reverie with sooty grey
                                    and stainless steel

A paint-by-numbers
        where no hue has color
                for there are pangs   doubts

The funny part is this distance is closed
        that seemed an impossible sum
                          of emptiness
If you ever thought differently
        the Valley's playing music
                        played by Arthur

Here is a crossroads
As profound as any junction
        GPS admitting multiples of union

Here   where the rest of wildlife's heartbeats
        repeat their staccato meters
        from hyper to leisurely
                while the space heater sun
                        is bulky
                        with all-encompassing purpose

Where it's green
Where the rancher's will
        has led to shade and comfort
And mutual concerns
                have fashioned neighbors
                        of disparate acquaintance

A strategic bonding
        that includes that single cabin
                stark-lonely for the foreseeable
Abandoned brown
        with a lease
                that was signed by the weather

There's a farm
Where always is heard, "Come back home!"
                                to the auguries of silence

    of cougars and skinks
     the calculations of Flammulated owls

The tight spots found
  by bushy-tailed woodrats
The softest caress of Valentine winds

205's a number taken seriously its whole length
Allowing oscillations north and south
Machining slowly so as not to miss a thing
  when you may espy the little ponds
  where the violent crime of predation's
       a minimal outrage

And the redband trout somehow manage
Swim their equivalent Chopin
   to a discount spawning

I'll keep your company here
And thank you for any tomorrows

Carefully word a book of my own
  to say we'll settle here
   in a way
    that's like the request
    to close one's eyes
      to increase surprise
The ranch a gift from the lottery of grace

And we'll bear witness
  to Catlow's performance art
Who knew until now   the sacred unseen

This coming spring
This going summer
  with a winter in between
    that is guesswork's snows
Like the next revolution
  frozen solid by its own decrees

The playback of seasons
  to include a chapter on us
   making it up
    as we go along the road to Fields

Past John Simpkins
His ghost town of Andrew's
                    begging for attention
The trajectory to include John's art at last

In a few days' time the best results
        of being residents of Catlow Valley
                will be known
                    like an MRI from native medicine

In a little while
        the petroglyphs we left alone
        will follow us to Burning Man
Their anime a cancel culture in reverse
                        and determined

The Northern Paiute persisting
Their excellent service
                surpassing the noisiest start-up

Cut in half is the disc of certainty
So that it may not be flung like a frisbee
And thus sobered
        the graben of Catlow is crossed
            without a loan
                from what is really happening

Guests of the Pleistocene just passing through
Not privy to its secrets exactly
        yet capable of learning every increased risk
Any day now the basalt poised to move again

If these were ordinary times
                    it would be scary

79. BARRIER

A thousand feet of the Catlow Rim

A barrier being a statement
Like diplomacy
      or something final that looms
           implacable
           carrying weight
Those layers of Steens up there

If I were a sheriff
      there'd be nothing whatever to do
      but recite the daily word of this bulk
A book that would show its every chapter
And publish   if it could
      the *whole* of Steens Mountain

The generations of its lavas
      calling your name
           in a bass voice beyond your hearing
           the decibels profound
And dedicated to the deep Earth's story

When the drawing was vast
      and a t-square favored ninety degrees
What fires burned that raised it up
And were a furnace's message
                to the surface of things?

There'd been no interview
      just the fault block's force and belief

"It's so easy to fall in love!"
      looking up the junipered slope
Erosion's essay on the angle of repose
When a rock's dramatic pause
           may not be for real

From the looks of things it's a cinch
      except for the rattlers
Just an afternoon's scramble
Or years on your knees

      like a slow-moving pilgrim
          come from the Karakoram
         uphill
         out of character

A simple inheritance is the barrier
There to exemplify ambition
      yet qualify its heights
One may be haunted by murder
   when the crime was mere indifference

Before the wall of the Catlow Rim
   I'm thinking the easy part's ascent
What's hard is stopping to do so
As if something last-minute must be dealt with
      and only good luck mattered

It's nice how the junipers on a hot day
    cool the climbing
      as you go from shade to shade
The short storeys that take you to the top
The sun corrected for
Little rests   brief lyrics
   until the wall's last challenges

Catlow Rim   the gentler Abert
When you summit
    pretend to reunite with the wildcat
      the one that transferred its felinity
      as if we'd made it a date to do it
      that day near to Pyramid Lake
    with laughter and applause
       from somewhere

The Valley's eastern barrier's
      a police state of rock
And bad as that sounds it makes no arrests
Unless you want it to
And then the custody's
   a kind of expedient confinement
     for the duration

Geology's moment in the sun your own
Being lucky to be near it

      and looking down
          from where the slope has taken you

The mystery of thought come to life
      and held for questioning
Losing one's mind
For the scent of juniper's money
                        power
                        and love

Its stiff branches wanting employ
          as multiple metronomes
The fugue state awoken
A chance to be horrified or happy
      a thousand ways
          for a thousand feet unknown to any till now

This random route
          part of a plan to invade all of Oregon
                                      starting with vacancy

80. HISTORY'S STRUCTURE

You don't have to do this
You don't have to read this
You don't have to find out
You can skip it
No big deal   no, really!
Never mind
You're not interested   never were

Or maybe you are
Yes, you must be!

You're part of history's structure
          as much as the forlorn abandoned
                what lingers past its function
The planks of a pioneer "tiny house"

History's structure is absurdly seen
And Daniel Higgs
    once wrote in a book at the end,
      "Who you really are knows you don't exist"

Make it history you talk to
History that was never a masterwork
Only the sordid approximations
    of terrified historians
      repeated in earnest
        till their heads bow down
        till random creep stuff
          is acceptable heroics

Getting rocks to tell a shorter story
              than their billions of years
Narrowing the blueprint
    to bluebirds likely to force a smile

But you don't have to read it
    or see any birds with binoculars
There's never an ending
    and that should tell you something

You must decide if you will read this
Or anything at all that's history
    that's history's bones
Its exquisite skeletons
    that seem so eager
        to explain themselves
        and qualify for welfare
        in their wayfaring afterlives

You can skip the natural radiance of entropy
The annals that end up as nothing
All of it being what we do
    and do ingeniously
      humans feel secure at times
        replacing one regime with another

Fair enough that laughter is possible
But never mind   just skip it
I know there's little interest
    in anything but being twenty years old

     and advertising your charm
     as Japanese cherry blossoms
       before their warlike fall

Perhaps it's getting something done
Though the crisis of reality is unabated

History's a parking lot
  for every make and model of aggression
And who you really are
  wants the keys without a down
  when you will drive away
   without a mind
    every gear a conceit

Thinking raggedly of structure
Sure the real thing is firm as rebar
   wanting a building
"Okay!" is your word
The rest of the world held up
   by at least a turtle

And being sure of this you can stop right now
At any period
You don't have to find out
I'm just the mystery announcer
  out to lunch on the pond of "I am"

A country of one without foundation
The court of all else is merely amused

You must decide if history's a LEGO for parents
A little smug
  about the uses plastic may be put to

The birds are sick of it all
And yearn for yesterday with every birdcall
For prehistory's formless seasons
  when the land was laid out
   according to what Nature's looking for

When history started
  it was the start of meanwhile

It seemed to contain   like a skyscraper
Yet Gaia said history was just a hologram
    and marveled at the joke
      or whatever it was

The white heart of the universe throbbed
     with lifegiving
You'll love the aliens!
They'll say the same things
    though their sentence structure
        might delay your understanding

Keep reading why don't you!?
It's better you know

And after you read this
     I'll introduce you to Daniel
        and the final chapter
The forlorn ramshackle
Abandoned   that was mistaken for history
      whose chronicles were scraps
          before their ink was dry!

81.   LAVA'S SUMMIT FOREGROUNDED BY TREES

Be that refugee who goes to the Catlow Valley
    and takes a seat on lava's summit
      Steens's westmost rock

Be gone with a view of homesteads
     your own home uncertain
The foreground trees in love with the soil

What town you're from is forgotten
As well as the language spoken *in* it
One can drive around so much of the time
      no address is the new normal

But the Catlow is plentiful miles

      so be changed
      and let a destination have a say
Your status uncertain till then

From your basalt chair aspire to clarity
The sun has pronounced the syllables needed
      to make a new language
           one the winds will understand
           and the branches it moves

Do you see?   do you realize?
This is ideal!
You'll be safe in all this living room of stone
Bring pillows to the pillows *lava* made
Be that kid
      that's grateful for this far
      and no farther

Think the next generation
      will have too many appointments to keep
          to notice you
          in this volcanic setting
              with its foreground forest

Though no timpani will sound
      yet the Catlow will advertise its welcome
With strings subtle as distant cicadas
      curious as to your whereabouts

Be a percentage of interest yourself
Somebody certain of what's worthwhile
Be gone with common sense
      telling tales of tomorrow
          that may not be frightening

And the future
      told rightly
          will enhance any sundown
          with the promise of layaway light
              for later
                  for anytime at all

The lava summit's
      like a song's level lyrics heard

            after the crags of instrumental

A pause in the unfolding of apocalypse
Poetry's as near as the Nature
      and it ebbs and flows
              with an easy salvage

No trail was taken unless resolution's that
With empty pockets go to the Catlow Valley
Be the foreigner that's orphan, too
        reminded of a family far from togetherness

Ascend
    to lava's throne of empty places
        subject to geology
Places where unrealistic thinking's rewarded

I think that what has happened
    will happen again
        because religion didn't work right
Bad economic numbers will not be recited
Nor the bad poem of progress

You can talk to the hawks
Your back-and-forth
    a new normal informed by amnesia
        your Geiger counter set aside

And those pillows from the middle Miocene?
Their formation's
    just an earlier-in-the-day thing
Somehow it's not good for you
The way time is not good for you

But take notes anyway
    you'll learn a lot before you're through
    and your flesh-eating past
        will try its best
            to colonize your soul
The atavist to find that nothing adds up

The heart of the canary
    its private song all that matters
        pictures or no pictures

All the art there is   or none at all

History's giving orders again
They'll be easy to follow   they always are
Fluid lava to Catlow's stone
     with its wooded foreground

You won't shop here again   one visit
     infinite shelves
The way you want to do it all
         in just one day
         as orphan refugee

My name is yours

82. THE BEST PICTURE

The Best Picture was taken
     when both form and content
        cried out together
        for their snapshot:

"Somebody love us before it's too late!"

The Best Picture was unexpected
A photo like a painting
     that slowed down the day
     with amazement

A specific framing
An accidental "click"

Wish I could say I had anything to do with it
But delusions of grandeur
     kept me in the back seat
        of art's demands altogether

Things appeared
     in the picture   exactly

        where the photographer
        would not have placed them

Lucky the gallery getting the print!
The "Oohs!" and "Aahs!"
    like a pleasant white noise
    making the owner happy
        and eager for a show

Too bad the Best Picture's
    so much better than the rest
The photographer's no longer sure

It is being readied   mounted
The Catlow
    its creeks and weathered shacks
      those windbreaks framing the ranches
Wide-angle   all-inclusive
      the lowest price of perfection

The Picture that had cost no gold but sunshine
Late in the day
    the last games of light played
      for a captive audience
      fighting for its sanity
The Picture was so different from all others
Because it followed a different aesthetic
One that was hitherto unknown
    non-human   yet revealing

Its pixels arranged
    like iron filings
    in the presence of a magnet
Whose mystery's acquired by the spectrum
        for a greater truth
    than mere appearance

The Best Picture was a concert rectangled
With a bonus feature of uncanny perspective
    that lasts well past the viewing

A technology shorn of purpose
One that just happens
    and ends up Best Picture

       though a single frame
The rest of the reel just imaginary cinema

A trip pic wanted by jealous National Parks
The clearest image of their aspirations

The photographer was tired
There were snakes
       and vultures up there
         wondering about outcomes

Getting real was the work of a camera
      when all else
      had settled on "close enough for jazz"

There was woodwork to it also
For one of the picnic tables
       had   carved:
         "Heidi + Henry"
    the Best Picture's best part

A tree's conclusion as puppy love
Oh!   it was there in the blow-up
Their embraces inferred
      with the help of the Swiss Army
And knowing the Swiss
       they'd never go to war
       those two
         with their briefest of picnics

The Picture said
     that what's everlasting
       will not trouble the living

But would the Picture suffice for a pastime?
The best of all worlds
     be that idyllic instant
       like a final word spoken
        with no expectations?

A specific framing
I wish I could say I had something to do with it
The dark room has told me to leave
     and leave well-enough alone

      though form and content still cry
            for unexpected painting and pixels
But I'm not quite that somebody sent
            before it's too late

A shutter's click in the Cosmos sounding its white noise

83. FARMS UNSEEN

Liberty was a farm

There were three of them
    more imagined than beheld

There was sleep between encounters
Pulling over
    before fatigue caught the driver unaware

Waking, he resumed safely
The miles continued
    past farms of one's fancy
Their storehouses and barns
    conceived as places
    where you may stand on your feet all day

You may live in the same body as a rancher
Intensely vicarious
    the hard work tiring all who think of it
        and lovingly
        as if a traveler might be a homesteader

What a word is "spread!"
And what a having   is *having* a spread!
The lingo saved
    for a sense of heritage
    that's always in danger of falling down
                    drunk with assumptions
What a grandpappy said would continue

It's better the farms are unseen
And their sketchy cows
      who've made a union now and made demands

If "whuppin's" still happen
      let them happen out of sight too
For the simple-minded century
            may not abide tradition

And change-for-change's-sake
      wraps its fingers about a plowshare
      and giggles foolishly   dust rising
A millennial's planted squash
Big deal

The ducks are cold-blooded
      and waddle   dissembling

Nothing's for sale
If there's a feedstore somewhere
      it's just for looks
Livery's lost its meaning entirely
And is only memory's minimum requirement

The market's faraway and over the hill
      that would care
      and not raise its eyebrows
            with bemusement

There were three farms
With sleep between
      each   spread
          more imagined than beheld

With uncanny waking
      one drives the miles it takes
      to once more get out and stand tall
           with vicarious wonder

Not yet are the farms finished off
And I'm unfrightened as a consequence

Bells improbable
      clang approval of the reckoning

84. THE STONE HOUSE

The stone was therapeutic and warm
Five abandoned bedrooms in the sun

Let's just say it was a desert's pile of rocks
    arranged as solid geometry
    a leftover house
        like a 3-D puzzle
           fitted to suit

What's standing stands tall and grey
And its windows
    though broken
        see the same as before
Their eyesight trained on the sun of the Alvord

As if to beseech it to offer faith
        that someone may return

There's a scraggle of branches lain
The winds' detritus strewn
    and the winds saying
        they'll "be right back"
        like Johnny Carson

The cottonwood's waiting
Its minimal shade
    a daily word of wishbone
        the letter "Y" upreaching
            to a blue jurisdiction

No need to break a door down
Old school's enough
    the edit of restraint
        is entry supposed
        and sufficient understanding

The interior that talks to us
        when "no admittance" is the rule
It's recon's relief expedition
The fortress stone still hospitable
            despite desertion

Go ahead   walk around
      the house in rotation as you do this
Discover the outside cellar
Similar   just as sturdy
            its usage a guesswork going back

Circling back
     out of a desire to learn the layout
         and further imagine
         what the old you would have thought

Right here in the radiance
     with noontime abeyance
        is your new favorite room
        you haven't even seen
           that waits upon a grand reopening
Going somewhere else is unthinkable
The next door neighbor of today
        is all over your overall

The world was put together like a stone house
Its dry garden
     gaining ground
     for a full disclosure of arid

No one needs a doctor
No one needs a thing
And ownership's a moot abstraction
              faraway as mirage

If there were anything that needed doing
     someone must have said,
        "It's not going to work
       not here   not now"

The town is Fields
     that might have included the stone house
When folks would have made house calls
Neighborly affection for keeps thus assured
     though all concerned go steer-crazy

The rubble is perfect   leave it alone
The castle keep

to show forever's possibilities
    owning every minute
    of long-lasting's style
The recommended stone of a biblical reprise

Start a history new to any past
See how it courts the centuries
    as though they were courtesans
The boulders beyond
    like a future found to be a sure thing

Their firmness *pertaining* to that certainty
    insisting the future's a building too

The town of Fields is a wayside
    with milkshakes
Safe as the twenty-first century can make it
Still   if a redoubt's needed
    the stone house is ready
    and might be a party
        a place for innocence even

Previous shelter repurposed   reconfigured
A small school perhaps
    with little boots on the ground

What I believe in already
Years adding up
    to a playground as vast as Oregon
    where finance melts like the snow

And what's always there for you
    is sturdy as yourself
        in the perfectly legal
            yet quite   wild   world

What not to say is, "What's not to *like*?"
In a bass voice full of soprano inclusivity

Although the stones do not roll themselves
    the cradle certainly rocks within
        albeit unobviously

Was it a shortage of silver?

Some war that somehow came across the sea
      uninterrupted?
Any day now there'll be an explanation
And   like a journalist   I'll let you know
        the stone house in the background

For now there are footsteps and silence
The place surrounded
     by the frilling of curiosity

Just as belief builds a house
     so a faith in roads builds to Beyond
          like the third symphony of Brahms
If it may now be heard!
If it may only *begin*   I'd settle for that

The *start* alone
     this space to pacifist wars donating
    when peace itself
        is parsed for relevance

When the entropy of stone is perceived
     in spite of all it's supposed to be
             non-drowsy
                   adamantine
               conclusive

Regret postponed
     until new stone is made
       and joined like puzzle pieces
And you take up residence there
     to be Oscar-nominated for gumption
                      a last minute homesteader

The roof's an angle with separation anxiety
Metallic   reflective
     its useless apex wanting attention
The compensation due for watching over
        with an attic's concern for secrecy
        and the tricks of coyotes

Reason walks
     in the presence of the last stone house
     that says there's nothing to worry about

    when nothing has no home
    or very much to say

Just one story at a time
  till the sun turns red
    and engulfs all else
As if it really cared
  for the extended family of *homo sapiens*

The species with a price on its head
   and in need of therapy
     beginning again to fill five bedrooms
      with exceptional children
       whose eyesight shatters glass

85. A YEARNING FOR THE ALVORD SPRING

From the junction it was dusty miles

Someone said, "See you around!"
  and went there
   but that was years
    before the crowds
    and the cost of a soak

When they all stand waiting
    inspecting the artifacts
The flat desert insisting there's nothing more

The energy
  and resilience
    the waters promised
These were canceled
     by the milling multitudes
      eager
      overwhelming
      over-socialized
       and telling stories

For there was a yearning to bathe in the Alvord

A demand for its healing
        as if it were a last oasis

No one's exactly impolite
They just won't go away
        and stand around
            bunching and babbling
                the city come to the country again
                              determined to handshake

What they *really* want is silence
And listening for the faintest gurgle of the Spring
But no one thought to bring duct tape
        and enforce a mute enlightenment

I overslept
        and let the bad guys do what they want
If you say "*we* want" I'd object
But to die in battle I need the Springs
If Western civilization *itself* is to perish
        still take a dip
             before deciding what to do
                        in secret

Let the water serve as a nexus
A solo moment   in some way
An Iraqi vista wedged
        within a stretching landscape
            called "basin and range"
                taking care of all dimensions

If they were only a tribe that stirred!
Their presence explained
        as a pause in a group vision quest
        then   talking to one
             would be like talking to all
              with communal parts of speech

A brand new Bible could talk about the Alvord
Tell stories right here in Oregon
                chapter and verse

But perhaps a single page is better
A Bible that's a poem
        but has a few "beholds"
                and rocky wastelands
Something beyond historic at least

And maybe
        the tourists at the Springs will get religion
                disperse and spread the Word
                      saying   one to the other
                      "See you around!"

I'm like a drunk from the fifties
Though the World War's over
        I'm wanting another
                whenever the caissons arrive

"Go on!   Begone, *all* of ya'!"

Razor-sharp is the blade
        that would cleave the wholeness
Even language   the pressure to employ it
            is unwanted glue
                and dull agreement
                        making sure

Each conversation a check to see
Like spouses' smooches
        just when you thought
                you still might be on your own

There they are
Uncertain yet loquacious
        the great prow of Steens overseeing
                perhaps a novena for *conversos*
Keeping it real as sunstroke permits

There are decades to a minute
With captions
        to say just why each and every
        and common decency
        trying to hide missing money

All discussion a flow of orinasals
                        intoning clues for Poirot

The night the comet pronounced its name
                in the western skies
                      its announcement
                          also cometary
       was a glow that commenced
                      as early as twilight

 Its subterfuge a needling murmur
      prior to the main show of extinction

The Alvord was hosting   then as now
The comet wanting solitude
      as much as the makers of dreams
Like the one
       where the celestial curve of the comet
           is viewed
           from the same hot springs
                      in a bivouac's seclusion

On a first-name basis with catharsis
        this year will be different
               the comet said so

It's possible I misremember
But *NEOWISE* it was that was a comet
      and it didn't disappoint
NEOWISE waiting
     like arthritis   for later

And therefore all is yearning
For an outcome   for weeks and years

Maybe all that's needed is a calling
One that offers more relief
               than life as a hermit

Why not simply pay
      and approach the pools and benches?
Why not join?
Then serve in some way
Administer the drug of independence

                                                                                                                 to everyone

A doctor from the Pleistocene
        who remembers the lake
        who's only upset it was so simple
    after all

A mobile church
A secret devotee
        who will work with awareness
        who is unafraid of fire
And knows strictest adherence
                to a novel urtext

Start a year of it
        as if trying anything
                that might a memorial make
                of your exceptional love
                        that must continue
                        as its source
                                and surface expression

Getting myself *killed*
        if it assured your devotion

86. DOG FOOD DELUDED

Before you dine
        just be sure it's legit
                intended for humans

Pay attention
Like you would in a foreign land
        or if a new planet appeared

In the crucible of experience
        things fall apart post-stone age
Get a good diet   drop the club
Determined to save those cells of yours

The project of living to be done right
Learning from before
      remembering   adjusting
                         adolescence

Mindful of prior absurdities:
When you thought that hot sauce was soup
                         in a Mission taqueria
Confused horse radish with apple sauce
And   in a fog of conversation
      absently ordered naked steak
      not knowing "naked" meant raw

Now on the Denio-Fields ribbon of gravel
      more blundering
A can of dog food is opened
A can not read in the grocery store
      remote viewing
          when supplies ran out
              and were casually replenished

It   tasted   funny
Not just bad but wrong
      unwanted protein

It was a long summer
A long playa and breakfast
      not in bed
      but at least roadside and safe
Too bad breakfast's intended for dogs!

"Labels?   we don't need no stinkin' labels!"

Go ahead!
Have some more
      while transitioning to canine
          and life as a coyote
The Indian miles to be four-footed

In this theater of carry-out
        one can was not made sure of
        being so on-the-go it didn't matter
Wouldn't make or break a career

A strange flavor yet you keep on eating
Make a meal serving Alpo to yourself
A dream vacation   a dream cuisine
                 lifesaving, even

The multiverse speaks of idiocy
Says it's a good thing   a food thing
Like a target weight
         lifted perhaps

But what were you thinking?!

Oh, for stevia now!
The herb with sweet-tasting leaves!
The treat far from home
       and so far from nutrition

"Naked and Afraid," the can is survival
       unless the can opener's lost
       and unglinting   in the sunshine
                 no dog or human able

This is the school of "How Not to Car-Camp"

Believe and belong
       having some idea
            of what even a kid wouldn't do
            to spite

"Dense"   an adjective
A part of belonging   I.Q.   the problem
An I.Q. of 4 but friendly
       but friendly's not enough goodness
               to stop the wars

I'm thinking with the brain of a salamander
Its wriggling agenda matters to me
And the look you get from a squirrel
       is the look I have
           not entirely sure of its motives
The raven's flight plan
The concerns of a rooster
       his loud ovations
       and irrefutable protest

All this did the can introduce

Let the catalog of questions
        include the stare of hyenas
                the goats' quizzical stance
All the "tame" life that takes us to be "wild"

Please!   the jury's no longer out!
The Jesuses of other planets
        are thinking the Word isn't working
                              on *this* one

"Umm!   delicious!
I think I'll have some more!"

Might there be an anti-anthem sung
                to density's wagon trains!
For those of you
        who may not know
                I'm now a rescue dog
                just wanting to help
                        with eight years of service
                        an affordable pup!

It's a full spectrum of dunce
When is the due date for common sense?
        when folks will not ask,
      "Are you okay?   ya' sure?"

The real issue   pay attention
Be wedded to discretion
To congratulations
        that a foreign land accepts you

The road was sunny
        and without provocation
Forever's sage was going on sale
                for the sake of a revolution

Things falling apart
        it was thought absurdity
                might travel "all over this land"
Like Peter, Paul and Mary
        and the rest of the party of free-for-all

Maybe sooner rather than later
      the Future will call on the Past
And say,
      "Be sure to read the labels!"

Things aren't what they seem
      and you shouldn't go "woof!"
           when you hear a noise in the night
Other situations   in turn
      have come to sit on your doorstep
           and patiently wait for you to open

Come when called yourself
To sip soup that isn't soup
And down apple sauce that's really a radish

Be "carefuller"
The *Scrabble* comparative that's allowed
      though your opponent might challenge

It's one or the other:
A wolf or the hominid that tamed the thing

And if it's the former then what version?
A poodle?
      a Bichon Frise?
           a Pomeranian?
                a Great Dane?
                      a Lhasa Apso?
                            a Lab?

A happy dog?
Or one that wants caviar
      and breaking into the grocery store

"Dog years" are not a problem
           nor is "needing to go"
Life will not be defined by longevity
Rather
      by the long hot summer
           of craving Alpo's juicy tidbits
                with a nearby water bowl

Roadside's made its bed for you
And after chasing balls
     it's great to lie down

Transitioning further
     poetry is now a scent
          the open mic an open range
          with carry-out verses
Lyrical as baying at emergency vehicles

Later   in Denio
     with unconditional love
         learn a new identity

In the unexpected multiverse of small town
     settle down to what you were thinking
         when shopping
           weightless and abandoned

With a wandering mind
     that wanders back
     as in the epic journeys of certain pets
         for whom state lines
           are no arrest of devotion

And faithful
As demonstrations for pain relief
     that are commercials for loyalty

As we are found in Nature
     so let us remain forever foreign
         yet native
          with cans and changing tastes
              in cuisine

87.   SLATS AND POSTCARDS

Fields   it's a stop

There are milkshakes and tables
And slats above that try to shade

The orders are hollered when it's time
       and strangers mingle   or do not

Right over there's a cabin
Might a European stay?
       why sure   but not today
       no matter how many say "Hello!"

And no matter how much you twist it
       Ficlds stays aloof
            and overcomes travel abroad
            with a one-off weekend

In case you're
          hungry
          angry
          lonely or tired
It's kind of a pickup AA
           no matter the sobriety

COVID'S playing games
And the inside's outside serving

There are cards to write
And today they'll be serious
       the way a virus is serious in spreading
       and burglarizes all the bodies it can

So let the slats be partial shade
       while the electric shocks I'm trying to scrawl
          are effortless correspondence
          with distant dreamers

I'll be out-of-line this once
That the rest of what I have to say
       another day
          can better reassure

Here in Fields
       all the writing
       will be high risk overexertion

    with milkshakes to go

88. THAT STEENS COUPLE, A REPRISE

It's a reunion!
Let's join them
  those mountaineers with the same ideas!

Yes, from Steens to Catlow
And thence to Fields
  and here they are!
    with the same dog, of course

And all of us who studied Kiger from on high
      are refreshed down below

There are so very few in the Outback
  with only one way to go that's paved
    crossing paths is hardly that
    more a meeting prearranged

It's an encounter group
A reprise of the East Rim's splendor
Nothing more
  but Steens is so very much it'll serve

It's a court of thirty minutes
Voices medieval superstitious
  the same that spoke to Jean of Arc

Such was the retro induced by the mountain
  we lost six centuries in one afternoon
  and attempted barter in lieu of coins

We might have traveled by cart and horse
In search of miracles refusing caution
Eyewitnesses
    to the Gorge
      with subliminal desires

        and obligations

Freedom's freedom
      every moment of what comes next!

89. A FIELDS LECTURE ON THE BARN

It was a story of elsewhere told
     with pictures
     with a reference to Peter
The man of all the hours spent
       wide open
         except for that barn

The Round Barn built
     and filled with horses in winter

A story told in the August sun
     that was news from history
Xena would be mentioned
     she who ran the Round Barn's gift shop
     mentioned   not shared
       I'd keep her my own if possible

In that blue-wide wilderness   horses
     the right way to train despite the snow
Peter French   he did it all
Though he failed to please his neighbors

No matter
     at this distance crossing time
His specific pioneer demeanor's unknowable

The story took a lunchtime
It *might* have made a better *morning's* tale
     when it's easy to imagine rising early

"You're making this *up*!"

"*Au contraire*! his name was French
        and he was good to his men

"Like all interiors
  the Barn's tried to exclude
    for the sake of confession
    for all that's intimate

"The light of cracks
  allowing the most fragile thoughts
     their due consideration
And you're right where you belong
    Peter's ghost notwithstanding

"It's a full service attraction
Shows you what the world was like then
       in Harney County
Please note the timber
How the center flares outwards
How stone *becomes* the structure
   flatters the wood
    asks, 'Where were we without this barn?'

"Barn where the horses danced in the dark
  and dreamed their horse dreams

"Think you might wish to trot your own self
If you saw it better
  than these pictures allow

"Help and wellness
  may be a barn not so far away
  just somewhere north
  before you reach the Craters
All that country
     and so very little juniper
       and ponderosa

"The boards departed places distant
They came in wagons slowly to the ranch
  where the Barn was raised
    in service to *vaqueros*

"Look once more
         while the pandemic seeps
                  into every corner
                           of urbia
                           suburbia
                           and exurbia

"Here in Fields
         working fast
         through the Station's signature burgers
                  know the hardships of January
Let's take a little test together
Break horses and ponies and ourselves

"Know how it ended?
Well   someone shot him
                  got away with it too
The jury's still out
Yet somehow believes
         its verdict will stand in their afterlives

"The short story's long
It would take past lunch to tell it all
There's a blues
         blowing out of the nineteenth century
                  trying to be born
                  to one-up the way it was
                           and turned out to be

"A movie set
         where you kind of get the drift of a Western

"Think you're ready for Xena?
         yeah   well   she's ready for you
Oh, you didn't know that?
You'll get a gift
         it's enough you smile at her
                  a dissembling tourist

"Kind who'd do ranching for real
                  if only for one afternoon
One like this
         being southward bound
                  yet resolved to return

                    perhaps to what's north
                                    and waiting

"The cattle?   they'll outnumber
Just don't count
        for elsewhere knows no math anyhow
        and the Pueblo Mountains least of all
The mind's built into the geography
            and the soul hears a summons
                                that needs no calculation

"Where's a piano?
The better part of promotion's
        those eighty-eight black-and-whites
Film noir's musical masterpiece

"Where's ballet   now you've found the stage?
Have you forgotten the "grand allegro" promised?
The ballet class's finale
        that used all of the floors' diagonal?

"The barre abandoned
        these multiple horizons
                vie to be your dance's destination
                with *fouettes* and *adagios*

"The Round Barn turns
As if a great spindle propelled
        the spirit world revolving too
The Four Directions melding
            sliding with a whirligig preference
                                the movie kaleidoscopic

"All the hours spent to pay for enchantment
The blue wilderness
        that would make Peter French
            a next door neighbor of today

"It's better mornings
Like a rehearsal for all you may imagine
        right here in famous Fields
            the milkshakes
                    made with Outback conviction

"This lecture   this confession   accept
Though you insist it's all made up
the light of cracks seen
        from within the barn
            should call your fragile thoughts
                                belief"

90. THE DENIO PIANO

It isn't a piano that wants to be played
Not at first   for it's shy
It wants to be sure you love it a little

It's a keyboard needing a certain touch
        one of understanding
            when the player makes allowance
                eases into discovery
                    of missing strings and hammers

Where mistrust of pitch is not an issue
The F Sharp that should be a C

And so   gingerly   a piece is played
The unfixed piano taking interest
The pianist careful
        and remembering
            where not to place a finger

An improv to restore the piano's confidence
        that all may be well
            until a technician stops by
                perhaps a traveler too
                    and decides to take it on

Restore the Denio piano
The shy upright
        that waits unnoticed at the Junction
            where 140 bends
                and leaps westward

                on the desert planet

There's the cafe buzz
       the piano would silence   if only
And the good notes hope for an audience
A tune to capture the crowd
A pretty piece to belie the soundboard's ruin
       the disappeared hammers
            felt
            and saddle straps

It's time the ancient found a voice
       to assuage the piano's depression
For it's a piano maligned
           disparaged
           dismissed

You want to *act*
Discover the constellation of usable keys
Make it a stage
       that was merely storage in public
           furniture at best

There'll be a laying on of gentle hands
To make the very wrong sound very right
Lonely strings
       needing the charity
       of hands softened for expression

In the out-of-the-way rodeo of weather
       dust's on a whirlwind tour
The talent
       to include a recluse Baldwin
           with reluctant pedals

What matters more
       than a concert grand in San Francisco
           the finest Bosendorfer ready
               for Mozart's B Minor "Adagio"
Maybe a recital in disarray
       yet obliging age-old arts

As late in the day as it is

        a spindly Nocturne play
The Denio piano a strongbox of affection
A music box reliving the twentieth century
                one careful note at a time

The good strings' free speech
                albeit out-of-tune
The best of Outer Space suspense
      climbing stairs to the stars
          with saloon sounds
              plunking uncertainty
A bar fights' accompaniment

I'll complete the feat of performance
            no matter the John Cage silence
Exclusive keys that promise mastery
That make it easier than ever
      to get a start
          in the middle of middle age

Planning for a family, even
The lonely upright
      to bring together all that's outlying

And Denio   named for Aaron out of Illinois
      is pleased to say he's listening
         and keeping time
           with the town hall
              of music in a zip code of wonder

What's on the program's
        not foot-stomping dissonance
              but a "prepared" piano

Oh! for a pilot light to brighten the planet!
I'm sitting by the window waiting on a ruby
      the right idea I had that fled
      and made me seek a patient shriver

The Baldwin's deserving
The acoustics perfect
A wooden room like an accidental studio

And it *might* be your boyhood piano

        trucked cross-country to Nevada
            to be a pioneer piano
The same you learned on
Same you lost track of
    the first hours of heading west

Ruby of finding once more!
Maybe that's why the instrument's shy
    thinking it wasn't wanted and when
And all the cubicles of music school
                      can never compare!

Relaxed into that police state
              that was departure
A thralldom chasing sundown
All the way from Massachusetts
    with its double letters and meanings

The daydream now is missing a doctor
The kind who reassures
    the way they used to in fifties hospitals

How much pretending
        before a truth is enacted?
You realize it might mean reunion
            with those broken hammers
            that once were bouncy
Find the story ends with restoration
Warming up to make-over and making up

Denio's little piano
    maybe trusting the grown-ups again
How they swaggered!
The civilians all skinny
    in the wake of World War Two
    having vanquished the Evil One
        just   barely!

The Denio piano will be guaranteed a concert
Will be embraced as long-lost
The reunion celebrated with mocktails
    to keep us sober
    and keep things virginal

We'll compliment the music
                with lipograms
                    the missing letters analogous

That artillery piece to come to life
        the big gun at the Junction there
New research
                to learn just when and why
                the thing was emplaced

Will the motel have room when it's over?

Publish the rebuild?
The job done to save the antique?
Meet the Greeks halfway to Atlantis
                  returning ancient lyres?

Offer improv on Denio's off-days
When rubies embellish ordinary sights
        and make five-stars
                of mere accommodation?

This is where patience pays off   patience
That's what the piano's had
        all the years it's stood idle

And now
        it has something to discuss with beginners

Would love a metronome again
And watching little hands enlarge
        to keep pace with assignments

Now the loose cuspids of keys
        are denied a dentist's lessons
Think it's too late
        for the Commonwealth of Massachusetts
                to study anything but survival

But I have my eye on the Baldwin even so
Walter Gieseking's make
        whose grands allowed
                such a pearly, pearly tone
Walter irresistible

His Impressionist sound said to be ravishing!

The boyhood piano could travel again
        down the Burner Byway
Be brought from the Junction to Black Rock
And honored in a place
        where art doesn't have to be perfect

The Baldwin as *recordanza*
Think the boy
        built into the wood and iron
              would like that

The *objet trouvé*
        you come upon
           bicycling the playa
                that's considered interactive
                with the proviso you're gentle
With a "See you later!" feel

Nothing bossy!
But demands it not suffer pounding!

I can see it from here!
A stand-alone from Attleboro
        the jewelry town with rubies all its own
A secret in plain sight in the sunshine

I'd truck it   all fixed even
Do it right now in advance of the revels
        so they find it waiting there
            as it was waiting in Denio for me
            with concert tickets sold for free

If UFOs are real
        let them not abduct this lonely piano
        but get after exhibitionist accordions!

The cafe's calm
It's close to closing time
        and nine o'clock
                comes early to the Virgin Valley

A few notes and then

        the first darkness after twilight
            to prepare
                for the conceptual
                the miraculous
                the imaginary

The final notes repeating like a motto
Or subject for a fugue state

Yes, a piano of the night
        that plays for itself
            all those moments of supreme confidence
Untroubled dreaming
First piano pieces played again
            to please John Cage

The pianist remembers
The first piano recital
        like a rehearsal
           for everything else that's kind and generous

Music as friendly furniture's comfort zone
        unless your desire's desolation

The question of audience answered
        by the bass-most string still sounding
            and ascending after that
                to a pingy treble

Keys maligned
            as a life not lived but talked about
By those who hear their story
        amazed this was even possible

San Francisco's perfection
        to refuse a shipment of concert grands
        in favor of Denio's traveling keyboard
Maybe such a preference
            may lead to immortality
                no matter the world's confusion

The sonata begins that's half silent
And proceeds
        to no conclusion or rocking chair

In the dead of summer
    the Baldwin says it's not a piano at all
        but something played by the wind
            whenever the westerlies come calling
        at Denio

91. 140 AND ITS ESCARPMENT

The rim is suddenly seen
The slide
    the monument topside
      historical   Langslet called

And downshifting's then a reflex move
Happiness gearing for a winding descent
Stateline Canyon having given its approval

For now
    Guano Valley's prepared to receive
        where Slide Spring burbles

The air's too heavy for Doherty's scheme
No hang gliding today
    the wind's the wrong way anyhow

Antelope Butte isn't so far
Sage Butte, too   an easy destination
Why not Round Mountain while we're at it?

Prove you believe there's truly no rush
    and the grade can wait
Encounter the drop-off
    as if you lived there in those thermals
        a bird of prey
           added to the flock of vultures

In other words   just be yourself

What year is it now
        that may be the last
                before Geiger
                        and his counter count down
                                or lose count altogether?

Go!
Cold-blooded as the rattler
        also at home and here to stay
        if only to appreciate the truth of silence
When media
        may nevermore announce a state line
                      or anything else

The Ice Age's gazetteer just blank pages
Let Doherty say if they'll ever be another
If Milankovich may resume his cycles
        or warm nightmares loosed
                seek the light of day

There's a slide begun
        whose waterhole's shy
        and wants a wetter plan
                than uncertainty

The spring has promised even so
And still awaits your dancer's toes

I've seen the pronghorn antelope race
As if what was after them
        were after them still
        swift lions at large
Extinction   has its ghosts all right

I'm invisible myself
        halfway down to Guano Valley
        with prehistoric steering
Hang gliding 140
            after a fashion of strange

92. THE PONIES AT ADEL

Were there supposed to be ponies?
Or did an hallucination
      crowd into the afternoon
         to overtake the natural world
            with thoughts of making it super?

Surely the carriage is real
And why not the team of ponies
      posing there as if to charm?

As if they'd be off to Fort Bidwell
Knowing the way so well
         no reins are required

Can it be a surrey?
Adel has made a parade   a partial parade
Saint Richard has blessed it
    the ponies
    the store
    the hot springs
        the school
           where Adel's steam of Hornets swarm

Perhaps a pool game before I board
I'd have the ponies take me to Shiloh Ranch
    that I may reach
        with others
           for meaning uninterrupted

Just the thought of it
A cowboy church   its doors blown open

The blue seats of the swings
     to make you moderation's plaything
A pendulum's dream of keeping order

Crump Lake's a little north
The ponies have been there too
       and wanted to stay
        the day being beautiful

English is spoken with the accent of Adel
If you listen carefully
      and you will
            in the ambient stillness it's easy
Each discussion paused at times
Just enough to arrive at meaning

Adel the town
Whose name was a cow's name backwards

The teachers teach ponies
      until it's time to ride
        being carefully carried
           from a four-letter crossroads
The Hornets playing keepaway
                with cares

The Kidutokado band
      of the Northern Paiutes
          to resume their petroglyphs
          and the building of hunting blinds

The ponies of Adel know all about it
And so will you

93.   O'KEEFE LANE

You're Irish on the outskirts
The skirts commencing
      mere yards from "downtown"
        where a store is that
           and not much more

O'Keefe Lane
      is a country road
          as short as memory may be long

There's a ranch in Warner Valley

A parcel that helps us to last longer
A black cow wanders
      with tags on her ears
            yellow and white
                   her stare is profound

What goes on outside goes on inside
Like a prime time doc
      concerning auburn landscapes
      and long-lived Irish families
          with as many apostrophes
          as needed
              to supply tradition with a plow

Posts and wire
The cross hatched acres
      like an overlain geometry

But O'Keefe has no more Irish left
The island having lost its way
      and gone rogue too many times
          to gain attention now
        when infants rule
            and notice only bright colors

All their giggling and raucous tantrums
      prevent any history
          from assembling itself
The unfenced bull is not more uncaring

So brief is O'Keefe!
The lane like a dead end accomplished
      just when the generations dared
                 to plan ahead

Faraway places
      have brought declarations of war
          all the way to the Outback
Their mindless demands
      made more *fortissimo* than thunder
Their words an ugly subset of babble

I'm saving up to see what happens
Which makes me just another looky-loo

But for now
        the quiet lane with its quiet cow
                is sufficient seeing

Only politics is missing
Or at most is a windstorm
        shuffling the tumbleweeds

Tough love has built it   the town of Adel
And no more than what stands distinctly
      or is that which memory provides
Though it's a very *small* town
        I'm Irish enough to know
              there might be big city trouble
              that no one will understand
                                    for decades

O'Keefe *can*
        and *should*
                bring peace if he's allowed
May I be granted permission?

Can this be North America?
Or an earlier-than-ever continent
                of two dozen acres?

O'Keefe has captured a town
But I missed his conversations
        and the friendly revolution of his ranch

I want simple-to-understand history
                            over biscuits and gravy
Never mind the antlers in the store
The creatures' glassy eyes

There will be no more understanding
        than knowledge of life as an Etruscan
A mystery's more comfy anyway
A zone more suitable for vagabonds
                              as long as the money lasts

It makes you wonder   counting

So far the car stops and starts

But somewhere in all that machinery
       something's   tired   needs rest
       or else!

What happens will happen to me
I hope it's here
       when   with the last of my strength
              I'll walk the path to O'Keefe
              knock on the door
                      and request a lavabo

I'll take words to his door as well
As candidates
       for the office of approximate wisdom
See what he says
       while the bovine bass of freedom
                          bawls in her pasture

For now   there won't be any fuss made
It will just be Irish on the outskirts
       spoken with reverence
       and whatever pioneer accent
                      that may be easy

94. THE BLACK-AND-WHITE PORCH PUP BOW-WOW

Too far from home
       there was a black-and-white dog
         In the tawny landscape of Oregon's Adel

As if a movie of visitation were hybrid cinema

Part-this and part-that
       assembled on a doorstep
The laziest of ideas just lying there
The still from a video's flow

There's nothing left to do but love it

No stranger disturbs
Nor any dog dream of chasing

Its paws are precious furry
      and the rest of him fluffs   agreeably so
If he's old   if he's young
      I'd take him home
    if somehow
        he'd not be homesick for the doorway

This spot   this afternoon
      the entire kennel of Adel

I want to know   how to say it   "Adel"
Know which of those two syllables is stressed
        but I'm too shy to ask

For the Adel dog there's no stress at all
      and things like calculus
        are numbers not known

Black-and-white's the proposition
Nature takes a nap with no one's permission

I'd wake him with treats
      but being so shaggy
        it's hard to say if he's really asleep

If "first thought" is still the "best thought"
And Ginsberg's notion's not endangered
      we'll just observe and report
        like a conscientious security guard

Completely disappeared is any ownership now
For nothing's affordable   even the pooch
    you can tell

To see him's a fine detention
You wanna' say, "God bless you, dog!"
      until you realize what that may mean
Yes, pick the god or goddess
      that hasn't been up to some creep stuff

Oh, dog!
Oh, black-and-white exception
          to technicolor crimes!
You're historic
     far beyond the pages
          of history's screenplays

There's a man in Ohio who might understand
A friend with friendly poodles he has
     cavorting
          or sleeping like this one
          knowing things
               that can only be guessed at

Although I have no exceptional powers
     to discover his dreams
          still I'll gaze at him as if I *could*
The least that may accomplish rapport

Perhaps black-and-white can be lent
The good dog brought to the Bay
     and allowed to visit there
          as I've been pleased to visit Adel
There is always someone
     happy to meet a new dog

"You'd like her!" I whisper
But he snores nothing back
     no bark proclaiming he's ready to travel

"More likely she'll need to journey to *you*
Someone will tell her
     she'll come here for you"

I know I can't forget him
          for money
          for anything
A fluffy vision so very close up
          Nature's inexplicably friendly side

And he no doubt expects
     with innocence
          the bones to continue

                    in afternoons like this one
Their further manufacture taken for granted

Napping   he knows   something
          not known or believed
                  by the world of color
But I'm willing to learn it like the sleeper
                  his expectation to be my own

Remember what faith was?
Even without it the feeling returns
Attempts to make amends to illusion

He's guarding *himself*
His siesta's all it takes
      and the peace of his repose
          will see to it
               the crossroads stay a junction
               and just the weather
                      of random meteorology

A government of two rulers
          where certainty and circumstance
               pretend to compete
Adel's dyarchy nothing more
               than mere wagging
                            especially on Sundays

If she comes here
          she may miss citified late night
          may at first say no to so much silence
But black-and-white
          would soon put to bed the spectrum
               and a new
                    and sultry discernment obtain

A canine persuasion that roams the sage
Before   during   and after   satori

Please be advised
      "go fetch" is for humans too
And the balls that are thrown
               may enclose a dubious rubber
                    moving armies

>   moving out

I'll credit the dog
Perfection's afterthought

Praise how one is stopped
           entering or leaving the store
When dognapping drifts
               through our mutual intentions
               albeit unhurriedly

He's a *sympatico* breed
Although "breed" is a hard word to say
             without blushing ever so slightly

I wonder if he'd like ice cream
             and if he was ever owned at all

If you get here in time for when he wakes
           you can help with the answers
                 and anything that's unforeseen
Like a need to raise a family
                  right here in the doorway

It doesn't have to be a *hadj* you journey
         it's not a mecca
And the prayers you say
         may be a beseeching all your own

Best wishes for what's lying there
A sprawl of pure understanding

So, "Loie, take a train
         and I'll wait in Adel   it ain't no far!"

95. ADEL TO PLUSH

Adel to Plush is an Oregon road
And you have to stay on it to travel

Though left and right beg for detours
        continue
It can be slowly of course
For the first encounter with the lake
        that seems to lengthen as you go

Adel to Plush is better summer afternoons
        when the western ridge
            keeps the road in shadow
            not asking for thanks
Then may contrast be all it can be
            and not be called a fiction

So far the landscape hasn't lied
At thirty miles-an-hour you'd know
        the speed beyond a covered wagon's
        but well below a desire to get somewhere

Going north
        will be going west
            when Plush is found
            and the highway loops to Lakeview

West after awhile
After seeing how melancholy clings
            to whatever it can
                that's still in the sun

Like right now   when slowing
        for the sight of bulls
        and how they wander
                profoundly uncertain

"Should I just lie down? it's over!"

They seem unnatural
Not quite right
They've too much time
        to be killed or allowed to live

Although they are massive
        their weight is merely *future* pounds
            their stares accusatory

As if they'd call you names if they could
Speak their truth to reprobates

I'm worried they see me
And remember the license plate

What's needed's a guitar   here to there
There's a field for humans too
　　　　but so far it's empty
　　　　for grazing's elsewhere
　　　　　　　and unaccompanied by reason

What's wrong they stay so far away?
What is it
　　　　that's taking so long
　　　　　　　that Nothingness
　　　　　　　is tempted to take over the world
Or at least get involved?

There's a page of history
　　　　that might have applied
　　　　　　　but someone tore it up
　　　　　　　and wrote a novel instead
Perhaps even put out an album

The universe isn't the same as before
There's worry
　　　　that discovery's only made it worse

Even if you hitched a ride
　　　　there's no escaping   nevermind
The Plan is unknown
　　　　and so far topography's silent too

Adel to Plush
Switching gears
　　　　to hear another way of travel
　　　　　　　the rear view sampled
　　　　　　　for the very recent past
Pretending New Year's could happen here
　　　　　　　　　　　right alongside Easter

What's office space
　　　　to Crump's amazing inland lake?

The fever of song and story
      has spread to every landform
      every temperature raised
            without saying too much

What's left is left behind   like pavement
This Oregon road
      driven slowly
           just to make sure of solitude's structure

It's good   and getting better

Like a perfect job
      that brings you to work and back
And the pay
      does not depend on widgets-per-hour
           but lets you play with your employer
Every afternoon in the western shadow!

Melancholy's easy
Something separate but wanting a paycheck
      if only for so longing to see you

It's a media-savvy route
Hart Mountain making headlines
      with the long lake
           writing editorials on Becoming

The sage so many journalists
      reporting the wealth discovery misses
Sage that stiffly moves with the wind
         but is a generous storyteller

All in addition to skimpy history
A promotion scruffy yet concise
      saying how much longer   exactly
         the Outback can stay out

Who I am is Adel to Plush
Only transiting this shaded shore

Make it a Father's Day
      for bachelors
      working to fix things

    like cars or anything else
           that needs fixing

The dominant culture's too tired to continue
I'm listening   looking for what follows
And what was in second gear
   that could be first
      because I don't want to get there
     well   not exactly

Just maybe
Until some pictures are taken
   as evidence
      in the case of heartaching surprise
Like when you first asked me to dance

96. SUPPLIES IN PLUSH

In the town of Plush while buying supplies:

He was drunk and making speeches
         like a silly politician

"In order to vote in *my* country
   you'll need much more than a picture I.D.!
You'll need proof you climbed Mt. Everest!
Everest in winter, naked!

"Not only that," he blathered,
   "you'll need very special skills
    like the ability to feed rabid service dogs
      by *hand*
       until they expire
And you will need an I.Q. of at least 200!"

He teetered he garbled he guffawed
It was weird
   and not expected
      in Plush's little store and bar

    with the dollars hanging
        tacked and signed

He kept talking

"And you'll need to be a drunk like me
And be monitored for insults

"Also you won't get to vote if you're too alone
Not only *that*
  in my country you'll vote by bowling
  and you *have* to bowl 300!
Do you hear me?!"

We did
  and his belches
    and broken bottles

Plush had made him a sandwich
A big one
  and it took some doing
    because he wanted the *works*
        with his triple cheeseburger

He continued drooling

"And you won't get to vote
  unless you can ward off the spiders
  the giant spiders
    I saw in my dream last night
That's right!

"And *further*more!
In order to vote in my country
  you'll need to get your picture taken
     with Santa Claus!
Hold a poetry reading at 7 am!
Be fluent in Hottentot!
With all those 'clicks' in all the right places
  that the language requires!

"You'll need to remember my name
    even if I change it every day!
You'll have to bathe in a lake of my choosing!

Abandon your cell phone!
Adopt a tone of hostility!
Learn the art of curling and teach others!"

I listened absent-mindedly in the aisles
      snatching SPAM
      and Cheetos
           from the shelves
Choosing drinks a teetotaler drinks
Grabbing peaches and apples

The "candidate"
      or whatever he was
      had even *more* to say

"In my country
      to be sure of your vote
      you must be sure of *me* and not doubt!
You must make an *airplane* of your ballot
And then sail it
From the *summit* of Hart Mountain
      so that it lands on the Lake of Destiny!

"And you just can't vote till I *say* so!"

And then
      with all the supplies
           that anyone would ever need
And while everyone whooped and hollered
While even the collie joined in with an "arf!"
      I gave a token hoot and a shout
                    and stole away

To a country of one citizen only
Where voting's completely absurd
      and just moot
           and mere nodding   of my head

97. ADDITIONAL BULLS

The foreground
      and background
           has filled with additional bulls

They just keep coming
They just keep appearing

As if some stimulus were in play
      for uncontrolled reproduction

I keep saying,
      "Just look at you multiplying
         like outsized cells
            romanced by God-knows-what!"

They are being bad and proud *of* it
And wishing *beyond* pride
      to accomplish *other* deadly sins
         and parade them
           all the way
               to Oregon's horizon

But while the world will have none of it
      the beef people laugh
      and *welcome* more bulls
           than they've ever seen before

Bulls rampant yet divine!
Bulls antsy to make more of themselves
      talking bull
         on the same page of proliferation

It is a same-day same-sex explosion
Unqualified by moderation or caution
And there is nothing in time to stop it
And the go-for-broke bulls
      make fools of the cowboys
      sent to somehow manage
         a herd of such proportions
         all of Crete would have said, "Enough!"

But it isn't B.C.   nosiree!
It is the west past its prime and prime beef
     so that the bulls of Crump Lake
       grow in number   grow in size
          and play footsie with each other
While the sky
     with dangling participles
         attempts to make sense of it all

Bulls in addition
Bulls mathematical
Numbers' message

They were supposed to stay just a few
      and far apart
       the spread still spacious
Maybe the summer blows out of proportion
The heat causing eyesight illusions

There they are
Eyes *closed* they are there
       a deep *field* of bulls!

Like cows they moo
     but there is snorting
       grunts galore
       and lots of bellowing
It is a "what do we do *now*?" sound

Oh, bulls!
We're so glad you're asking questions!
Even Sartre would be proud
     of your existential baritone vowel
       which   as a chorus
       sounds
          in the ruthless countryside

The recipient passersby are thus serenaded
     and qualified for amazement

"Them bulls is smart," says my neighbor
"I saw them
     studying their multiplication tables

        when I drove up!"

There are so many
And so very suddenly
      there hasn't been time to take
           or take stock
They'd be a strong military
      should they choose to stampede

I'd like to know what metaphor they are
What symbol
      that strives with numbers
          to inform the languid

Force them to wonder
      what else is akin to this spectacle
          what drama's found example
          likes its chances for acceptance

Perhaps a ruling class
One that can't get enough of itself
      and so the God of Cattle got involved
         spoke truth to power
            and filled a foreground
            and background

With bulls
Bulls in addition

Or perhaps a comedian
      with magical powers
         who thinks magical thoughts
            wished to bring to life
              an alternative "vast majority"
A vastness just getting started

I'm feeling beastly too!
Something different going on
A sense of "This is it!"

A kind of inflation
      where it takes more and more bulls
      to make a pasture

They're kind of cute in spite of their size
There's no reason to kill them
            you'd interrupt the show
It's admittedly weird
But I'm calling former friends so they can see it

And now the furthest bulls
        are further away than ever before
What we love about expansion
I'm sure they've shown up
                beyond the distant dunes

At least it's occurred to them to go
Their hooves
        are a footwear from ancient shoe stores
            when "cloven" was a novelty

Uncontrolled is the herd
        though it mostly just stands there
                tuition-free in the College of Cud
And they *mingle*
Like students cramming for a final

Well, they're graduating
        though the world will have none of it

Their sins are yet to be committed
True rampant   true antsy for a doubling
        their prime numbers crowding

There's a message
            think I get it   but summer keeps me dumb

One last look
        and then the road again
But first a little sleep
I'll make it a nap 'cause it isn't the night

It's so much bullshit it must be canceled
 And   unconscious   it could happen
        when daydreams manage populations

And one prize bull

        is left to snort insistence
        that things are not as they seemed
            but somehow
                were close enough
                    to the jazz of menace
                    to play on a *very* sunny day!

98. LAYERS OF LIGHT

"May it be a brief summation, m'lord
Though what I wish to tell you deserves a novel?"

"Thank you for sending me there, sire
        to the Edge   to the Layers of Light!
        dark blue to faintest yellow!

"Thank you for Crump Lake, your Excellency!
The *sine qua non* of aesthetics!

"May it please you
        to accept a single sentence, your grace
            as my words did refuse me?
They'd said,
        'No excessive hysterics
            it is only sand and water
                and a zone of flora
                    so shut up!'

"And those words
        of my words
            I'm compelled to tell

"Pretty-please-with-sugar, m'lord
      do forgive!
I don't know why the words refused
But I'd consider it an honor to stick around
        find out

        if your majesty's budget
           might allow for an extended stay

"When new words may obey
                like   'limnetic'."

99. HART'S HAZY DISTANCE

Some came by Greyhounds
      and Trailways
Were even supplied pillows for the journeys
Close friends and newlyweds

The routes were many
But there was never a ticket to Hart
              the Hart Mountain Refuge

It was just too far to go
       winding on gravel to level highlands
           and their elevated antelopes

Even now   here in the haze
      it seems unreachable   legendary
                   broad daylight not withstanding

Like a love lost
      that was in need of attention at the time
A quick phone call at least
      to address "First Things First"
      in the aftermath of hurtful insults said

The amends
      that require you make them right away
      because sometimes
           the gods of all that's good demand it

And no money offered to get your life back
Just a timely admission of error will do
Never giving up

    for it may be enough
      to gain the antelope's leap
       in the country of our wanderings

Where we heard the classical music
    played as soundtracks of certain Westerns
      with a principle at stake
The MGM lion lending his voice
Like a guarantee of freedom

Now   trying not to say goodbye
And before getting there
   I ask where   where is the treasure now
   that once was everywhere apparent?

What combination of luck and sunshine
     will lift the veil
     that mists the mountain?

The Hart not mistaken for grief
   but allowed to shine
   in spite of the strange darkness
     that's boarded a bus somewhere
       and rides in search of refuge

100. THE DUNED SHORE EAST

It was so restful to see it
The colors of a desert
   in a temperate playground

The dunes seemed a life insurance
   better than some policy devised
It might have been the pristine sands
     angling to the shore
       of a lake named wrongly
        the English not to be heard at all

A bad headache was left to cobalt blue

And one's entire mind put at ease
As when Lawrence reached the Canal
      and reassured Farad
         saying, "It's all right…"

No ship will pass   and Arabia's a rumor
Even David Lean did not believe it

But here are the dunes
Oregon's Suez
      and beyond it
           the child's play
              of unboxed freedom

Where "Nuthin' doing"
      is a quest for Mohammed
To see if he has any further plans
Or whether it can stay a playground
           of shouts and babble

So restful the breeze!
Like an assurance of life
      despite its overthin span

Life has found a landscape
      that meant it didn't matter
      anymore
           than the correct pronunciation of a sigh

101.   JUNIPERS' SLOPES

The junipers waited   coniferous
Their species a series of illusions spaced
A managed acreage
      far from horticulture's whims
         its inclined soil
         beyond all expectations

No one had been kissed goodbye

Rather   persuasion left farewells unsaid
And so we traveled together
     to emergency medicine so scentful

And though the junipers are found in high-up Tibet
     it's enough they flourish in the Outback
     their airborne pollen
          spelling allergy as many ways
          as the word may be said

But really   why *not* get close?

Though completely male versions
     rate a "10" on the Ogren Scale
          the female's a "1"
          and considered an allergy *fighter*
So you might get lucky
Going near you might improve

Can you say "*Cupressaceae*?"
How about "*Tracheophytes*?"
Neither can I
     but allow yourself the climb
          through this aromatic forest
          to harvest its berries

Let an evergreen fantasia
     qualify your conscious waking
     with needle-like precision
The hard-shelled seeds to soften reflection

May you bloom in every autumn
     like the *Juniperus communis*
          your juvenile foliage full ranging
          without flowers or fruit
               yet gifting even so and silently

En route to Plush
     be fanning out
     to reconnoiter the balcony of plants
Like an ideology of patience on high

The slope is an angled planter
Tempting children to get lost

        or at least do some hiding

It is a playable game and acceptable hooky
Their mingled sopranos
      like the Old Days somehow

We'll find the right emoji to summon them
One that's ambulatory
    and   smiling   good at roundup

Like you
      the juniper encompasses open spaces
And is always seeking them
      with their attendant moths and butterflies

Blowy Oregon awaits
And *has* been waiting with all its junipers
      monoecious and *dioecious*

A sixth sense to follow
Constructing bows
      backed with sinew for hunting
The ghosts of mammoths remember as much

Now in the sun-dark glen
      no fragrance compares

I'd saved some peponida for this
The fruit for seeking the fame of juniper
      and how it will stay the whole night
      delivered to your new home

Someone had said
      "See you on the bottom rung"
But there were so many rungs
And the ladder was so long
      I lost interest
        except for a dilettante's interest in botany

It's stayed that way
Junipers now are the main attraction
      what we talk about and highlight

This hill is our choice

Newlywed we'd invite our friends
        and celebrate the vows
          without distractions
Filling our *quaichs* with Scottish beverages
            in a *zipcode* of botany

What happens now
        depends on computers
And it may come to pass
          that *machines* will marry
Everyday unions spic-and-span with circuitry

I'll continue to fight for otherwise
Just to get attention
        that the transition to unfeeling
           may be less than cut-and-dried

The real world is what you say it is
Or shout or gesture
And working hard for a living
          is slaving for a tyrant

Adel to Plush will make it plain
        the junipers remedy the unlearned

We're brilliant without warning
Delightfully taught to see an ending
           that is foolish optimism
We will be going to elsewhere's delusions
But the grandeur
        of these scruff evergreen will linger

The seeds of an overall comprehension
That starts with handholding
        and otherworldly attractions

The junipers
        were not expecting anyone today
Certainly not ourselves
And our herd of lost quaggas
        far from their South African range

It's nice to be so newlywed
        we know not

    what it means to squabble!

102. THE DARK BLUE THAT PULLS YOU OVER

It is not the police this time

It's hoping that   losing one's faculties
    it will be sight
    that's the last sense to fail

Even music
    cannot be this color
        and say so many things
When photons
    the *carriers* of color
        find the wavelength of light
            most suitable for serenity

A dark blue
    suggesting black
        has an upside hue
Like a project begun by the Cosmos
To see if something may be made of the Void

Truth is
    the Lake of a certain Crater
        cobalt's uncanny pigment
And the near-shore blue of Crump's body of water
        means nowhere else perhaps
            need you look
            at this time of day
            on the way
                to midnight's certainty

It's a challenge
A good job done by the universe
    to dazzle and set in motion
        a rage to possess such a blue!

Begin back-and-forth artistry
The brush with furious purpose applied
The very best argument for blue
                lying lengthwise

A final decision before arriving at violet
The freight train of "ultra"
        delayed for the sake of a canvas
The institution of the rainbow
                to show a preference

Long before this
        the brain trust of scenery's gods
            said, "Behold!"
        and made it so

This blue
        had been a dream allowed
And in its slumber the level lake appeared
Just as this dark blue has
                that pulled the traveler over

As if Nature were freshly remodeled
        for a later age than this
And whoever should see it joins the future
                              ahead of time

Thank God the color has no time limit
Says only, "Just a minute, I'll be right with you"
As if it were an appointment
           one that required a co-pay
           a dedication to deep blue
                    and not merely noting it in passing

Still friends with the idea of dropping out
        there was further absenting
             a freedom
                with behind-the-scenes knowledge

If one says it's not to be missed
                it would be going too far
The wonders just one valley yonder
(Yes, think "yonder"   make it familiar)

The wonders there as many as here
                      you're fulfilled either way

Give it another name than the map's
It doesn't have to be "Dark Blue"
Can be any name you fancy

Walk with me   keeping things just right
      as you'd have to
          with any small business
                  all day any day

No music can be this color now or ever
No matter how much wishing
No harmonies of Franck
        will contest its melancholia
        the last color
            being the easiest to see

Not doing anything
        this blue takes care of everything

It's said the planet's out of time
And it's true enough you seek a color
        to say it right in the hills and valleys

All the violence there is
        will be yet to come with indigo's brain
        the mind of Newton
His color wheel lurching in fits and starts
Supplanting homegrown intuition
        the shorter wavelength more succinct
                              for a descriptor's purpose

And were this the last chronicle
        mention must be made
        the dusk to shorten its life
            as if by a snapping of fingers

Nothing in the night
        may tell of the sun's cycle complete
Yet imagination
        once more

            fills a need to know it all

How a pigment
      turns out to be an esculent devoured
            for its flavor of Infinity
            or just the thrill of novelty

There is
      at present
            no realistic expectation of privacy
            the world collapsing inward
Last glimpses of one's very own scenery
      serve as finale

As reflection
      upon a poetry that stayed readable
      up-to-date
The quandaries of the past examined
With stanzas of the many forms
Villanelles   pantoums   sonnets   sestinas

Failings pored over
Wars parsed for the inventions they sponsored
Who has ever been ready for that?

Dark blue will cover dark acts
Even now   what is seen is how evil is not
An aquamarine
      that glosses over and readily
         a real estate
           of water cooled down
                to a desperate concealment

This survey is suspect though
A purview itself colored blue
      as many varieties *of* it
      as in professional pages offering paint

The Cosmos   right here and now
           proposes a closer inspection
Is no longer content with human assumptions

Oregon's Crater

Mazama's perfect pool
The West has given names
      but let's stop saying them
It's bad enough
      that   once assigned
      they're impossible to cancel
            like acts unforgivable

Every day is a chapter in blue
You wonder how it does that

The heart
      has not captured love enough
      to survive certain colors
One's life is let go of
         to explore what it might
              without arteries

Find a place
      where someone cares enough to say,
"You better get some sleep
Slip into something softer than cowhide"

It is a color metallic
And may be the reason its beauty yields unease

The sun-damaged world
      needs a sketch of this outtold story
A fighting fool would dispense with philosophy

The deep past preening
And nobody cares
      in the overcold overture of what's to come
For once   no fighting can change its color
      lively for all the solemn chanting

The time of day telling of the days
      down which
           like stairs
              the present descends
The very best afternoon
Like a final decision regarding the rainbow

For the sake of the gods proclaim "Behold!"

    though the millions hear not

And while the level lake
    is stirred
      that holds the blue
          the brain of the planet knows best
         and consults Nature
             before any remodeling

There's nothing to be scared of
"Just a minute, I'll be with you" means just that

Brahms is not a part-time musician
But always is sending symphonies to Earth
        dedicated
     to this dark blue absentee freedom

And you're fulfilled with the unnaming

Are you suffering still?
What balm beyond this blue
     is not uncertain shuffling in a fixt card game ?

You'll not know the reason you die
       and repeat the same life till now
All the violence there was unpreventable
                        the prison of a loop

Books to school again in the cold blue morning
Where what is wrong's once more delayed
     among the wonders of just one valley

Or at dusk   and after that
      when the night adds its *polish* to blue
         awhile
         until a candidate star appears
            and Infinity
           seems a plausible pigment

One to be applied   and liberally
    to a canvas
    that stretches
        all the way from here to the moon
Be the artist no one saw in time

Expecting publicity
      in spite of an obsession with privacy

The wars were poems enraged
      and barely spoken words at all
            just guttural sounds in blue combat zones

I'm still friends with many other ideas
But they phone less often
      and leave no forwarding

"Whatcha' gonna' do when the well runs dry?"
      answered with screeching!
Whatever faculties have flown
        have left their universities
        hoping for easier assignments
            than science and medicine

And they whirl away from responsible acts
When photons fierce
      seek the center
      of Crump Lake's sidelong expanse

What's next is color-coded
      and so far the code has stayed unbroken
The overcold past
      has yielded present-day obsessions
        with what may be seen
        as far as may be seen

No surprise the landscape has a hit single
A thorough treatment of dark blue
And you see what happens
      with just a color to think of
We're going to see exactly   see truly
        straightened
        like the shore

As if blue would force a decision:
"Now that you know
      what will you do
          besides causing problems?"

If you insist you don't understand

      we'll camp out   give it time
    time   it turns out   you have
Like waiting on hold   tireless
Not minding this view of perfection

This is your summer
       augmented with philosophy
Sure of the road and where it may go
          into soft and chilly illusions
         nevertheless structured
                    irresistibly

Like an *industry* of knowing
       that other people in other rooms
      will listen to Mozart
          and wish dark blue to never cease
Having happily been pulled over too

103.   WHAT'S HORIZONTAL'S LEFT TO ENTHRALL

What's horizontal here is left to enthrall
     though gravity-flattened

Open the Outback
    like a newspaper
        wanting circulation to keep it known

Live to see the evening edition
The editorials concerning what is transitory
Save the cartoons for after that
     and save some work for yourself
        summarizing futility
       physical gold
          fought for and squandered

The only news in this ancient place
     the latest touch of your hand
        that brings history up to date

And makes of it a present tenderness

By the look on your face
        I think that dharma's shown up
                to underlie appearances

Kinesics is all
What it means to be on the level
        when the horizontal Earth may enthrall
And although I'm a nonimage
        sure of nothing but your angel's grace
                            the contact celebrity suits

There is to be no brooding
        in a broken-down pickup
It will start again if you say so
                and with just your hands

You appeared out of a planar reverie
        ghosting Crump Lake and all its basin
                                  lyricizing delight
The failed structures of Elsewhere deserted
Almost unexpectedly
        the wilderness is in charge of marriage

Think that psychological changes
        are swiftest in the outdoors
                when your true desperation
                              may be revealed
A clarification to match the untouched mirage

Your subscription to gravity's pages renewed
Live to see what's left to enthrall
        and what dharma says to do
                in the dusk of all attachments

Your kinesics studied
        for good meanings the angels allege
                and strive to make known

104. FROM THE WET SHORELINE

Without a single course correction
      Crump Lake was found
        putting faith in crash landings
The waterlogged shore quite lonely till then

Green's a wet color
      wanting thorough inspection
        and mostly it's been waiting
          for a drama's slow motion

Just getting started's
      the end of a long siesta
        the Bureau of Land Management approved

Just getting started's
      learning to say "endorheic"
        knowing the ghosts of Warner Valley
          are watching
Watching over the Greater Petroglyphs
            and so much more

There'd been an island once
Right there in the middle
      destroyed for artifacts
      souvenirs
        of no comprehended tribe

The arrows   the relics
      however meager
        had to be found
        the island dozered
          and reduced to nothing at all

It is a goal to find Deep Creek
Twelve Mile, too
      and the waters of Pelican Lake
And study the flow of everything

Like going home to a meadow and marshes
With voices saying,
      "We'll send you more if you're stoic!"

The sodium and potassium
       attest to elements dissolved
              for the sake of chemistry alone
And staying busy with the periodic table
The nutrients' narrow wetlands
       are recited for *Scrabble*
             "phosphorus" and "chlorophyll"

Perhaps a redband trout will explain itself
And the cougar
       bobcat and mule deer
              reveal their plans for the future

Should the mountain chickadee tweet
The orange-crowned warbler
       and the spotted towhee misdirect traffic
And should the tundra swan take a liking
The American bittern change its identity
The swallows and nighthawks come when called
The whiteface ibis grow confused in migration
       all is made even green
              with flyover assured

Oh, Captain!
Captain William H. Warner!
       what happened to you in the dew of 1849?
Did you get too topographical?
Was being an engineer not enough?

They say it was an ambush
Bows and arrows
       too bad and very sad
You were as young as I want to be now
Putting up with ambush myself to make it so
       for twice thirty-seven's inconvenient

What?   he went to West Point?
    okay
    well, so will I
And when we travel to Crump Lake's shores
                                that'll be it

No further than the marshes

       and family photos
We'd be done and just tell stories
For it's possible to be a pioneer there
   a rancher botanist geologist

As soon as Simon says
   you may regale the company
     lost to urban geometry
Speaking of 3-D informed by flora and fauna

Perhaps your wish may be their own
And they too
   will seek the soft wet shoreline
   here presented in the dubious Holocene

The brain works well
   in shallow inland seas endorheic
Even a duffer's better-balanced then
   No stumbling no problem

In the low-lying places
   waterlogged
     and profoundly flooded
       with rushes and reeds
       and all the herbaceous plants
             no sinking

Rather you lightly go
A furtive spirit's reconnaissance

North of Adel science goes to sleep
   and dreams of an ancient animist realm
Joins superstition's quest for a higher reality
All creatures lucky or unlucky
   are yet safe for sure from experiments
   where "intelligent design" is a laboratory

With the net worth of homeless
   I want this a chronicle
     of when
     and where
       prehistory appears
A better life than predictable downfall

Ladies and gentlemen!
Can you   for once in your life
     just cease and desist?
     be truly ladies and gentlemen!?
     live up to those plurals?
Even if it means you're stuck in the West
       with wagons and mules
                      and handcrafted clothes?

Your new start to stay a piece of advice
Taken like shaman's medicine

There is a damp passage
The sponge of the ground absorbing travel
     all belongings strewn with arrival
       when you form an opinion
       and allow for semiotics

All the benefits of a symbolic terrain
The sign a pool's your very own plunge
That watery swale the way to hydration
A heartbeat's promise
     you're not in too much trouble

By the time one's course is correct
By the time a faith is found
     and the topographical engineer Warner
       is saved for later
        the arrows averted
          deflected by lasting peace

When loneliness discovers children's games
And joins in to get better
     then the world will be encoded
     with some percentage of gratitude!

Like a pleasantness uncovered
Just when you thought archaeology was done for

We'll run again   not only walk
Run like a candidate
     nothing knowing
       until his puppet self's informed by sylphies
Their table of contents spilling all over

New petroglyphs are stirring
       that would tell the whole story
Even the first
When the wetlands knew a hunter's presence
       and that of the gatherer

Their infinite patience north and south

I'm hearing the same birds
Learning the catalogue
       of light and dark coloration
       to conceal   or dangerous appear

The projectile points to settle accounts
Then the going home to a meadow
       which the flow of everything permitted
       and just now
         when you think about it

When a species
       not yet introduced to the wild
       still discovers its wherefores at least
And thus is no grand conclusion made

105.   SHADED TREES AND FUTURE GROVES

The trees that would be shade are sheltered too

It was a theme the desert sun had sung all day
       so in-and-out of the clouds' powers
       were all the plains
         and hills
          below their summits' arrest
           at the hands
            of a ragged *posse* of cloud shadow

A scene not easily imitable

Even CGI must fail
        though it's likely the techies who try
                would attempt something else

The cedars close by
        and those further groves
                attest to indirect lighting
                arranged by deities
Those gods that would misguide

There's an alphabetical order to the beauty
It's like coming to a home before it's built
        all the ancestors yet to be
        and some devil let loose
                          to wreak havoc beforehand

Get something out of its system ahead of time
Before any drum is heard
        or ideatic cloud is darkened
                      and others
Midnight suggested with just that piece of the day

It's about the dimming
And how we get a feeling
        that's both relief and foreboding

You stop playing horseshoes to consider the sky
And maybe there's more of a breeze than before
The air moving
        in accordance with the molecular
The shade some sober recollection
        needing timeout to make an impression

Something delivered
        that's determined to satisfy
                despite the doubt attending
And capture those trees further off
As if that *something* were going around

You want to suddenly turn away
Even though you'd been throwing "ringers"
        and love the clank of that connection

Someone says to finish what you start
        but that was in the bright sun's moments

Let a biography begin
        with these near and far shadows
Each chapter to be an illustration
            with trees mostly cedar

 Imagine how much better the colors can be
        when the sun's tyrant yellow
        is toned down to subtlety
            and not allowed to constantly surprise

Being left alone
        there's always more incentive
The best results are
        every day
            the trees that shade
                are sheltered too

The shade seems to whisper,
"We'll see about that!"
        as if it truly believed
        in its umbra's better picture
The big picture of the sun
        left to burn in the sprockets

Shade on a payroll of unvarnished truth-telling
        with a crossbow's precision
A facepalm moment the emoji intended

One hundred percent of calm is required
With surroundings seen
        and those imagined

The rustle of a novel's pages turned by the breeze
The plains and hills
        repainted swiftly yet carefully
            detail's import fully grasped

There will be a cloze
For reading comprehension
        the book and panorama both
                wanting perusal

What the clouds have tutored
       I'll turn over to you
             who slept the noontime through
It was how to get rich without gold
The G2V star above our heads
       thwarted *just* enough
             by cotton's white islands drifting

A persistent marketing plan for all terrain
Whose obscuration
       lessons the lucky ones who know to wait

Plush knows   and daily endures
The only bar
       patient as the dollars that change hands
           or hang
           with initials
                from the ceiling

Plush
Whose interior spaces
       resemble the shade exterior
             wanting only a little appreciation
And further towns are also eclipsed
Gone to bed in the little night of the day

Of course it's a game of the cumulus
To cover   uncover   like horseshoes
      connecting or not
      before travel's resumed

There's not much to it but air
Still the clouds may a story start
        with the least hint of moisture
           and all else
              with a preference
                  for minimal belongings

It will be CGI's repeated tries
And coming close but no cigars
Those pixels
      in the end
           refusing to assemble

       their minute mosaics

And the devil confined to *attempts* at detail
Still determined to satisfy his lust
       but unable to start
       or stop
            his drinking

106.   THE GOLDEN LINE

The golden line is weather-dependent
The summer's underlined Hart Mountain
       all of its base defined
       the above and the below
            levelly divided

Thinnest crease you may imagine
As if Euclid's early constructs
       the math of yester
          were brought to the present
          and offered to the sense of sight

Like something earned and saved for later

And gold
       like a sealant
          separating land
The lofty antelopes from life in the green grass

Whatever Western this is
       the music's *adagio* for the stunts of frogs

Those things you were saying were strata too
Like a composite learning
Layers of meaning
A need to water   hey!
       where'd the marshal go?

Never mind

>   it's a matter of aesthetics
>   the natural order nicely seen

What you were saying illustrated thus
A lifetime warranty for lying flat
Just a camera the proof it's possible

Severely or tenderly think of it
That golden in-between
      scarce as the metal
          yet fully supporting the point you make

The fault block of Hart
      and its almost secret spring on high

          beautiful
          delineating

107. SUNSTONES

Can't find them
Can't keep them
      they'd even be lost
      they'd be mislaid

Don't even want them in the first place
Better someone *else* get hold of them
      bring their dazzle to parties
          be no fuss that way

Sunstones
They sound hot just being pronounced
      their plural courting greed
         something shiny to show to others
            energy in the share
              as if a search for more were ongoing

The display of treasure an urgent intermission

There's copper in the stones
        the geologic story
                hard to appreciate

And there's the story of best friends
Gone looking and gone missing
Please *someone* say why
        why anyone strives for the sunstone at all

Maybe it's a love
        that gets started and can't be stopped
        love for a plagioclase feldspar
                a triclinic crystal system

System of *sparkle*
Which   once beheld
        takes you places
                you never thought you'd go to
Southern Norway and Sweden
The basin of Baiku
        and the shores of Australia

But maybe *most* of all
        the sunstone will send you to Plush
                the Oregon town
                that's nearest treasure
They say *its* crystals are the largest
The copper *most* eager to dazzle from within
The hues most contrasting
        when the sunstone's turned

The sense of sight made the most important
Yet suggesting there may be more
        than the sense can make of it
Chemistry's astounding credentials
        not letting on right away
        it intends to use them
                to get you to say
                      "That's mighty pretty!
                              how much?"

It is the madness maybe
        of personal vicissitudes
                that present as commendable modesty

I'd suffer the irrational greed
Journey to Plush
      where I wish to be anyway
And think of it as a large village with cars
      that people then get out of
        and then start walking
             and looking at the ground

The time and space of it wanting perusal

There isn't a gate but there could be
Since some say it's paradise
      and paradise has one
        sufficient to enclose

A district of shine
Where certain stones
      contain the seeds of other suns
And ecstasy may be held in your hands
      while you call out loudly with discovery
        as if rehearsing for Shakespeare
        and lassoing the moment

In the forever home of Plush
      it is not their fault the gems so arrest
        and signal the strength of a star
          where interiors burn so intently

Too bad I can't find them
But when I *did* once
      I couldn't hold on to them
        after the lucky improbable day they were found

Don't even want them   really
Like much else meant for others

It's no one's fault that plunder's afoot
      our species profoundly inclined
And even country music can't calm things down
The itch is continuous scratching
And the ground must yield its sunstones
      to modify personalities

You didn't ask
And I didn't tell you I went there anyway
    to be in the *wake* of discovery
                      onlooking

Went to Plush to complete stealing dollars
      off the walls
      and ceiling
           of the only bar
In lieu of actual prospecting

Hoping the sunstone hunters' blindness
    will miss my avarice
    before I'm found out

Should have listened to you more carefully
You   who have more ideas than merely human
It will take a few years to course-correct

Still I want you to have one   maybe a few
There's no obligation you *accept* the sunstones
You could even throw them away
    or gift another

But they just feel fraudulent in *my* hands
Like some sort of loot
Maybe what attracts is the word
    "sunstone"
        and what it should be
        and cannot be entirely
            unless suggestion counts

Call it a mineral's aspiration to resemble the sun
Or the mind's runaway concept
    Pythagoras to explain
        what Nature imperfectly displays

Perhaps early success
    may assuage the demons that sit
    transfixed themselves by glitter
Beginner's luck to quiet the cravings
Letting souls turn inward
    where they damned well belong

Now it's the sun and sunstroke
The unbalanced state of assigning value
  and rescue isn't every day deserved
    putting on a *tie* for the sunstones

It was the peer pressure of interest
        that made it formal
And sure enough
  there they are
   glinting wanting to be in your hands
    in the back-to-back season
     of more of the same

You'll know what to do
I think this one here's a record crystal
  and it grew
   just to fit your finger and enthrall!

108. SMALL HOUSES, BIG COUNTRY

Small houses big country

No matter the mansion
  and the changes you wanted
   the country downsizes
Eastern Oregon's dimensions making sure of this

The noble Outside to temper that Inside
The future results
  as far away as the see-past horizon
  and depending on the fresh sage of patience

The tiny house tries Immensity
And aspires to cloud land
  the forms within a form familiar
And generations brief as sudden instincts
   strive
    in a vastness

I want to sleep in small houses
        sampling minimum shelter
Though a Bosendorfer *grand* be found
And multiple stairways
            still it's luxury's illusion
                an emergency appeal for comfort

Life-threatening the vista
Those ridges and the empty mountains
        like a flawless newfound planet
            whose dangers are not fully understood
                like heart failure

I'm yet unborn
And so survival's a moot proposition

From the plains to the coast
        a cityless land has allowed small mansions
           where the wayward are welcomed back
                and recruited to farm
                with the ghost of Barbara Stanwick
Her Big Valley filled to the brim
                with Old Western thought

I'll help you discover
The schoolhouse   solitary
The play school that's a whole university
        all of it enrolled in a higher education
        provided daily with every single sunrise

Tickets at the last minute
And the price of admission
        to the so, so big country
            and its cute little houses?
Just your smile
The amazing value of your modest appraisals

Nothing in the night
        may so favorably illumine
                as your candle

There'll be a house
Perhaps a former ranchero
        part of the incomplete empire

Spain had to lose

Some Laura Ingalls would like this
And save for later   for you
A "little house"
      that might be splendid and sprawling
          if not for the spread of Oregon
              where everything's a tipi with blankets
            really

And any piano's made pianissimo by the westerlies

I would stand this ground
Place where I can even see my mother and father
And there's a gramophone
      long-playing the classics
      all the moments different, too
              lengthy as clouds

There's a lens that lets you see
      what's large and small at once
      and human kindness guides the glass

Before dawn is the imagination prepared
For our own private day
      with a beginning   middle
          but no end
When you stay and study
As if for a report card
      where deportment's a code of silence

A conference dispersed
      are the dwellings in a go-forth theater

The bankrupt prairie's a Far-Left graveyard
Where the ghosts of their bad acting
      yet seek approval and acceptance
The raving Right is buried too
And   phantoms *themselves*
      go as banshees about

It will go badly   this afterlife messaging
Where Left and Right in the extreme tie the knot
      and are canceled each in the combat

I'm merely drowsy
   and check the weather with you
We are making no predictions ourselves

While the latest technology's put back in its box
And I'll run for the office of nothing at all
    campaigning on whispers' innuendo
    and rumors

It'll be fun to see if anyone votes!
The country's so big anything's possible
When they ask if I did
   I'll say I just wanted to help
     make a few waves
     concerning a theory as policy

We'll decorate our mansion not visible from Space
Think of it as sod and start *over* again
With Thanksgiving even

And then
   at least flip a coin
    when it comes to judging creep stuff

Top of the world's a ground level lid
Though you search everywhere
        you'll never find it
         for the realm
         for the expanse

"Environment"

Too many syllables   just be quiet
Accept the gift of square miles
   toy houses
    their Lego walls and doors in place
Solid as geometry may be
     and get by miniature

The whirl of construction like an E5 vortex
A tail-end disturbance
   in half an acre of want
A major city's seed that stays a single barn

When violent crime's confined to rusty nails
                                      and hay bales' bundles

What is your opinion?
No pressure   but how much more persuasion?
Even terror hasn't a chance
     if your prowess is known

Come out of Oz a little while
              to be a midwestern Glinda!
Surely you'll wave your wand   and tellingly
A highly educated witch
     you'll hold nothing back
          in a Land of Doctors
Modest in spite of your own degrees

An elsewhere queen
     of can't-wait-to-do-good

Montana should know
And Colorado   Wyoming   and Utah
The rest of the square states relaxed into
     their available beauty unbesmirched
If I can say that word's three syllables
                             and stay serious

Contrast's the exclamation point
Those outlying farms   the all-inclusive sky

The best price is none at all
Nature's estates
     are said to be real
          as wildest dreams' discovered talent

But not so fast!
No summary
     no sound at all
"I never knew I'd need your history class,
                        Professor Goodness Sakes!"

Close your eyes
And when they open
     it will be to treasures
          neverminded till now

To new words read   "parritch" for porridge
We'll need notebooks to keep up!

There was a resort
      just dying to disappear into mirage
Perhaps we missed it
It could have left early
      to be not quite observable
            in the big haze yonder
            out-of-date and out-of-mind

I've brought a *robata*
      for next time we cook Japanese
      as new neighbors in one little house
The country will ask,
"What's the big idea that's just a bit shy?"

Looks like memory must take it from here
The beat of a tabor to help the pipe to play
                with ancient intent
And a song to say "we'll be right back"
      when the ad for civilization intrudes

Let's make sure of something back home
Were it a tower of Dubai
      the blue sky says "No!"
            and sends the dunes to disguise
The outdoors in charge of indoors

And it is *easy* for immensity!
Every house a form within its form

Instinct says so
And *brags* even that it *must* be so
      unless   and until
      a Type I civilization evolves
            make that a Type II   Type III
                and counting

With worlds of Bosendorfers waiting
For *your* fingers too!

Luxury now is a camouflage incremental
Its stairways barely ascending

to restricted emergencies
flawlessly resolved

Just the menace of open air
Ourselves unborn
    and accustomed to the Void
        yet following a plan to appear suddenly
        and be welcomed back

Never mind the specifics
Our theory of chaos is enough
    and it will cover all possibilities

Wait for it
Might take years
    and more than one appointment

Big Valley's Stockton's lost its outline
Has no appreciable profile
Dangers understood to lie elsewhere in time

Yet that Old West's eager
    and waiting on a signal
            a land rush
            Oklahoma!

Grand is the illusion
Invisible   in an every day way
    perhaps we are too
But we do have our tickets to be seen someday

And when I want security you'll smile
In all this open space
    that's made miniature its towns
        ancient Spain
        whispers' wishes for hegemony

Hints of a shaken confidence
    that the land could be held
Our private day
        must yield to a very public geography
            that's all business
            and distance to travel

The beginning and middle of a journey only
The rest to "puzzle the will"
    with Hamlet's DNA inherited
    like a farm

Maybe you've thought about freedom
And call it the pursuit of happiness
Well, we're mother and father
    to all mothers and fathers before

Every moment
    a different length of human kindness
The imagination prepared to receive impressions
              and consolidate ambition

Dispersed are the dwellings
Their ghosts gone abroad
    still drowsy from hauntings
It will be fun to see if they find us!
We'd certainly want to play   whatever the game

It's Thanksgiving all year
In this realm and expanse a Lego world
    that follows the science of empty Space
       building on that
           so that it's a quantum settlement
           and certain momentum
                minus confusion

Waiting to see what's next
As if it were a train from the nearest horizon
A rusty locomotive
    with doctors from the past
        urging retro cures for evil tomorrows
Doctors going house to house
        with the CDC's blessing

You were desperate, I remember
It's why I brought you
    with borrowed ballet slippers
        to choreograph the opposite forces

See how modest accomplishments
    in small backyards

>   make the cirrus take notice
>   and all the mountains tilt
>   to allow for stairways

Believe and belong   borderless

Yet loving the sounds
     of saying the square states' names
Having history then constructed   vocal

Being reminded   who knows
The way you looked at me forever
     the years gone by
         out of touch   out of reach

Let's find the porch again
And watch a hawk's lazy circles
     spelling "Rodgers and Hammerstein"

109. SLAVE SHIP

It was worse than hard to watch

The takeaway took me to sea
    myself in the Middle Passage
    squished in the hold of a horrible ship
And it's not working out   I want to die

It all started with a channel
A documentary
Who would have thought
    the channel could not be changed?

Perhaps having company
    might have broken the spell   maybe
But there would
    have been more
        than one captive then

The power of suggestion
        had yanked me out of Africa
                made me a slave somehow
                      the motel room leaky
I was *en route* to the Caribbean
                with a useless remote!

I was helpless
      before a high-def vortex
      spinning and sucking!

A little history before bedtime
            was more than I could handle
And I found myself pining
      for a tribe I never knew I belonged to

I wanted the ship to turn around
                      and take me back
It was a kidnap such I couldn't move

And   transfixed   I stared
      a creature of the flat screen
And for all I knew
          my neighbors in room 8
            might *also* be slow-drifting
               to the Americas
Having stumbled on the evil channel themselves

Pure and simple is the boat
Only the strong will debark
The fresh sheets and pillows
      complimentary shampoo
          the towels so very soft
                        are moot luxury

And did the manager know?
Was the motel a nest of voodoo?

The ocean was slapping
There was lightning   I saw a body splash!
It was serious
My shackles meant I couldn't itch

I was black but I was white
        in grainy black-and-white
The director fresh
        from Lisbon's spic-and-span palace

The special effects so real
        that salt spray dampened the double bed
        and seagulls settled on the nightstand

I thought
        if only I'd not hung 'Do Not Disturb'
            there might have been a chance for rescue

But the door was bolted
The waves rolled sea sickness and dread
Too bad the road trip
        had to end in the middle of the Atlantic

For once I wouldn't have minded a commercial
Even a pitch for Cheetos
        I'd buy a year's supply

Or a tease for an upcoming Mel Gibson
            with him yelling "Freedom!"

110. THE REVOLUTIONARY WAR SPREADS TO OREGON

It was such a lonely place   Oregon
Peaceful but sad
        and needing some excitement

It wanted wigs and speeches
Wanted indignation
            bluster and resentment
Needed flags and fifes and drums and stuff
Needed uniforms and boots

It just didn't know it

The list was long of what it wanted
       for Oregon was especially empty
       and had never heard much yelling and screaming

Oregon was an "I Am Curious" virgin
         waiting on the miracle of strife
Oregon had not really *known* any, really
It needed the American Revolution
         and the Dark Side's deceptions

And when it came
      it would be all the more shocking
          for Oregon
            whose shape
               was both somewhat square
               and squiggly

The Indians must have sensed what was up
Intuited quarrels and the hubbub to come
      for they were having many councils
         and the shamans were working overtime

There was of course a circle
A *circle* to the Revolution
      which   once unleashed
      would seem familiar
         as if it had all happened before

Even now and then
Somebody   anybody   a nation
        loses power yet pretends still

Washington's mixed up
He's crossed a western river
            perhaps the Willamette
He thinks Trenton's a cinder cone
      of the shield volcano
         known as Newberry

Sees the horizon of the many wrongs and rights
They will time travel slightly
Bring Enlightenment to past and future places
      the years like cards dealt and shuffled

The overall mood is, "Let's gamble"
The French can be found
    though their king and queen will soon be lost

The Coast Range is not used to cannons
The volcanoes seem to be jealous

The rivers float the man-o'-wars
        with their Union Jacks
Red coats are the color
And the concept of many years ago
    has shown up in the Northern Great Basin
        to pester the present
           with Eighteenth century discord

The Midnight Ride
    to happen in a semi-arid countryside
                with rattlesnakes

The tea's been dumped in Coos Bay
The Stamp *Act* went unnoticed by the salmon
The Klamath tribe
    has not chosen sides
Gravity *itself* has not made up its mind

When the Revolution comes to Oregon
    Benedict Arnold will be *caught*
He *doesn't* get to England after all
Does *not* find safety
    but is taken to a prison high on Steens
    closer to heaven
        where he'll try to apologize

Funny   but the two sides seem the same
    and anatomy can't tell the difference
The bones that bang together in battle
        know not their species' flaws
        know not that you must be a mob
                and nothing more

The last question asked by anyone is "Why?"

It's just theater   nothing more

Puppets in a Rock 'n' Roll universe
      remembering onstage
      and this Oregon is that

The Revolution's like a tease
Gold glimpsed and craved but never held
And warmonger minds
      network their nerves
           and spark conformity

Just now the wind stirred the juniper
Like a *policy* of waywardness
The Revolution's drifting too
           rootless and tumbling

"One if by land   two if by sea"

A ghostly refrain
      in search of a suitable geography
         the real deal
         a date with Betsy Ross
And now   improbably   Mozart's shown up
After all, it's *his* century too!   why not?
An Oregon Symphony may come of it
      but it's going to be weird

Those German Hessians
      feel just as out of place at Crater Lake
      as they did in New Jersey
           but at least there's scenery

By the looks on their faces
      they seem about to make a statement
          maybe quit the war altogether

West Point's been brought so far west
      the Hudson Valley's forgotten

There's a Constitution all right
But it's all about the penmanship
Thomas Jefferson
      Benjamin Franklin
          all the principals are here
          and they don't wish to go home

They're tired of the Colonies
      the wars that are never over
Wars which
           even with surrender
              promulgate the science of violence

Grow it like an evil geode
Its crystal unseen
      yet whose animus
           grips and tightens
Every future imagined in lonely places

Peaceful
Except for the first stirrings of strange passions
                              barely understood

I'll bet the Revolution rides out like Revere
However uncertain
      to a greater conformity
           than Lexington and Concord

It's raining
      and the parades are getting soaked
Well, the Pacific Northwest's *like* that
All wet
      and determined
           to dampen dry cerebella

The injuries
      and torments
           are amended
An awkward transition to derangement
           and unstable demagoguery

It was a final hope
Just like that
      outdoing the Greeks
           far from the Aegean
Improving on those black-and-white pebbles
                              tossed in a pot

A lot of conversation mistaken for a party
A room of gamblers determined to lose

      let worst-case take hold
            and barcode the chaos

The cotton gin is still to come
And though no one's free right *now*
      the gin will take those cotton seeds
           and seed something worse
                      all over the place
With no timeouts for the consent of the governed

There's resistance to the Crown
I'll be hiding in the Malheur marsh
      I *think* I remember where

Spain's a part of it
They want Florida back
Such Halloween!
      and no one said a thing
           till the very last minute

The lodge at Mount Hood's involved!
Stanley Kubrick's to blame
Perhaps he's set this phantasmagoria in motion
      made Jack Nicholson a general
      a "shining" to encompass revolution's ghost

The way it is now
      Shelley Duvall
           is posing as the Statue of Liberty

I'd actually pick up a musket
But the Pendleton Roundup
      has bigger plans for me
           set me on a bull and said, "Ride!"

The Crooked River has to be crossed
The voice of geology's trying its best
      though science
           is now a secondary sound
               to the crowds' "Ooh"s and "Aah"s

The war came to Oregon
Why should *one* coast have had all the fun?

Now is history balanced
And the bashful West   just met
      accepts the East as if it were a date
        a prom with certain risks
              moderate to severe

What about provisions?
How about shoes?
What to wear
      to a rebellious marriage

The same language
But no longer at home
      with those who speak it now and later

I wanted to turn on the heater
      though it's still midsummer
         for Valley Forge had chilled

In spite of the military taking its time
        no one's been caught
And garrisons   *all* of them
          show blockbuster movies
            while waiting for orders

All of the troops are stuck on stupid
Thinking they fight for Walmarts to come
                      and tents in Portland
There's that duplicate Salem
      declared an open city that no one wants

Flyers have appeared with the new Constitution
      an occasional "s"
      looking just like an "f"
They flutter and land
But the rate of literacy
        does not permit comprehension

They've learned not to care
      and assume it's just bad news

I've had an allergic reaction to the wool
                        but at least it's a uniform
Please don't shoot!

I'm part of a sports team *only*
     with a life expectancy of thirty

The coroner's a nice man   very patient
He thinks what we have is a stalemate
          isn't that a kind of truce?

And will it hold?   yes

The English
     the French
         the Germans
             the Spanish
                the Colonists
                   the Klamath

Held in place like fragile glassware
          conceived by sand

111. "YOU'RE SET"

She said it succinctly
Something concerning survival

"You're set"   meaning
         locked in
         protected
         not in need
         no worries

Something sure enough and lovestruck
What's next become a beautiful extra

"You're set"
     is every step it took to summit
         (the verb that was once a noun)
Let's get rid of it   say "secure" instead

And let the quotes explain "set"

When no worldwide emergency is even imagined

"Set" such all currency is yours
The tipping point
    when dead-even yields to prosperity
Like a scaled-down lottery known to a few

Or the only apartment left in Berlin
        the war years over
A job consisting only of what you want to do
Saying hello to strangers
    knowing you'll never need their help
A secret smile
    reserved for an afterlife
        that overlaps the present
A changed name
    to go with a different fortune than before

She said, "You're set"
    as if surprised it happened
        and a nicer person deserved it

I should never have listened
For ever since I learned I was "set"
    the truth of struggle has eluded

112. DINNER BELL CAFE, "THE OCTAGON"

It was eight sides similar to something else
Psyche's home in the Black Rock once
    her life insurance
    and airy gazebo

To call this octagon "The Dinner Bell Cafe"
    is to *distance* the installation
        from today's optimistic morning
        with ordinary windows

And they calm the passion it took

          to make those *other* windows
                  in the sun of 2001
                              Year of the Towers

Though the Bell has conjured Enya
      the music played
            on approach to "Psyche's Windows"
Let her "sail away" this morning be silence
            the better to let the day get started

Here in Lakeview
        the octagon reimagined as basic hospitality

For there's only so much mythology possible
          this far from the bed
                that was Psyche's home for awhile
Her windows varied and illumined
                with fiber optics
                    and electro-luminescent prayers
                              for safekeeping

Here in Lakeview's dawn
        simplicity will bring us up to date
        and let geometry be all it can be
        without summoning too much melancholy
                      for this time of day

113.   WHERE'S GOOSE LAKE?

Where's Goose Lake?
Where did it go?
Gone for the summer?
Gone for good?

The lake that floated logs to the mill is missing
Maybe saving itself
        for the later ice of Milankovitch
            his cycle to kick in
                and provide depth once more

Right now
      the lake's just hyperbole
            uncounted oaths it's really there
                        and not a figment

Look
And think you see a certain dampness
      far off
      and darker than the rest of the plain

The slanted shore's an incline
      of homes and farms
           that are missing their Goose
           and wanting the waters to rise
And asking,
"What kind of gun should I get
      for a goose in case it returns?"

The town says it's a view   a Lakeview
But it's just ideological
Even the Christians don't believe it
                and they believe a lot

If the Sun came out
      would there be any blue that wasn't the sky?
And would there be a parade then?

But no question's good enough
So relax
      letting 395 take you south
Don't get started
        unless it's down that highway
        or the Yellow Brick Road

No active shooters have heard of you
Survive as Goose Lake has
      its entire history told
           with one foot on the accelerator

Be inclusive
All its lake levels known
Every episode of falling rocks from Space
      splashing

      or thudding the dry land of a drought

It's nice to be near the Goose
Forty-five minutes maybe an hour
A map's name repeated like a very short mantra

Until a monk somewhere
      looks up from the rice
        and says, "That all ya' got?"

"Where?"
The worst of the W's perhaps
      for it most pertains to loss

"Who?" "when?" "what?" and "why?" mere mysteries
      having no specific addresses
But "where?" will stay away
      till fright is mastered
        and loss is something gotten over
            like a shoreline's expansion

The day has requested more than idle curiosity
There are still decisions to be made
How many home invasions
      bank robberies and stolen cars
        a small town can handle and stay cohesive

But wait!
Hold on!

There's a glint
      some reflection
        to qualify as Goose
          the Sun just right for this!
And even *geese*   goose plural
      in perfect formation
        their telepathy reassuring:

"Don't worry about a thing!"

And I believe it
      as I believe in their migration

114. THAT SHIFTING BORDERLINE

The states' border was shifting
    north and south
        until someone put their foot down

Whatever reckoning it was
    the wandering minds that made it
        had to stop
        and fix California
            fix Oregon
Make the states fit a narrative

East to west
What the survey said
    and averred
        with tripods
       scopes
           and squinting

In the early decades
Long before a Dollar Store might be divided
    the Oregon aisles of household
    and the drinks on California's shelves
When checkouts are taxed   or not
        in a town of mistakes

Things not adding up in 1868
In the decade of many wrongs
    a drunk draws a line
        between Oregon Country and New Spain
That special state of affairs
Of owning more than anyone imagines
            only to see it slip away

I'll mention his name   Daniel
Daniel Major   the surveyor
It was the equipment
    maybe
    or   Daniel *had* been drinking

Who could blame him?
Think it was easy   the line

           supposed to be perfectly parallel?

So was Haydn supposed to live forever
His parallel life to complement the future
Accompany the signing of treaties
As if his music belonged
      and should be a part of pioneer doings

The 42nd parallel proved elusive
Adams-Otis   1821
        a straight line
        a thought

The Southern Empire
      barely born
         flawless
            conforming to latitude
              last night
              this morning
And every afternoon of your reckoning

We're sure Daniel worked really hard
Everyone in the 19th century *had* to

But this survey would be different
        not right away apparent
        for the land was beautiful
D*istracting* it was
      where the borderline went

I wonder if he was a soft-*spoken* alcoholic
Whispering his way
      from the coast to Goose
      while his zigzags were drawn
Must have been a tricky adventure

Three servings of fruits and vegetable
      each day
This could have made all the difference
And Daniel Major might have gone straight

There used to be more open space
So a border didn't matter that much
Now there's a town

        albeit a tiny one

And this town wanted to know
"Exactly *where* does that damned line go?"

What would the delegations do?
Those Sacramento guys that were sent
Oregon and California both
      gently rocking the community
      trying to put the dispute to sleep
                      before any fighting

The streets more or less
And a line more or less
All of it official
      quoting Indian gods
      choosing which ones wouldn't mind

The magic of frontier turned to stone
And being stolid in a land of Medicare

It's well the border kind of creeps up on you
As if it were entitled to deceive and shift
Wishing to share uncertainty
      the 42nd parallel
      a memory of spherical geometry
          wanting whiskey for everyone
          drinks all around

Who's running for mayor?
Still want to stay there?
Are we any closer to the truth?
      it takes travel to know

Five hours from the Bay's pianos
      there's a line to cross
      but where, exactly?

Evil's courting error
      having not so far to go
And the truth
      on life support
      says "See you soon!"
          then skedaddles

What governance likes
        and does not wish to push past
                a border

We're still waiting all afternoon
        for the authorities to show
I heard they're pretty matter of fact
But there has to *be* a fact
        for them to come to life and decide

Napoleon's to blame
Weakened Spain could not keep the coast
Nor could Louisiana's watershed
        bulge into Canada
        with so much promise

Napoleon just had to do it
Worry Spain with ruthless invasion
        the New World becoming Old in a hurry
                the vice royalty to falter
The borders to start all over again

I have even heard
        the lines do move when we're asleep
        like politics' shifting bamboozles

When what you think a party is must be revised
And narratives silly with contradiction
        enter the spillways of the mind
A lunatic liquid in places it doesn't belong

Want to find out where?
All of the downhill?
                bet you do

I'm already there and will tell you more
All the folks of New Pine Creek
        and well beyond
                are forthcoming

I've been in their homes
Where the line
        creeps past a fridge or a sofa

      and sometimes leads to separate beds
          and broken marriages
Preventing the dogs from knowing the cats

I saw the border lurking
      in backyards and front
Saw it stray into a cemetery
      and raise only half of the dead

Oh, I'm sure it had the best of intentions
And so does a drunk

The line even came to volley ball
      and stopped the game for a time
Tried to be good news in a very bad world
But there wasn't a which way to cross
              that would be risk free

To the south
      live the angry ghosts of conquistadors
And what's to the north
      are the phantoms of the fur trade
         whose afterlives
         are marked by pelt reenactments
            done on a diet of too much salmon

Do we have operational control?
Is geography running wild?

Make it Christmas
And gift the shape of things to come
      as well as what became of kings and queens

And make it Hallmark including what's rude
So that Christmas has verisimilitude and bravery

I want a vault for what's left of blank countries
Their beforehands
      stored for safekeeping
         beyond the grasp of mapmakers

But if there *has* to a be a line
      let it be as thin as a mastodon's whisker
That hard to see

Whether you like it or not
              next day and the day after that

A baby shall draw
One trained to draw straight and not scribble
              no matter the tantrum
You just give it See's candy
              before you give it a name

I'll see you don't trip on this borderline
Even if it shifts when you cross
              and makes jump rope necessary

I am putting my foot down
En route   in passing

Sure that mere reckoning is not enough
And believing the two states
        were always figments
              that took possession of Daniel Major
                  got him loaded
                  long before AA
                      and the book "As Bill Sees It"

As it turned out
        Daniel saw nothing but flattened zigzags
And hoarsely proclaimed their provenance

I'd have gotten him to a meeting
        even if it turned into a drunken brawl
Spoil his border
Spoil everything
        the nineteenth century to pick up the tab

Even the birds of the fresh air
        seem to belong to the line
As though its thin property could outdo the stars
And make their migrations its own adventure

There used to be more leeway and gentle rocking
But the cradle's too crowded
Too many disputes
            which Indian god's the best
            In the land of medicine

Where you count to the 42nd parallel
And stop short of 43   a primary number

Korea's been stuck at 38
Where tight-fisted guards glare back and forth
          and wonder
     what sex with each other would be like

When reunification comes
     will they at least kiss and make up?

Little New Pine Creek is not a Zone
Let alone one that's demilitarized
So won't you stay there
     find out if the line truly varies?

Get close to the truth   or uncertainty
Can it stay a frontier
     with a flat screen to watch
          along with the line?

And   while we're at it
     can we say something's "down the line"
          and applicable to borders?

It will take some travel   and travel in time
     coming to life like Napoleon
     making sure things get done
If the lines *do* move at night he'd know
Make use of his metric system
               to determine how far

Could celebrate the brain and all its matter
     that takes such liberties
         conjecture rules
         and conjures a line

Any spalpeen can move it   rascals historical
Phantoms you notice if you're sensitive

There's a payroll somewhere   a train
It may be robbed in a Western way   a holdup
Cross the border afterwards
     New Spain to the Oregon Territory

                                                          we'll see

The engineer suffered a flesh wound!
Get a doctor!
Oh, and a shrink
      in order to learn
           why in the dickens
                they used slow locomotives!

Maybe in order to get a better look at the line

And savor the crossing beforehand
      or behind with babies
      and birds overhead
           Daniel Major riding sober
           and waving to all them townsfolk!

115.   FANDANGO PASS ABANDONED

It's said it got so cold
      they danced a fandango up there
      to stay warm going over

It was Lassen's route
But say it completely   using the hyphen
Lassen-Applegate
      the serious departure from the California Trail

Longer
      drearier
           and dangerous through the Black Rock
           going hot spring to hot spring in the sun

The Warner Mountains were the last of it
      if you'd managed the rest

Now   heading *east* from Fandango
        wind down to Surprise
          the Valley   the graben

Today   the fandango's a dance too difficult
        the gravel dance floor a treacherous prom

Lassen's dead
        and it's late in the day of do-nothing-stupid
I don't know any good guys
        the wagon's missing a hitch
And there's such a thing as too much of a stranger

Can there just be a wagon again?
Though it's 1848
        a magic engine, please
                and U-turn from Fandango

Let the key once more recover its purpose
Take just enough control
        to find a firmer pass
                with a little less history
                        and no privation

116.   NEW PINE CREEK

Your life may be threatened
Best you hightail it
We'll drive you north
        all the way to Oregon   or almost

Make it New Pine Creek
You'll find a safe house straddling the border

There you'll lay low
        say you're a tourist
        told this was the place to buy junk
G*ood* junk   antiques   collectables
Something for the shelves
            and conversation   *you* know
                the pieces for that very thing

You will dye your hair and wear platform shoes

Find some old clothes
        and say you like to shop for knick-knacks

Whoever's after you
        will never know where you have gone
And   your outfits complete
        you'll never be recognized

Even   if by chance
        the villain that's *after* you
            should go collecting
                in New Pine Creek, too

You'll have a beard and a cane
And be mistaken for a tall and scrawny senior
        instead of the average millennial you truly are

I'm concentrating on your security
No lunatic will find you

And look at it this way
You may find something you like
        among the backyard displays
        or deep in the store called Just Stuff
            a *famous* place

What once was a grocery store's
        gone beyond perishables
            to house all the knick-knacks it can

And chances are
        while browsing its bins
        and exploring *deeply*
            all its recessed treasures
                perhaps you'd forget the threat

Lost in contemplation
        of an ancient doll or toy
            no worry will have you

What's that?
You're wondering what's being done?

Well, the whole team's involved
  but so far no prevailing theory
Might be envy   *jealousy* at some level

If we could see *something*
    then a plot
     a pattern
       would emerge
If there were only physical evidence to go on
A cell phone   footprint   DNA

But the assault on your bodyguard was psychic
One minute he was reading the comics
The next he started babbling and wouldn't stop

It was touch-and-go for awhile but he *did* recover
In time he'll resume his duties   or not
      the whole thing kind of freaked him

I tell you
  whoever's responsible's being clever
  and using sophistication

Best guess?
It's mistaken identity

Have you made out a will?
I'll arrange for a lawyer and live-in priest
I know you're recently back in the fold
  in   case   there's   something   to   it

But don't get *ahead* of yourself
      no need to rush forward
Let New Pine Creek be your haven from care
Just a stroll in Just Stuff

Should take your mind off death rays
  and James Bond villainy
You'll be behind the scenes of your anxieties

And do take the stand
  in defense of your innocence
    albeit here
    in the privacy of New Pine Creek

Having faith you'll find an exit past this exile
You'll be driven   there'll be no rental
      no card or ID

They're watching closely a phantom
Your first amendment guaranteed
There's not enough science
          to know it's to New Pine you've come

However deadly
      and powerful
           you think they are
              Just Stuff is not on their radar
And there are no psychics so evil
      they'd offer their services to your enemy

Your friends and family are out of the loop
Only perfect strangers have been told
      and their disinterest may be counted on

As for legal action
      you know better than to wish upon
          a star
          a badge
          a court
You are not to wait for a morning alarm

In the remaining seconds of your sanity
      agree to be taken
Failing that   the military *shall* come by
        some said they'd look forward to that

The Other Side's for later
This side still has much to offer
      starting with junk and yard sales

You must strengthen your interest
      in 2nd   3rd   4th hand and counting

That candle holder
      the ancient X-mas decorations
          the choo-choo
              the rocking horse

       those *games*
        Scrabble
          Parcheesi
            Monopoly

Puzzles with missing pieces
Books from bygone
  geodes
    bicycles
      pottery
        pin cushions
          transistor radios

And   lucky horseshoes!

Until further notice
  you'll be walking in the shadows
There'll be friendly ghosts who'll welcome
With little else added to their greeting
      but the "whoosh" of air hugs

Your travel expenses?
Free as the air you'll breathe in New Pine Creek
A town that still has Nature flowing through it

In far-off New York City you *can't* say that
  though a mere three hundred years
    have elapsed since Europe's arrival

There's a chef who will be cooking for you
What's happening
  what's waiting
    and simmering on the stove
Beyond the border but just a little

There's kindergarten here
Your kid will learn to start to read
  learn cursive later, even

You'll come to love the peeling paint
  and the rust
    that says the roots still spread
    in the remaining seconds of summer

A family that's a town
        hard at work   but slow-talkin'
            well out of the box
            before the box was solid geometry

There's a road
And there's a goose
        with a lake named after it
            and you wonder which one
            with migration

Everything that's wrong's flown south
Not you, though
        You're going the *other* way
You won't care about street crime   or *any*
You won't need a hospital

The road to New Pine Creek
        shall give your body and brain a respite
            with colors and styles
                among the racks of used clothing

Wayside Salvation
        where the Army retired
        and sits there now
            in rocking chairs of welcome

How to save you took a lot of time
But I was needing a project

The bad guys will be hypnotized
            their parents impersonated
                by old folks in empty nests
                    who *still* wish
                        to be moms and dads

And soon enough
        your threatened life
            will be returned to normal
While the Lords of all the Flies are spanked
                              and sent to reform school

Lay low till then
And thanks for all your poetry

   your writing the reason
     we're going to all the trouble
We're here for you
   and waiting the way you always waited
   for the right word

And I'm thinking
Just Stuff and its hand-me-downs
    are each sestinas
      and pantoums
       wanting good penmanship
        and recitation
When New Pine Creek gets ready
       for some shut-eye

117.   RED JEEP AND A PEPSI

It would have been cheap   the gas
If you'd *needed* gas

And surely
   and also
      if you'd wanted a happy hour
     of shooting the breeze
       this
      would have been the place

Perhaps you would have thought about bowling
Where to fish
   and whether Uncle Mike will run for mayor

Place would have been *open*
The white paint fresh
   the pumps completely filled

For now   and later
   the station's a *virtual* fill-up
     the still life of a red Jeep
     and a Pepsi machine

Something to teach your child concerning change

All its aches and pains

Could be a junk Jeep and soda
Time has simply folded its arms
Then it steepled when asked what happened

Perhaps the station closed
      after someone heard Rodgers
      and Hammerstein
           say that a certain night
                was "too lovely for words!"
                      and resolved to sell

Get a future in place
      that is paradise ahead of time
           and not waiting for Sunday's promises

Perhaps it was getting late
And a long distance call had come in
      from a State Fair starring technicolor

Of *course*   the garage
      will experience something new
           despite its being abandoned
           with clean grass
                reclaiming the Jeep and the Pepsi

But return it to cross-country
Like the mountain east
      you were left to imagine
           may be a mountain made of numbers

The years   the height   the temps
The snowfall and sunshine since settlement

May we discover the history of everything!
The number of pines in New Pine Creek
The Creek's volume-per-second
How many times the Creek ran *dry*
                    or ran underground

Distinct is the Jeep in telltale red
Empty the cradles that held the Pepsis
The money-back cup
        a moot coin return container
                for nickles
                dimes
                and quarters gone extinct
                        that changed the dollars

The old folks are looking for ways to start over
While the young 'uns
        are willing to let the white paint peel

It was a time before people 'blew up'
                      on social media
The price of gas was ridiculously affordable
      the future way off

Although this story's not *your* story
        far-and-wide
                brought you here to near-at-hand
                      *any*way

Be great to open the station's door now
Naive as when the climate talked gently
        and kept the ice cold

Be something to fuel those fifties fins
            that would later disappear
                    when the truth came out
                    that they had no purpose

There's nothing for sale but Nature
The way it's rusting the red
                      the red Jeep prized
And tipping Pepsi to make it fall over

What if all this stuff still worked
        the station   the town
                the *boat*
                that ferried timber on Goose?

Not to be current
        but simply to reprise

           all the buildings that built New Pine
                as if construction's sacred
                      and not to be disturbed
In the atomic days and nights   normal

The Jeeps olive drab in Korea with MacArthur
But a mother saying sweetly,

"Have I got a surprise for *you*, my son!
You know   you *deserve* to be happy!
Remember that time
      you told me
           you wanted to play
           the big piano pieces
                while you were little?
Well, I know how hard that is to do
So here's the key to a brand new Jeep!
It's your favorite color too
      and we'll both have Pepsis to celebrate
Drive slowly at first   promise!"

It would have been a Sunday she said it
The *red* day of the week

They *all* had colors
Monday white
      Tuesday blue
           Wednesday brown
                Thursday green
                      Friday black
                          Saturday orange

And Sunday always *always* red
Her child's predilections honored
                          remembered

So that her own *singing*
        would also be remembered and fondly
      not only her songs at breakfast
            but every time the table was set

Performance as much as Monday paint
        applied to a brand new service station
            before all pronouns knew of cancer

A little building born
      in the menace of assumptions

Would have been fun
Barely illegal   thought   word
      and whatever *deed*
            you might have been itchin'

118.   "KEEP OUT AND KEEP AWAY!"

It was something we would never do again
      we *thought*
            wander far   and fenceless

Oh, it took *time* for the land to go private!
Took awhile to draw the lines all over
      the lines the fences would follow
          silent-deliberate
             as a Christmas love story
                that ends
                    with barbed wire and shears

Love just couldn't come along
Figure it out   when it came to neighbors
So "keep out" came to mean "stay out"
And "keep away," "*stay* away"
    with no go-to
    to get inside

And now we'll digress
      from the concept of property
         and perform home
         and ranch
            invasions

What a sad day the cattle couldn't *move* anymore!

What a *worse* day the cattle came at *all*
    to pester the frontier

           with heart attacks
           and "gid"
                  that disease of cattle

Is it human nature
      to patchwork a wilderness?
      make a quilt of it?

I am tugging at a gate
      in spite of everything
A performance piece in the dark of night
Getting down to the business
      of being a human herd of just one bull
          determined to trespass
          and be all I *can* be
              in the wide open spaces of yester

Though I'm already engaged
I'll break the date to be with you
      where you are   imprisoned

What are you doing?
What are you doing this Christmas?
Had anyone said,
      "You! keep away!   we don't want your kind!
      you're kind of weird?"

Were you warned to keep out of sight?
Stay *out*?
Stay *away*?

Look at this map   zoom in   closer

There!   you *see*?
     parcels, lots, ranches, cemeteries!!
Would you look at that subdivision!
     those acres of cars!
And *there*!   a military base
          bet *that's* restricted!

How far you think you'd get in the vineyards?

Before the maze of days and days
     stood the castles of month-by-month

      and before *that*
      the wilds of aeons

Too bad the gods stopped paying attention
Because suddenly the 19th century happened

They called them "spreads"
"Been to Bob's spread?"   or
"Bob's got a spread…"

They called them "places," too
"Hey, I was over to Bob's place"

Or simply "Bob's"
      where the apostrophe serves to say it all

"You're on my land   now git!"

This would be a farewell note to North America
Some day it'll be back if destroyed
Big, maybe   and One Place again
      no such total misery as now

With the squares and other geometry
      that's seen best from the air
With the steers contained
The growing up confined
      to the lanes and veins

"Which way ya' headin'?"   you don't know

The price of Today is unpayable
No estate is *real* enough
              to interest buyers
"By golly!" not rural enough for deception
     and no one believes in the "Yesterday"
                    The Beatles lived in

The land had to fracture   break up
Never mind the failed romance
     there is no "place to hide away"
     neither tent nor tipi will do

The boys and the girls don't understand
Their wishes
      are not the commands of the mighty
          their complicit mothers and fathers

And so   the most a backyard could ever be
      was a bordered realm
         where Laurel and Hardy were not allowed
           and rehearsals took place
             on how to be grownups

There is likely to be signage
      saying more than mere "Welcome!"
All entry proscribed
And every departure a lawsuit
      both coming and going
         to tighten property's grasp
        when easy and obvious
             have a harder time

Power's pressure to be its best self
All it can be   as if a recruit
           the feudal to *displace*

A god's country castled
A Middle Ages looking for trouble

Hah!
"The Sum of All Fears"
      is nothing more than a movie you miss
Warnings downplayed to mere suggestion
        that a range
         if not a country
           may once more open

A favorable report to come out
If the law's unlimited talk
      may not naysay the freedom

The business of ancient villages
All right with gold   and silver sequins too

It is summer's urgent appeal
      for winter to slacken its too formal lasso

The ballet lesson's performance art
Like trespass in a land of weapons

In the remaining seconds
        borrowed from minutes and hours
                stay keeping out there
To see what may come
        of next time's next year and century

The cells are perfect
The body is whole
Can it be the holding pens and prisons
        hold a baby's preference for belonging

That something larger
        that's a policy of mothering

And so   connections
The walls and omigosh gates and locks
Those cyclones silvery
        you find in the woods
        their mesh in the moonlight alluring

"Stay out!"   "keep inside!"   "don't try it!"
No in-and-out   or up-and-over

The slightest motion means you're wrong
        and don't belong
        bionic or not

Something goes bad it's the end
And even a palace has a dungeon just in case

But the parts have reassembled
It's called a "collective"
        free-ranging as any past frontier
        the future
                strangely to resemble
                      a kind of wide-open capture

A sameness of minds
Thinking non-fractured   non-partitioned
        with "keep out!" a moot proscription

A wilderness and spotlit darkness
      where tyranny casts its beam
            in search of dissent

119.   THE HOLLOW BARN

"Barn"

A very *old* word for a very old shed
Something as simple as shelter
      raised on a wheatfield's slope
         the truth of its future unknown

The barn is hollow
I would find out why and fill it
      with hay and horses
         for there's plenty of room in there

"Barn"

A longhouse
      a stone house
         round barns
In all the history that's happened
That seeped out of Europe and went West
      to age in the sun and the moonlight

A sleep expert's found the loft
Has curled up   and dozes
The large size of dreams to come
        will let the spirits take control
        their jinxes studied
           like blueprints for mischief

The hollow barn
      in a land of holidays
        tilts just a little

As if it would pour its ghosts out of hiding
To encourage superstition
       with flirtatious oeillades
              in this unlikely place

"Take care of yourself or we'll take care of *you*!"

The faith of birds
To trust their syringes to sing their notice

The adult construct of infinity
The loneliness of farms gone silent
       like the faintest idea of what's to come
             missing imagination altogether

It's not so much the shingles are worn
The timber cracked and letting light inside
The roof that would settle and cave

The ruin's irrelevant
Take care of the *vision*
       that strangeness might persist
       and its index be improved

Fascination becomes you
And I've seen you so many times enchanted
       it only seems right to show you the Goose
           and all the bottomlands
               that border the lake

When it was time to say goodbye
       reality began its journey to ruin
Like a special edition of despair
When you want to fall asleep
       and *stay* asleep till it's over

The miracle for us is remembrance
All the music of Ravel's "Sonatine"
              to soothe our separation

How like a structure is recall
These very old words for a very old barn
       that could use some pleasant rural prayers

Nothing personal
    but the boonies
        are now too much about today

In the year 2020
    it's hindsight you want
        with 20-20 vision
            twelve *months'* worth

This is a search
    for a history that's up-to-date enough to matter
        even if it's only banter

I'm a kid at risk for cancelation
Might a telethon follow what's hollow to renewal
The helping hands of day dreaming farmers
    more than enough
        for a barn re-raising
        worthy of the big screen

The flowers are wilting
    that grew the colors of faith forevermore

You must concentrate now
Midday in this cross section of land
        almost too shy to show itself
The beginning of the end of all geology

Age eight should see this
And save the barn for a place to play hooky
And learn the Dutch that started the slang

It is a back-to-basics barn
    hollow until game time comes along

A still life
The concept
    taken well beyond shiny bowls and fruit

Never mind the motel
Just self-check
    into the immensity of hollowness
        and spend the night
        as a one-time buddha powered by rice

Spend twenty-four hours
      where magic's motion-activated
           by the smallest offering
Perhaps it holds a manger

For some as-yet-unknown salvation
        one with only limited ambitions

120. THE CEDARVILLE CORNER STORE AFTER 6,200 FEET

If only one could find what's wanted!

I'd stay in Cedarville until the town was canceled

Stay in that corner store
      looking over the inventory
        making a search that's thorough
           as befits a strong desire to acquire

And why should not the corner store
                have everything you need?

Descending from the summit
      that's 6,200 feet and more
          in a car well-suited for the century
Remembering wagons went through in another
      certainly any provisioning
        should not need more than Cedarville's help

It is a small enough town
      the bad actors were actually detected and expelled
The residents' lives are *righteous*
Even nuclear war would let them sleep

On the shelves the cans are in English
No one talks fast

    and that can be a *good* thing
It isn't Congress but governance anyway

And at a sweet elevation
    where the graben is that held the lake

Families have time
   to count the hours they want to create
And the tourist's trance
    and strange gazing
      is harmless response

Main Street and Townsend the crossroads
Where treasure is the four points of the compass
So very *easy* to understand
   especially east
    where 299 persists to Nevada
     and loses its pavement
      suddenly
      au naturel

North is Fort Bidwell
South is Eagleville
Finally the west from whence
   the fandango's dance steps learned
     on the Warner's mile-high dance floor

No blues will jazz the junction
Unless the poles that support are considered
The color in tandem
   with the store's exterior brown

A sign says "hardware"
You wonder
   how much of a good thing it is
      to take steel for granted
There can be no inventory taken
   without the say-so of citizens
      your listicle to be approved

But the town's repaid its debt to visitors
Taken the sting out of rural interaction
   when you have no idea of what's appropriate

We'll Always Have Stockton

Steve Arntson

As far as anyone can tell
    the corner store
        is sacred as the Dome of the Rock
Though not much of a fuss is made of this
The Church of Five Minutes Ago is provenance

Brown and blue are the colors of this commerce
They keep working on improvements
    but a chain seems unlikely
        no matter the supplications made
                to the gods of capital

Living life to the fullest
    means telling truth to the powerless
        strengthening their resolve
            to succeed nevertheless

They know the nation's karmic chickens
    will not just be coming home to roost
            but to peck our eyes out!

Every Thursday
    there'll be stories told after closing time
Which
    while the storytellers
        may be averse to Edgar Allen
            yet their yarns
            are tinged with apprehension
                the country's chatter
                    distilled to foreboding

There is no information to be had
No further messaging than rumors
The streets stay straight
    no matter the crookedness at large

At Main and Townsend
    the temps are more extreme
               than any points of view

Nothing will disrupt the flow
    this Day of Judgment's preview
        that promises a next morning anyway

Never have the End Times seemed so peaceful
No worries   no pressure
No music that isn't 3/4 time
Bread and cheese   milk and butter
Pasta   fruit   potatoes and corn

Not merely a market
          there was much *else* to buy

Call them "goods"   perhaps "*sporting* goods"
Those essential fishing poles
The hardware those letters proclaimed
Blades   tools   and doorknobs

Luxury too
Soaps from the city and even perfume

There's a dog at the door
          and somewhere a cat
                    whose goals are a mystery

I was surprised it was secular
The corner store
          and all of Main Street
                    in support of a low-key pilgrimage
                    featuring laziness

The solo doctor stares like Rasputin
The firemen are wary of fall
          and only the gas
                    may be said to be a bargain

There's a kind a of *final* feeling here
Think there may be a bank
          but there's been a run
                    and Fred Astaire's been dancing
                                        to keep things calm
A prolonged choreography, with Ginger, of course

Try every trick you know
And it's nothing
          compared to their hoofing

Let sameness dress to be saneness
As much as Haydn's start in the Land of Symphonies
      is D Major in the cedars
           so-called classical music for shopping
The essential strings believing in harmony

The Bureau of Land Management's closed
I was hoping to make memories there
A cracked open "Can-you-imagine-that?!"

What satisfaction
Being able to help people
      and there are questions yet unformed
                      a need to know

The Bureau like a store
Where you go
      to find out
           how much land is to be managed
           and for how long into the future

BLM's first meaning
Before the city fires began
Before the letters were enrolled in politics

Before
      when you wanted to be everywhere
        all the places the topo map revealed
Walking all over those contour lines
Setting foot on every *square* foot

Shopping Old California
      till what is found is what is wanted

Perhaps it will it be treasure discussed
      at the corner store
           with gossip interspersed
And I'd buy the wheel
Go back in time
      with a strong desire to settle in Cedarville

One of the first
      deciding streets

       and shoeing horses
Learning all the steps
   to that summit Fandango
      so that travel's assured
        in Warner's mountains

6,200 feet of it not so lofty if you're limber
The cold is canceled till you're over
        and safely

How many honeymoons
   managed and watched over
     by the bright satellite itself?!

Good actors and actresses
   who'll need supplies
     for sleeping in at the height of the Cold War
And waking with no after-effects

I'll be shopping while the graben lowers

Be nice to build a fire later
Pour some coffee in the morning
   the likes of Richard Boone
    to say what's up
      and how easy it is
       to get by in the Valley
        that was a surprise so long ago

The drive time to the playa's a known duration
No burden no others bound
The crowd will be missing
   for it's 2020 and Burning Man's been canceled

The traffic died down to local

I miss the preliminary buzz
   the proof of attendance
     the cafes doing business
The ambient excitement
      of a vision on their *own* terms

And the store at Main and Townsend
         barely enough to outfit

Maybe something last minute   sure
As they count the hours *until*

Ahead of time
      the week of fire
           commences like a ceremony

One that praises preparation
That glories in anticipation
      almost as if the solar plexus
      were most nurtured then
Its many butterflies proof
      that *this* is where they belong

Tomorrow   beyond the usual tomorrows
Making new places out of old
Like Cedarville
      that qualifies contentment
           with sudden alacrity
A prelude missing from the rest of the year

Even now   in these August days
      that would see electric caravans pass
      and thoughtfully pause   never mind
They've stayed at home without a destination

Yet my own resolve is a solo tingling
      much as before
      in a trance   albeit lonely

Except for purchasing
Except for brief exchanges
      with Black Rock energy

I'll be the crowd myself
      that would have been without COVID
I'll be COVID disarmed
      as when a thug is apprehended
And say Cedarville's the beginning
         of one's very own nostrum

No date may find it
Nor any online dexterity

From now until the desert
       is a natural immunity powered by mojo

It's almost an education
       this taut deception
       some shortcut taken to bliss
             when the universe wasn't looking

Renegade angels
       offering true time away from chasing survival
Maybe there's time
       to buy treats for the ghosts of Fort Bidwell

Consult a list
Consecrate a corner
       so it dominates
             just like the Dome

There'll be a chip
       that cancels ancient plans for enslavement
             and starts things over rightly
Simplicity allowed to move up
And run nothing but open-air

Forget about the chickens
They'll merely roost
       and not bother too much the *status quo*
All depends on smart money's indifference

Poe's in the basement
And Nietzsche can't be bothered
       for the Day of Judgment came and went

Pilgrimage means a military holiday
When Fred and Ginger dance a fandango
       in plain sight of the thirties
Teaching Cedarville
       how a Depression
             improbably affixed taps to shiny shoes

Haydn's shown interest
       and adjusts his symphonies to Swing
                   D Major glad to accede

Wait!
The Bureau's gotten into the act
    and you can shop till you drop
        in topography's corner!

121.   THE WAGONS AT THE CEDARVILLE GARAGE

What purpose?   and when?

Are repairs required?
Are improvements desired
    on this first day of September?

With 2020 hindsight
    another first day of September's considered
A summer ending with Poland ending
And well into fall concluding

The day the French stayed home
And the English
    imagined the Maginot was enough defiance

Will the wagons before us suffice
    for an eighty-first anniversary?
Might they be construed as German caissons
        or carts for refugees?

No more questions!
Just take their picture
    buggies only   belonging to Cedarville
      for now

History's been kind to America
The Axis couldn't manage
A voice in the Valley of the Shadow said, "Stop!"

And it was so   and dreaming continued

An original song in an old garage
        whose chorus captures repair and restoration
Display that doesn't insist on travel
        the going or coming implied

And just now
        a non-profit sun
        says to just sit
            and warm up to renown
It doesn't seem to happen much
Buckboard's fashion prolonged prior to getaway

There are two of them
Stationary transport a broken heart of timber
        pieced back and wanting newlyweds
        That wants to ask
        but guesswork's a better tribute
            almost   a better comprehension

I'll be put back together too
        if only you'll join me in Cedar
Just can't imagine a finer reunion
Because getting over you's a wagon too squeaky

In gingham appear!
        the same girl
            that charmed the poets in North Beach!

In Western dress be driven 'round Cedarville
Some Sunday the tourists are featured
        and thanked
            for the trouble they took to get here

Two buggies   for that is what they truly are
The red one bedecked with floral arrangements

You come closer it's a buggy shop
The blue one's also white
        and borrows red from the other

Purpose is a modest affair
        with an honest end-of-the-day to it
            and the work is set aside
                to see the lake rise and fall

Repair's a trust
    that September 1st
        will never again mean 1939
Though the pages of time
        are scanned for the foreseeable

The improvement desired
    is a segment of hope
        that seems to have a better chance
            in the Valley of Surprise

The need to understand, to include 2020
When hindsight merges with here and now
And eight billion people
    fall in love like *we* did
        and go for a buggy ride

Be nice if Haydn were part of it
Be nice as well
    if summer had further plans for us
            besides transport

The nick of time was not enough
We needed months   needed centuries
    if we were not to be examples
        of some principle adopted by nations

What time period's planned
What original song you'll sing
What renown that's yet an understatement

The Sun is a temporal star
    despite Akhenaten's devotion

The buggy's secular relief
    makes world war simple
        if that is what you want
The technicolor town prepared to beguile
With flowers at the honest end of days

All September's reenacted
    for the improvement of hope

        knowing rehearsals
        are the best perfection to take for a ride

Just remember
        purpose *itself* may need repair

122. THE STATION

A station in life

A Station in town
        closed just now
            its espresso shut down

And   even open
        there's a cloud of doubt they'd get it right
            this far from Fourth Street, Berkeley

We've come so far only cows answer questions
The flag has different colors than ever before
And Betsy Ross is unwilling to work to make it right

It's a good thing the sun's out
        and there's an American dog, too
            used to the street and all its strangers

Laura's waiting   it won't be long
Right now she's just a premonition
But soon you'll see her
        guardian where a Gate would be

Someone's released the pressure
        and "Everything gonna' be all right" was heard
        like The Sandals' resort enticement
Cedarville to substitute
        for a trip to the Caribbean
            where paycheck-to-paycheck
            still permits decadence

The Station will open
       with coffee and calories to burn
                       and best friends to make
All you need is to be ready

Funny it's a Tuesday
Feels like Sunday
             a "Glad-to-know-ya'!" day
When what's left of religion
       puts out its hand
             so that a town's *adagio* all day long
             and the New West knows peace

If it's Tuesday
       the Burning Man that was canceled
                    is three days old
Another church that may be empty
We'll see whether young fury decides to attend

Just as the espresso's unattainable
       the same was thought
             about the streets of Black Rock
A city out of sight
The Org convinced there was no way

And the few of us who truly care
       just as convinced "Somehow!" must prevail
             and be a better word than "No!"

Should have put stamps on a thousand invitations

But perhaps it's better I'm entirely solo
               except for you
     when they get there
         if they get there
         the way I did when they were a throng

The Event like an emergency kit for later
And that stealing not *noticed* till later
Burning Man one's very own caper

Right now it's the next station after this one
       that's only closed if you *say* so

You know, Cedarville's a far-enough town
    a consider-it-done place
You might shake your head
    and wonder why anywhere else

Gravity there's the same as Paris
The espresso *can* be as serious
    and regarding any Burning Men
        plural   to come
            it was always the mind's recreation
            and will be again
            the mind *guiding*

Thinking it through in an after all way
Shuffling past The Station
    thinking of a second marriage
    though marriage is what we have
        and whatever we need's
            just a hallway together

It's just The Station's starting over somehow
A reset intimate
    without the wide world of politics glaring

A cloud cannot be doubt
And *other* language twist with loss of meaning
Just hope the *senses* set you right in spite

The cows concede the humans won
    but insist the victors
        should stand as still as they do

There's plenty of *room*   just look around
Middle Alkali Lake *alone*
    whose eastern edge is the start of Nevada
And the main drag's
    the drag of Berkeley's upscale 4th

You remember
    we decided Betsy Ross needed work
And perhaps Surprise Valley might suit
    for her all-important purpose
    sewing with a sense of humor

She's been called on again after so many years

The Sun's out a second time
And The Station?
    well, it won't be long before it's opened
        like the Gate where Laura stands
            and waits for those who care

A kind guardian
    who will be given espresso
        on the brink of the playa

123. WOODY'S

Woody's wasn't all
The *other* stores were *also* nice

But I *like* saying "Woody's"
    the way you would referring to film
        Woody Allen noodging his co-stars

So to say "Woody's"
    is to say more than a store
        with its welcome's stones
        and maybe a bench

Though it's open   it's for later
And Woody's
    will be a one-word chorus
    sung on the street of companion commerce

Old West Coffins
    The Wholesome Goodness of Mercantile
        with old bricks
        and new white paint

The false fronts
    of the Gift Shoppe

    and Country Hearth
      the restaurant
         with breakfast
         lunch
         burgers and pizza
      its bakery
        with donuts
        and ice cream

Ah! but Woody's chorus says it all!

124. IN EAGLEVILLE WE ARE WEARING BLACK

In Eagleville we are wearing black
   though the town is green with children's lit
     all the pages
       turning
       picturing
       teaching

Let's talk about making things easy
Talk about the eagle
   how it flies to advertise simplicity

Talk to the barn as if there's work to do
   that will just have to wait
     though this threatens the wallet

Clapped my hands
     because I'm happy and I know it
In Eagleville going public
   with a drink called lemonade
     taking no big chances with hard liquor

Came here early to get a feel
Find the streets though they be empty

There's a son somewhere as lost as his father
There's a priest whose sermons are always the same

And maybe a Paiute
       still stunned
             by the speed of western expansion

Funny how where you live
       is where you are   if for only an hour
            distance being a destination

You know everyone
       just driving the highway through
            feeling so much better
            for having made their acquaintance

Wonder if anyone in Eagleville ever said,
"Talk!   or I'll beat it out of you!"
       the way they carry on in bigger towns

No!   there's a meeting of minds
       in the meeting hall with pies and coffee
What's going on there is what I'll be about

Blending in as a temporary chameleon
A Boy George changing color
       for the sake of cultural appropriation

It's not too hot
Nor will the playa seem so
       without a throng
            for the Sun beats badly down for a crowd
            when empathy's communal

Will wait to read a book instead
While the scenery of homes is known
Their post-apocalypse repairs
       imagined to be a simple affair

Perhaps Eagleville still remembers
       Joseph Floyd Vaughan
       who settled here after getting famous
"Arky" to his friends
Maybe they still grieve his drowning
            in Lost Lake in 1952
               the baseball star
               who batted left

                but threw with his right

Somebody!   *Please!*
How do you *do* that?

Well, I'm part of a home run
        by coming to Eagleville
           and wearing black
              as if in mourning for "Arky"

Despite green children
      turning their pages so easily

125. THE GREEN HOUSE SO PALE

There's a house pale green in Eagleville
Its cube of two-storeyed vigilance
                is a privacy set aside

A house in the dale
Where lobelia grows
     in a meantime manner

And this slight acquaintance
                 will have to do
An almost punitive brevity
Short shrift given its example

The sight to recur and be recurring
Travel's seen to that
      whenever the road is this way
          past the pale green house

So that there's a "before" feel
Subject to recall
      each time a new edition
          of the *book* of pale green appears

It's not so much the wondering who lives there
It's more when will *we* be moving in
That one day that may be a solstice
        darkest day
        or brightest
                when extremity's most noticeable

We'd have *kubasa*   the Ukrainian sausage
Even if the Russians arrive
Go some distance in the mind
      to be in Kyiv   I don't know
          because war's all the rage

But even if it's over
      having once happened
          it *always* is happening

That one day the pale green house is ours
Those windows framed
      by a deeper green
          which folderol saw fit to ignore

And the awning in summer
      added shade to what surrounds
          all of it emerald
          a jade to *enclose*

The Warner rimrock's
      a grand suggestion you stay
          even if it's socage
          even if the Russians show

Ruefully perhaps we'll call it a *dacha*
Be done with distinction
The least likely to say
      that things to come must be just so

The enemies are tired drunks we'll be driving home
As we drove ourselves to Eagleville
      our own pale bodies to pamper

It's not a mansion
Just a straight path in
      with maybe a drawing room   we'll see

And make it a Thursday we see
That day of the week that's also green
        somehow   the way the days are colors too

Our own "Dance of the Hours"
       starts with stopping by
             if not walking in
                 with Amilcare Ponchielli holding our hands

Lime green is the shade
       that's shaded with poplars and cedars
Can I say the light is win-win?
An advantage to all?

No better security than being right here
Between Summer Lake and Winter Ridge

The pale fire burning   season to season
      everyone getting home
        to houses others own as well
Slipping engagement rings on the entire population

Life together on the way to Gerlach
The usual route adjusted
           for a brief sequester
           and even a wedding
Green's half-light to grace the nuptials

Beautiful as red Sunday's thought
      in the almost middle of the week

The question is
      how do we stay when we've already left?
Eagleville a lingering acquaintanceship
Town whose green house so pale
          is the very gist of hospitality

126. WEATHERING'S WAVELENGTHS

Eagleville is peeling
      it's all paint past protection
Eagleville's disintegrating

It's not enough the structures lean
They must settle and sink
      the only option after so much neglect
And more is on the way
      much more than what we know about

You need to help
You might stop the disappearance
      just walking its streets with reason
          or accountability
Getting to the cause for a culture's decay

Rescue's in the mind
Like a show business
      that never takes the stage
What tradition needs to survive
        to stay in place
        and apply fresh paint
           wearing suspenders and gingham

Renovation's a dream this summer morning
A starving animal looking for treats
To make it new would take reenactment
      City Hall to supervise
        if there's really a hall
        let alone a city of eagles

Strange how once-upon-a-time tries to stay present
A tiredness that still yearns for relevance

The colors there are
      do justice only to wear and tear
And brand-new's a premium concern
      that tries to rattle the cage of neglect

Town whose high is over with
      and so it curls up in withdrawal

                    run-down attuned to sparsity
Whose program of recovery has no Big Book at all
       just a few scribbled poems
          fading into the future
Still rural   though uncertain
Like gangling teens
              in the presence of hardened grownups

Perhaps a *koan* applies
Or a riddle might serve
          to improve enlightenment
Or a paradox that's end-of-the-line
              but still a sunny place

I'm persuaded the peeling's illustrative
Their delicate petals a question of time
                    that's answered with patience

The fair-minded among us
        want an explanation
             for the frailty of a town

The wavelengths are local
The colors a spectrum
        of longitude   of latitude
            their specific sadness
            defined as nothing of value

You are kind to accompany
And see if this weathering's for sure
              and not just a pause

Wandering these streets
        a kind of scapegoat glow
            prepares the mind for belief
We'll celebrate that barn   that storage shed
And the light of white paint   disappearing

As if concentrating we'll choose eagles
        and use their talons
             to seize upon a century's center
              fiercely shake its contents
                    and nidify thereafter

Nights and weekends
    there's time to scrutinize this capsule
        wanting action
            spurning the decades since
            that worry the past with irrelevance

Depression seeks the late afternoon
    when these same pastels may further fade
And I'll need you then
To say that the ancient doors before us
    may still be opened
        to let town doctors resume their practices
        Eagleville the instrument played

How far behind is the welcome
    and all that spilled so easily then?
The twenties   thirties   forties
With token distrust
    moving things slowly enough
        to sort and sift the nitty-gritty

It's like we know in advance
    that to stay would mean rebuilding
            into the next *life*, even
The cancers that started and ended
    moot concerns
    as medicine yearns for bygone caseloads

Will you excuse the delay?
Believe the interval of our knowing
        to be another way of learning?

It's like something you want to figure out
        before a journey resumes

The town's a delicate container
A trained eye sees the *art*
    of weathering
    and reversion

To be here is to live here
Involved and worn away appreciatively
I'd say to Laura, "We're on our way!"
    but that's all

    for the way *here* was important too

Our childhood backyards
  become a compensation of farms
  and favored eclogues
    let's walk the highway
      as if our intention's a country lane
        the leisure of bucolic

With wit and sagacity will you ascertain the sun
The star's plan for Eagleville
  as it is *warming*
  and proud of its craftsmanship

Weathering's wavelengths are shy and reserved
Imparting those same qualities
    to those who understand
      the better speech of melancholia

Let in this light
Accept free tickets to a vision
For there's an identity thief at large
  where Earlier's robbed
    and put in Later's cupboard

A story of faith disturbed

Neglect is a location
  a belief gone into hibernation
  and inviting the curious to follow

Will the weathering insist on complete erasure?
When Surprise Valley reverts
    to be a basin nameless?

For now the telephones work
  and rest in their retro cradles
And cats still roll and drool in the heat
What we have found here strangely inspires

And let's just say
  sometimes a photon's tired too
Light's leukemia wanting it knows not what

Like saying goodbye
    in a street that's a long, long road
        thoughtfully designed
            for sentimental journeys
                to the "peak of empire"
                    a time not noticed at the time

Town's a reliquary
All of it containing Unknown's religion
    the final version
The one that says,
        "I ain't done yet
        and you still need a church
            standing sideways to change"

Isn't that your mother calling?
Isn't that everyone you ever loved
        waiting on Main Street?

If ever the future gets its way
        it would be nice if Main survived
        as the main idea
Sensible in spite of wanton destruction

Main idea of running out of time
When you sell a home as is
        including the cushions

The rain and the wind *love* the project of weathering
As if given a job where the work will be noticed

Laura's waiting at the edge of the playa
We'll leave
    and hear her welcome
    to the sketch of an event
Black Rock's empty Burn
        when COVID came to wear away attendance

Shall we tell Eagleville we're here?
That we are also peeling and pale
      our own outcomes relaxing into disintegration?

Though cancer's been told to stay in in its corner
The extra lifetimes allowed

          double the age of Schubert's
                are those of unreasoning culture
An *approximate* wisdom
                and not good enough

So rescue's all in the mind
Its show business non-stop and once-upon-a-time

Fugal   like Bach
              yet discordant
              rundown

A paradox of dissolution wed to beauty
        that summons the exactitude of Rudy Jon Tanner
            who still yearns
            for another season at Pyramid Lake

And   oddly
        everything points to revival
            based on pastel shades
            and sagging lumber
Like a weird suggestivity
            comprising nothing of value
This street that's a road!
This ville of eagles staring
        in avian disbelief
            that a century's center could not hold!

Renovation's a raised eyebrow
        that insures the fixing stays intended
            a reverie governed by nostalgia
            just the way it is
                this day of docile wavelengths

Depression seeks an afterlife here
I'll need you more than ever
Your easy grace
        to neutralize conformity
        and restore the fast-fading veneer of privacy

Indeed how brashly
        does far behind insist on scrutiny!
No peasant rebellion came
Nor emigration

They're all still here and waiting in slow motion

We are knowing in advance *and* later *on*
      though teaching no interference
Starting and ending for now
This time that knows no clock
        with its piquant intermissions
          you and I have made together

A town unveiled
Something we will figure out
      like the art of weathering
The many backyards hereabouts wanting usage

We could stay
      the better speech of children to learn
      and proper names forgotten
We'll be a focus group of just two travelers
         lost on purpose
          with black telephones ringing

The final version of unobvious visitation
Thinking rain and wind and all that sun
      will be non-stop peeling abstract art
        to Bach
        and a chorus of neighbors waving goodbye
More than what we knew about or trusted

I'm wearing suspenders for the duration
And please!   oh, *please!*
      will you wear that lovely dress of gingham?

127. THOSE BELLS IN THE CHURCHYARD

Why should *not* the bells be separate?
If congregations go to sleep
      then all the world may be left alone

Though iron has no home in the belfry

And silence sings the *birds* to sleep
      yet the churchyard wants a ringing
      wants dualism's "clang!" to sound
            in the aftermath of worst-case

I'll be religion's understudy
See if mercy's made of metal
      and claps in time to a summons

If this is Sunday
      could Sunday School be on the way?
The other side of what is possible

There's no other place to "go-to-meeting"
Open air are the bells in a region of sound unheard
      a separation anxiety
      sustained by stillness

Faraway places share the churchyard's spaces
A hologram's overlap
      where bells apart sponsor repose

It is apparent that
      even sober   attendance has dropped
The little cliff of the skeptic
            is now a Yosemite everlasting
Would it take a funeral to fill the pews aqain?
A hasty wedding?

Perhaps there's been a Rapture for real!
An incomplete capture
      that took only a few
           bundled them up and   *voila*!

Someone took trouble though
            to separate the bells
      one is smaller   petite
Companion bell for an otherwise orphan
Both backgrounded by that house of God
      its red roof and steeple
      saying things I have forgotten

An architecture's sermon too
There's the cross   of course

    plain white
        can I say "unprepossessing?"
        don't want to but will

The cross an appeal lost to runaway reason
    always *just* around the corner
Something heard at age six
    that sank *in* but stayed unknown

If Handel says it's okay I'll listen further
But the bells stay put like sentries
            very still indeed!
Please!   the message came loose
    and went flying

Even history can't be bothered
It's a denomination needing too much help
Something's dismantled that lost its balance
    and teeters

Now unnatural worlds have sought the sun
And they orbit disbelief in place of assurance
Should you behave   there's no reward
    and too much gravity
        has brought the bells down to Earth

Their ringing on hold for the sake of complexity

Or at least some honest answers
    why simplicity should not be taught
        church as home on the range
        or an acre of wilderness allowed

Where Christ forgets his name and roams
While purposeful winds
    blow novel scriptures about
        in a catatonic landscape

Heavy is the iron since
And it saves reverberation for some day distant
    bells apart

As genius flees the capitols

          and finds repose in solitude
So the transfer
      steeple to churchyard
          replays the flight of talent

Gone to sleep is the doctrine
      that shall reawaken some spring of the planet
      when birds insist on a message

And with all the world left alone
            a pealing is possible
A double tonality
      understudied
      understood

And if Sunday should find the time
      then reassembled is a congregation
            no longer far from home
A "go-to-meeting" feel

Though a scripture's pages are blank
      another faith can fill them
Just the record of good deeds done
      in lieu of any doctrine

Guess we'll find out
When the first hologram begins
      like a First Alert   Second   and Third
          however many it takes to awake

Let sobriety continue
      that the churchyard bells may attract
          and even promote
Saying things I have forgotten
          as wayfaring orphan
            deaf from false clamor

The percussion of just these bells
      to be reinstalled in the steeple
          for a Rapture based on sticking around
And no recourse to magical thinking

Save the cult of All is One
      that's found in one place that's yours

128. THE TOWER

It seemed a lookout
      for some recommended vigil
           that Rapunzel should perform
              when she wasn't letting her hair down

Outpost tower
      and southernmost wood of Eagleville
           the *right now* of yesterday
Solitaire's attic

From which approach is scanned
So that the residents of Surprise Valley
                      are never truly surprised
And all are familiar before they arrive
      the southern side of town to see
           by those who never were a danger

But If Eagleville should fall to invaders
           the town might simply adjust

It's nice to have a tower three-storeyed
Maybe attached as an afterthought
      some weekend of communal design
      with black-and-white-and-green

Have you seen it?
The center of town's the *edge* of town
Could have sworn I once went in there
      and once inside
           there were sweets   coffee
           and happy talk
                like the news   only better

A piano had leaned on ancient planks
And some of the keys could even be played
But the loft's the interest
      that tapering   to a point of order

Maybe Emily's aerie
      when she wanted to know
           who was coming down the road

        to see her   in Amherst West
            some fogless morning of poetry

The wonder is it's a home to squirrels
No human ventures to stay for long
    despite the view

They have no time for a vigil
And search for grandstanding
    and chirring
        the muddled business
      of "getting over"

In just one minute the tower impresses
With sufficient appraisal Rapunzel returns
    Saint Barbara
        The Brothers Grimm
          making sure their folklore's
              found a place in Eagleville, Oregon
A father's caution leading to disaster

The third century hints she's real
    think about that?   sure! wonderful!
But the castles there are don't add up to Germany

They only attest to American small town
    and friends in houses of wood
Together they seek to be neighbors
    and throw spaghetti feeds from time to time

Their tower's an allegation of farsightedness
Seeing something south that's coming this way
    or just staring from a certain distance

I'm a ribald   without vocabulary
Still some attempt should be made
        to gift the reader with elevation
The best of the things we were talking about
    to suggest this may be possible

Maybe just move in
Evict the squirrels
    and contemplate Emily
        even insist the wallpaper's hers

        its roses inferred
            from a bygone swatch discovered

Just strive for refinement
Though Mozart didn't *have* to
    made it seem easy
    as if the notes
        were already suggested
        by the God he loved
"Amadeus"   after all   what it truly means

I'll be Jimmy Stewart losing his fear of heights
      without causing Kim Novak to fall
The tower to be a studio
With ungodly art too dangerous to see
The art show
    to stay a private obsession
        with those alkali lakes
        reliving their discovery
              from a tower

Being all in with the Ice Age
And guessing the lakes' deepest moment
              with independent thought

Climb to the tower
Seek its third storey
    the last place they'll look
        if the law takes an interest in this getaway
        and why it was necessary

Crime tried to follow the rental
In such a way it wasn't noticed

I'm sorry
    and say it to the eagles
        if they care to hear me out
An eagle myself up there
With paint affixed to occult canvasses
    a partnership of brushes
        moving pictures surpassing cinema

Who's going   who's coming to town
    where the southern tower commands

                where you check for trouble
And contemplate long hair   1880
                Alfred Hitchcock
                    and concepts of narrow popularity

129. BALES

They were not *precisely* Euclidean bales
Neither was spherical geometry complete

What's certain though is
        they were round
        the way cylinders are
And stacked   symmetric
The hay a spiral within each bundle

The heart of a harvest
        unmolested by usage intended
The hay brought to dubious justice
Rolled up and rolled away

The skies of California showcase the feed
The bales
        that went from cuboids
        scattered in yellow fields
            to these same circular versions
Just when is not known
        unless you're a farmer

It came to pass a better plan was made
But the *squarish* bales
        the more *traditional* bales
            used to come to Burning Man

Back in the nineties you'd see them
In the shade of Center Camp's parachutes
                hay to sit on
                    recite your words

It was a novelty to see the bales in Black Rock City
Here and there
       and comprising the platform too
          where stood that wooden figure
              revered for its delicious absurdity

But the bales disappeared
        there were never any cylinders either
                the desert lost its hay

Guess we'll do things differently forever
In *spite* of granite's example of age-old
        the petty crime of staring not likely to matter

The Stockton cop is back at work
But I think he'd break the law a little his *own* self

There's no particular shock value
The pale bales are restful
       like morality accepted
           at least in principle
There's order in the countryside
Well-rounded bales belonging to hereabouts

Spirals fulgent with a sunshiny glow!
How long ago is the mood
       despite the modern look of things

I'm *tangential* to the bales
           no sex worker beckons
             the city itself unthinkable
The hard cider of zen's preferred
        in the presence of Van Gogh
          his swirls contained in the hay bales'

All this what I wanted you to hear   however later

The landscape   with its harvest
       is nude enough to satisfy a photographer
       if not Euclid himself
           in his quest for perfection

130. THE BURNT LAND

The burnt land is land remembered
The black an absolute   taking liberties
And the ashen hills debating with color
      on whether to return to the rainbow

The land is yet to transition
As if the trauma had been too much of a bad thing

And boulders that had been concealed
      lie naked-*noir* in the scenery
      a frame of film
           from a time when shades of grey were all
           though the movie were an ardent romance

There's something about a fire's conclusion
      that belies the bright flame of what came before
The yellow   the orange   and the red
           not having meant it

Being insincere in conflagration
      black-and-white's the consequence
           the soil itself reduced

In the heat of the day
      it's hottest here in the burnt land
      where its barren rocks
           are almost *illegal* with exposure

If it's purification
If it's a fresh start   a rural reset
      still sadness attends
      a hint of unintelligent design

What's remembered's more than these few acres
      the lands along 395 once
      the devastation selective
               capricious
A fire's out that couldn't stop
      on the north-south highway then

A tenth of a second to see it *here*

Out of place
        the gold of that furnace quietened

Have the boulders cooled?
Can you say "scorched earth"
      as in war
            when you're losing
            and have to burn in retreat?

Yet fire's a destination now
A pursuit to see
        if the non-event that's Burning Man
            may still see The Man's immolation
            albeit downsized   symbolic

The burnt land left and right remembers and imparts

Puts in mind the memory of a midnight arson
        seen from a road like this
The car drifting forward
To a fire that was a home aflame
        a department's engines deployed
           to douse what was left

On approach it had been distance aglow
And after slowing to 10
        it was the same in the rearview
                      with acceleration away

Other fires   other ages
A forest engulfed my father brought me to see
And   weirdly   I'd thought he'd set it
        all because we didn't get along

Such was the *poverty* of the burnt land
        you'd go begging
           though to do so would have no meaning
                      beyond reflex survival

There could be dancing in the ashes
As conqueror
        or more simply
             out of joy unrelated to devastation
             happily losing control in the lap of nihilism

                its only child with a mind of its own

The "number of the beast" unknown
Forgotten   the better to foster defiance
The earth uncapitalized
All *else* lower case
      to lower the expectations of mythology

It's so much more fun to live in a pretend world
A world remembered well
      one that was spotlit
         with playday's beginning, middle and end
The good story told by a favorite teacher

Think the brand-new body of a child
      the best hope of understanding the burnt land
For youth will demand an explanation
Will want to know *exactly* why
           there's a blackened field

Will hope the answer's a surprise
                like the Valley
Will not be satisfied
      with some monotone of boredom
         and obfuscation

Today is one day closer
      to the total timeout of Burning Man
         as if it were a pool
            with a Stockton cop
          though the water's in its table
              and thoroughly unseen below

Invisibility beginning
      where the Quinn   and other rivers
         strive to run time into the basin

The burnt roadside's good information
Though my brain is full
      and I'm raising my hand in fourth grade
                  wishing to be excused

There will be no prayer vigil
Whatever war this resembles

will have to wait till the *film noir*'s over
and any pictures taken
      show a sprig of green at least

Whoever's neighbor to these acres
      will have learned "close call"
        learned "live and local" like the news
Bulletins without preliminary chatter

Can black be forgiven for scarring?
Be welcome back to sable innocence
          unaware of terror?

The darkness seems volcanic
Indistinguishable
You're in the presence of eruption
      if only through suggestion
Out of a database of black
      many visions are possible
        some state-sponsored
          and seeming benevolent even

If insanity knows ignition
      then a wildness comes
        that the winds will find and draft all else
On a mission to do so
      with the westerlies fully involved

The smoke that   not so long ago
      brought about the red sun's mystery
        is here reimagined
         driving to Nevada
So soon to come it's a near*by* border

Red mystery as misdirection
Just as the burnt land fools with analogy
      will not let it alone
        but teases onlookers with ash
And the ruined ground
      purports to summon time and space
        and freely associate both

And silently   as now
Impactful

        like a document
                everyone feared would determine the truth
The black-and-white of it explicit evocation

In advance of arriving at playa
        the burnt land's a preview
        and accelerant scene

There is nothing mainstream to it
No matter *how* much of a study is made

The heavy rocks
        may be settees
        for contemplation
You   The Thinker   modeling for Rodin
In the burnt land
        that's a battlefield's charity of insights

Perhaps the dark's the start   the Ideal
after which
        the delusion of luck and good fortune
                seem glorious exceptions

What death is more annoying
        than the contemplation of ashes?

It is some demon nihilist's charcoal assertion
        that demands like-minded acolytes
            redouble their devotion to nothing at all
                but the chronic joint pains of the hominid

Mind if I just phone this in?
I do *not* trust the narrative
        and so may set it on fire
My two best friends will understand
And possibly try to talk me down
        from *film noir's* trance state of media despair

The burnt land prefers the nightfall
                when Earth's shadow
                    is then a commensurate shade

Greatness seeks its own dissolution
The top choice that oblivion is

Prometheus   Titan god of fire's been by
        his gift to the mortals
            the subject of debate
The outdoors accepting his Fahrenheit
               as well as the trained eagle
                  sent by Zeus to punish

It is trauma to say it
How Prometheus was bound!
        and even Shelley had to work hard to free him!

Before moving on
And before color's restored
        let the black-and-white of uncontrolled Greece
            burn a hole in the sprockets
               like an ardent romance with celluloid
With no conclusion therefore possible

The bright flame of what came before
            is now the heat of the day
               greeting a barren Stonehenge
               random-strewn

This could be 395 drunk on road rage
Winding   capricious past Bodie
The long-ago town   population: 2

Remember   if you can   the gold
The gold that caused combustion

War is a picnic laid
        a non-event that's zero-down
            a house of embers
               the shiny red trucks in retreat

Having once happened it always is happening
Like history that goes begging for attention paid
        even as arsonists lie in wait in virgin nations

Is it father among them?
Or has he had enough
        and just wants to lie down now
            be a lower case dad
               and no god of the Greeks?

The best hope of understanding
      which can be *another* child's concern
this one is blank
The way Will Dodger said he was that   "I'm blank!"
      in Polk Street Beans in San Francisco
          one night of blank verse
          and communion with words

Today is one day closer to winter rains
There may be more fires
No worries
      for Lucifer's been caught
      and says there won't be more
            than small *bon*fires

Resting here in the ashes
      I want to meet the neighbors to this battlefield
Find out what they do and how they do it

Would it be an acceptable inquiry?
Or one that was awkward
      given we're all a little cautious
          and not really forthcoming now?

Maybe the fire *itself* was secret
D*espite* the wildness the wind will find
I'd show the flames to my father
      my own sparks flying
      preemptive

Ahead of his time
          and whatever he was up to
            so long ago
This *summer* on time
      with space to explain the rest

131. THE SHEEP

As they seem content
And quietly graze
     the herd shifting randomly

As they are studied and admired for their softness
     the fluffy wool
        a sense of compromise
            and gentle reason

Can a question just as harmless be asked?

For a question forms   ever so meekly
A wondering that will not go away
     and must be addressed
        in the commercial mind
        in the idle moments
           after money's changed hands
In between shearings perhaps

"Could a sheep have a leader like Kim Jong Un?"

132. NEVADA, ENTERING

It's just a line

Sometimes the pavement changes
     crossing such lines
        funding
         maintenance

The lines are precise in theory only
Sometimes they move
     the surveyors roused to reconsider

Then suddenly
     Four Corners

          down there in the southwest
               isn't where it *should* be
And the four states' crosshairs must be repositioned

Or not   depending on resolve

Nevada's coming
The land of the playas
      Black Rock   and Smoke Creek

It's not every day you come here
Kind of keeps it a View Master's world
      with each new vista's 3D
          clicked and snapped

We'll exit the Valley now
      Surprised and pleased

Soon enough
      will the distant profile faintly appear
The Granite Range
With its lofty central pyramid
      whose millions of years still say "Good Morning!"

Into Nevada   once part of Mormon "Deseret"
Nevada
      the state with the bent border
          angling down to Vegas

And although it's   just   a   line
      there's power to it
         toying as it does with the intellect

133.   FRANCK'S QUINTET AT THE CREST

There's a pass you can't pass without a pause

And the Buffalo Hills that tantalize
      may do so   nearby and marvelous

>   though because they're remote
>   a visit so far has stayed a desire

The crest of the pass will suffice
With Franck's solitary Quintet spinning in the player
>   dramatic as it wants to be
>   great and honorable
>   between the engines coming and going

If there are to be buffalo now's the time

And briefly walking
>   the 4-wheel track
>   to lookout rocks
>   Franck's piano
>   is prominent as they are

The pause to exceed the Quintet's measures
To capture the silence that follows
>   becoming convinced
>   the high ground's short-handed
>   but far from prison

The pass is a place of heavenly scarcity
The descent eastward
>   will be a second gear's cravings
>   and swerving

And   it must be said
>   descent with a certain reluctance

Perhaps the buffalo will follow
At least for awhile
But Franck has sworn to stay with you
>   teaching F Minor forever

134. PARSING "SQUAW VALLEY" AND THE ENCAMPMENT THERE

As far as it is possible
       to be perfect
              and perfectly correct
                     "squaw" will have to go
                agreed   it is wrong

No matter the music of the word itself
Especially that *vowel*

If history hadn't named the wrong
       and taken offense if "squaw" is said
              the *sound* is innocent
                a morpheme wishing its independence

We'll get to the encampment and why
But the valley's former name wants attention paid
The detective in all of us summoned to proceed

"Squaw Valley"
       might have been the last of the
                           "squaws"
A holdout stubbornly insisted on
And then
       with a pen
              "Squaw" went away in Nevada
              the Washoe tribe respected

"Smoke Creek Valley Opening"
       "Too Kapu Tawaka"
              "Deep Hole Spring Creek"
                     "Granite Mountain Reservoir"

New names going to work on prejudice
And that word   barely one syllable   is lost
      but not the meaning

Were a language unknown heard
A flood of foreign vowels and consonants
       how much exception might be taken?

Perhaps the strange tongue
       is enough to trigger
              something strange to one's nature

But "squaw" can never be right, now
       and its prejudice must be unlearned
Having once happened
       the voice will arrest itself
            before it happens again
                try to hide something
            that can't be hidden

How much of a tribe
       is gathered as a Second People?
And what fishing is started   or camping
       the lake staying calm
              and unassuming?

Nothing personal taken
       beyond the energy of ripples
The encampment too is mostly oblivious
Says, "How dare you!" if questions are asked

Privacy allowed an access
The wealth around had relaxed its hold
Decided to share the reeds and bright water

There's a dam
       the reason open to interpretation
            the dirt tracks many and connecting

Before the pool was anything at all
And the Washoe were still *en route*
       this   "opening"   to the playa
       this oasis undisturbed
            was just the consequence
                    of a spring upwelling

All of this was a dream you sent to me
              one night of serendipity
And I said we could find it
Like another planet of prehistory
       pristine with anticipation of our landing there

Yet such would be our usage
        it must stay a virgin world
How not to colonize but merely watch *over*

There is no death
        the Deep Spring cannot take apart
                and scatter like pollen
Your minstrel self to activate the afterlife
        that's not just sleep
           but enlightenment's dawn

"Squaw" can be a whisper without definition
Right now "sol" is not only the sun
        but the fifth tone of the scale you sing
           the *forever* note of all the rest
With Granite Peak
        the background for your recital

The years are slowing
They don't want to be over with
Time itself has sympathy   *and* patience

If time could stop altogether it *would*
        but a higher authority
           insists on centuries to come

We'll go for a swim   make new friends
        even if they're cleaning their guns
For hypnosis only takes a minute
        and scrap metal has many uses!

Here at the lake
        it is easy to think the Earth will survive
            without money, too
The reckless cities
        to be the faintest of notions

Instinct can settle down
Divorce the brain
        be as brand-new as it *wants* to be
The highway a number forgotten
And the "squaw" that's buried in "squabble"
                have linguistic life of its own

The Granite Range is adamant it must be so
Its firmament of crystals glinting
      with resolution overriding
            the lesser geology of fools

One life at a time to come 'round
The way the comatose revive and resume

Beyond the cows
      the start of the Buffalo Hills
            those terraced lavas   who knew?
At elevation and peaceful for all their basalts' beginnings

We may not see the entire plateau
Nor anyone else before the end of the world

Meanwhile a word is drowned
      gone fishing
           hiding in the tall grass
                learning to make sense
A Washoe maiden reclaiming her people

We'll take her with us
Speak a common language of telepathy

Green and brown
      has brought perfection
           to the court of color
The jury took two minutes and the judge then retired

History's been hanging around
But so far has left us alone
                not minding the babble
Its *own* detectives
      prepared to give us a pass

Say "Too Kapu Tawaka" and return
Say "Deep Hole Spring Creek"
It's the morning show
      and there's a wedding in the sage
           ours
              a certain   *déjà vu*

Let's be conversational
Parse the lingo
      our tongue strange enough
          to start a new religion
Our voices to arrest who hear us say, "Behold!"

Or simply ask "What's up?"

Though everyone's welcome at water's edge
It is privacy sure seeing only *your*self
    as if
        finding the treasure of solitude
            is improved by your presence

The wilderness is saying,
"Now listen, and listen *good*!
    and the mostly silent scenery will talk!"

Nature making its case for misanthropy

Just be in the Deep Spring drowned
      knowing "squaw" is a contention
         that outlasts solutions
You want to make important calls to unimportance

Settle on usage
All dialects and sub-tongues censored for politics
Wandering minds
      allowed the vagrancy
         of thinking there's no crime
         if you're an animal
And "knowing better" is just conceit

Precision's a folly pushing through the dictionary
With meanings shy and coquettish both
      "squaw" reluctant to yield
         stubborn for sure
         content to be offensive

I can hear it in your singing
Whenever your voice
      finds the fifth degree of your scale
         and says the water's cold

                but let's go in
For it's the perfect temperature
                for making sense right now

And if someone wants to fish for *us* that's fine
Time has time for *this* as well
Is patient with the presumption
      the spoken word is to be trusted at all

From now it's noise
When they say "Smoke Creek Valley Opening"
      and insist
           that everyone's happy
                joyous and free
                because it's *called* that
What to do next will not be obvious

You're my single friend double-jointed with affection
And so   you have heard these concerns
      for which I'm grateful

Forget about a warrant
English stays unarrested   reckless, even
I want that divorce
      and permission to understudy the Washoe
Discover their own misdemeanors   if any

The Asiatic conquest of North America
      to resume
           one life at a time
                arriving at the Granite Range
                    and the unceasing spring

And oh!
What a prayer of thanks there must have been
      upon discovery!
What relief!

And the Washoe   well
Did the tribe have words that weren't quite right?
Equivalent to "squaw" so they had to go?

Perhaps it would be better
      if the hominids say nothing

        only stare knowingly
        like Bubba Free John in the end

John *Cage* getting his way
Suggesting a silence that catches on
      the free-and-clear encampment
            a mute R &R

And the real deal of Deep Hole sufficient finding
A little universe of well-meaning bubbles
      that need not be explained
A first-of-all place beyond fussiness

Etymology yielding to hydrology
      and geology
          the big questions posed by the rocks

The reservoir's a special case
      of catch-and-release logic
          any baptisms
          brought to the attention of animist shamans
Who may or may not take the plunge

Too bad the squabbles have distracted
Unfortunate
      that language turned out to be
            fighting words
      and "holier than"

The knowledge that was power
        squandered on pushing and shoving
          and missiles!
What someone said
        learning to make sense
            making war!

What disrespect!
That roused antiquity
      to mess with the present tense
          and tell it to chill

Be perfect as far as it is possible to be
          and perfectly correct

Yet wishing in a way for a language unintelligible
                                        a glorious noise

135.   WRONG TURN TO BIVOUAC

The length   width   and depth   were wrong
And so a wrong turn to what was familiar

Nevada fooling with the traveler some
The desert telling little lies to perception

And so it was a rancher appeared
      to make known the truth of the terrain
      and how his spread
           would not be taking guests that day
How the creek I sought was further

He understood of course
And perhaps   now and then
      Nevada told fibs to him as well

A trickery adjacent to wonder

Thus a turn too soon
      was yet the right one for a good conversation

136.   MOSQUITO GLEN

It was shelter and refreshment
Where the water ran from under
      and the trees meant
           the sun should not be wake-up
                but indirect lighting for last-minute dreaming

Accept the sins of any animals near
And not mind too much
      the mosquito's interest taken
         despite repellants
All felonies forgiven

In the morning the creek is a conspiracy
      insisting the desert's a paradise
         well-watered
And shimmer's an outline's belief in oasis

Call it a glen that's off the beaten
      having no capital letters to boast of

Once again was bivouac made
      car-camping the night away
         meaning something cozy
            in spite of open ground

It doesn't matter   bivouac it is
      reclining in the rental
         wrapt against the night winds
         enclosed even
The windows cracked one inch or so

While the planet turns you turn *yourself*
               in proximity to gurgles
A home you leave reluctantly
For slumber's neither left nor right
      politics no purchase makes
      and vanishes

The evening's a better brainwashing
      that might stick around
         the crimes of the daylight to uncommit

If the creek is identity theft I don't mind
It means a brand-new mind is possible

The carriers of malaria will fly away bloodless
      thanks to chemical dependency
I'm a country of one whose border's a bivouac

Its colonies are many
The invasions unnoticed
And might the surround sound of whispers
      signify approval?
The susurrus of drafting instill conviction?

So far from war
      the atavist comes to life
           to embroider boredom

Ripples   and branches of the cottonwood
    are an ideology
        recruiting the stranger
          to see all the corners of a country
As much as may be easy

Call it a glen
Disowning the rush
     that puts us well past a wayside's accomplishments

The morning begun at noon
     the shade has made a mirror
        blotchy with reflection
Like staring into secrecy
          its entire repertoire of meaning

The pool   with surface tension
     implying
       "Look nowhere else!
       here is safety and concealment!"

A crime stopper creek
Where still water hides
     in a mottled glistening
         far from any town

Planet X is nearest   up the road a little
That place of pots and vases
     where a little business thrives

Planet X that's next today
         will turn the volume up
         with exceptional ceramics
That art may loudly call your name

There's nothing to buy in the glen
Whatever lottery there may have been
       made tracks for a future of barter
            where Burning Man "blows up"
            and a comprehension of value obtains

A fixer-upper culture begins with bivouac
The skinny mosquito fully involved

Now   whatever words have the power
       please present yourselves
       for service to the truth
A simple overnight spent in hiding
         can seem a luxury's appointment

And "Mosquito Glen?"
Sounds like a resort
      place where a hebdomad
          could discuss the Seven Deadlies
         though all is forgiven

Wildlife's late to the party
But goes about with machinations
Think I'll join their late morning
            of rustle and bustle
       having a chance to be a part of things
       and break no promises to space out

We'll walk the creek before departure
The rural sun postponing discomfort

No other campers came
Perhaps some superstition
      or aversion
        to those slender and segmented bodies

The *culicidae*

The glen sending love notes from the Cretaceous
      letters heretofore unopened
Late morning's conspiracies abating
           in favor of an ordinary day
              of wayside shelter

      and refreshment

137. AN EASTERN WIND

What is the east wind doing?

It is a contrary breeze that opposes the westerlies
A civil disturbance of atmospherics
  that gently chides and cools
    doing the best it can to raise questions

How much you can hold in your hand
        cupped to receive

Whatever the east wind seeks
    its search will soon expire
For it is some *errant* reversal of the flow

Just for the day there's an air of protest
Whether low or high pressure's uncertain
    irrelevant

In the swirling is a hint of exception
And the playa kites will face another direction
   the string inclined to the distant Pacific
     where balloons attempt to travel too

Is it the world's rewinding and revolving anew?
The direction of its turning changed
        to suit a different faith?

At least revision's escorting us by the hand
And pleasant zephyrs from interior places
   are calming speculation
    helping to lay to rest concerns

Meteorology's miles-per-hour
   a balm in the palm
    that brought us captured Colorado

        in its non-stop flight through Nevada

Obviously some Tilt-a-Whirl's reversal
        spun by a mischievous carny

Just now
    a dust devil's kind and considerate cyclone
        has formed
        and likely lifted a praying mantis
            some inches from ground level
                but not much more
For the east wind's well-mannered
And does not wish too much to disturb

The east is wafting
    around the corners of the Granite Range
And whispers names heard only now and then
    if ever

Revelations saved for such a day as this
One that's uncertain
    so that Franck is summoned once more
    his *Les Eolides*
        like a recognition *of* this east wind
His apt expression lending credence

Every hurry will be slowed
Anxieties relaxed
    as if one is in good company for sure
        and for the duration

It is a transaction proposed by wayward barometers
    certain their measurements matter

What is the east wind doing?

Telling a story counterintuitive
Documenting deserts
    to share them with the seashore

And as long as it wafts
    so will the clouds make their way
        and willingly conspire
All in all an easing of westerly coercion

Normalcy's roar and relentless messaging!

And Gerlach to come
        will add this eastern interlude
                to its history so far
As fences and doors are mildly buffeted
                                at no risk of failure

And the east wind's so good
        you wish it would happen again
                in spite of the jet stream

Nothing morbid attends
We'll savor this calm rebellion
        stirring the grasses
        or invisibly twisting solitary trees

The longest week is concluded
In the hotel of open air
        the east wind is renting spacious rooms
                          for the price of poetry

Perhaps the ghosts of the Pony Express will say it
        however dubious their recollections

The east wind's uncovered suspicions
        that were one-way *buried* by prevailing
A delicate search engine prepared to fully forgive
No matter how uncivil the skeletons

There are the kites again
        the string let out unraveling
And those balloons
                that follow the future   inflating
                a possibility that still exists

The devil's in the dust
And so far well-behaved and-learning
As if longing to be larger tornadoes
        with a willingness to change
        if they are gifted

The east wind has left
Think it only wanted half an hour

      and that would be sufficient finding
          like a music close enough to jazz

Weather wanting the best
Blowing through the sixties
      and the folk songs that started it all

138.   HOW EASY IT WAS FOR EVIL

The abandoned mother
The sunken child *en route* to Italy
Africa mined for batteries
All the crimes in desert places

The lizard's struggle
And the limitless atrocities of sealife

The canceled future

Religion's tour guides   Dante's Beatrice
Minor-attracted popes
Allah's hum-dinger zealots
Ganges bullies amidst the crowding
The persistence of caste

Repurposed toys
The impossibility of getting truly acquainted
Chemistry's trance state savaged by distrust

Nuclear *anything*
The confusion it loves
The expectations of irradiation

Thinking someone's out to get you even in the arctic

A lifespan's surprising contradictions
The guesswork of friends

Mussolini's poses
Stalin's smallpox
The fuhrer's flatulence
Hirohito's obsession with starfish
     while Nanking lost its life

France's "sitzkrieg" and refusal to fight
Chamberlain's "peace in our time"

Korea   MacArthur
     Hanoi   the jungles
          Mao   the posters
              Uganda   the gators
                    Rwanda   the machetes

The Old West
The enabling media
Mobsters as pets
Hospitality's deceptions
The centerpiece of culture gone twerking

All night long the vagaries of *science*
Its clipboards *and* resplendent smocks!

Music made inaudible
Shinto made the summit of pretension

The way war waits in peacetime, dissembling
How English and every other lingo
              is just conformity's lube job
The certainty the life you live will be repeated forever

Climbing Everest and not *staying* there
Saying you've had enough
     and craving enough all the more

The way cities are stage sets for creep stuff
How democracy's now a slippery slope to fascist gloating
Perfection's seduction that puts you in prison

Living longer than Cro-Magnons did
The *de rigueur* of sleep as escapist
                            desperation

How easy for evil   when
     before you know it
          outrage is a *fait accompli*

Sex an invention with a patent
Drug landscapes and seascapes
Knowing *animals* know that something's wrong
                              except for the cats

Fathers forced to be boys
     and obey the whims of the state
Everybody knowing nothing
Singing sarcastic melodies to poverty
Myopia like a sport of CEOs
Nurseries expanded to include every genius
Snitching competitors
Recreational arson
Computers that will actually breed
Failure actually taught

"Save the whales!"
     "the planet!"
          "free Tibet!"
Unfortunate mantras
              mumbled in a dope haze

The frog in the pot dissolving
     to be a clueless broth oblivious
Paranormal news and legal enslavement

How easy it was is seen in the stars
How odd that simple good looks are all that matter

Evil's clinched it
Even Stockton's cop is helpless to arrest
I may be the only happy customer
     buying the bad guys dinner
         to better understand them

Evil   the umbrella term
     for when it's raining daily doses of bad opinions

In the House of False Hopes
     is a smirking chess master

            sitting *za-zen* with a strawberry shortcake

Fake wrestlers
      vying with "slam poets"
           for the prize of demise

For once the fish refuse the bait
      and Norway goes missing from the map

All pillow talk downgraded to reporting
A journalism the senses can't accept
And so   stuck on stupid
            procreation's a desultory ho-hum

A measly spirituality overturned
      by the slightest flick of Lucifer's pinky
Heavy breathing an asthma of not being sure

The brain of the crowd
      that "Ooh"s and "Aah"s
           the selection of chance sacrifice
              the hive *abuzz*
              with communal approval

Security's four syllables of fear
The hippie "flow"
      become a sinister flood of rundown
      with gravity the only god
And insanity's politics the sticky aftermath
                all muddy and grey

Say hello
And recognize affinity
      with the bullet's show-and-tell adventures
      in the body

Not grasping the horror
      you make a funny face
           of "not so bad"
           and "who's next?"

Evil's a five-star spaceship crash-landing on Venus
So that Love knows a foreign body's touch
      and the attention paid to futile orgies

There's a last-minute plan for everyone to sober up
But even Mahatma Ghandi's pushing a shopping cart
    on purpose
        in a south-of-Market reincarnation

A fifth column's flirting with the other four
And they were *easy,* I tell you!

See no   hear no   speak no   didn't work
The holy blueprint's running red with repurposing

Being nice to cartels
Going along
Seeing in the dark
Allowing
Condoning
Meekly nodding
Talking agreeably as fast as possible
Cheerfully excusing
      and the rest of the present participles
          that are synonyms for acceptance

That's why evil's had it easy
Once started   it accelerates
      as if it were the greatest truth
      and need not sell itself

It even has a secret it will never tell
And lives on
      where Left and Right in the extreme tie the knot

The end run around sanity
So easy evil's now an administrative state
The end of the day that starts an endless night

When arguments cease
And mental sharpness is blunted by surrender
"Addiction" the only word that applies

And so   unstable is the planet
      the universe's a showcase world

What came before and used to be
       is a stand up joke
              without an audience to hear
The comedy's "material" in search of Madonna

A funeral attended by the happy-go-lucky
       where the eulogy condemns those who died
             and *all* that is defunct

If it's a game the Cosmos plays
       will there ever be an intermission?
Is it all reenactment?

I want to be ready
Dedicated to oblivion
No one has a name now
       and even the collective signs with an "x"

And having made its mark
       reruns all the atrocities

Do *you* understand?
Or does New Stuff so bedazzle
       you will not recall Caligula
            his dollar sign usurped
            and one-upped by machine guns
Your peace of mind based on the last five minutes

The highway
       and the birds that told this story
The technicolor rocks that provided details
The poolside reverie that led to commitment
       however unstylish
The action taken by a local rancher
            to rid himself of strangers

All of this is like a jewel
       a diamond's assessment
            of enormous pressure
                applied to reason
                    so that it succumbs
              lies down beneath outrage
            and begs for more
Like a seasoned whore!

Evil says, "Easy does it!"
    in the homestretch of conquest
        and takes credit
            for every record broken for murder

Okay, okay!   you're walking away
But don't go too far
           are you sure it's not true?

Identity theft is chums with stolen souls
The piolet come to the tropics
           to bother Amazon tribes

Whatever's elemental knows a beautiful momentum
Has obstacles removed like Ganesha
           in the service of the Hindus
Who can resist?

Even traveling Nevada
        the Mongols have set up roadblocks
           demanding tribute or else
And rewinding history won't help

Turns out those Nature specials
        speak of millions of years
           and never a time
               when there wasn't predation

The web of life controlled
        by a spider bemused by the uses of silk

How important is a mother abandoned
A child drowned
A father shamed
        if the species that went insane
           finds madness so enjoyable
              industrial, even?

No civil war I see
Rather   a scheme
        to make docility far-reaching
           that the centuries may slide
           undisturbed by any progress

The finale   just   finished
The last lies of individuality recanted
There can be no explanation

Just the metaphor of flocks of birds
Their swirling migrations
Flights both scintillating *and* Orwellian
Their togetherness a feathered totality

The ironic freedom of soaring aloft
                 even guided by the stars!
    their benign twinkling
    a distant teaching with no graduation day

From the nuanced north
    to the extravagant south
                 and back they fly
When changing direction's no change at all

You may disagree
But first a toast
    to the patience
        that let you hear so far

And for letting me live
    with these international complaints

As for "so far"   it's been difficult
For charisma
    which makes *everything* easy
        hasn't flown my way
        only evil's

139.   HAPPY FOURTH OF JUPLAYA!

Don't think so!

Another gathering?   another party?
Nah!
     even if Bruno's Country Club is part of it

There's the ad
The gist to come a-runnin'
The invitation to an ATM
     free wi-fi
          veggie and salmon burgers
               and
                  their world-famous ravioli!

Bruno's notwithstanding
     "Juplaya" we will skip
          or any Woodstock at all

That Rainbow Gathering?
Forget it!

And there are other ones
And what you *think* you would do
     until you think some more
          thinking twice
          and then some thrice

Might as well be football   those events
Has to do with the first person plural, the overwrought *we*!

Burning Man?   we'll get to that
Didn't forget and *will* explain   just wait
                               awhile

I'm too lazy to list all the get-togethers
Suffice it to say
     the giant bubble of a crowd
          is unacceptable capture

Whatever the season
     the crush of numbers is awful
          a Colosseum's worth
              of *reductio ad absurdum*
                  that makes you weak
                  when you think you're strong

Juplaya the 4th?   think differently
Let its non-essential footprint in the desert
    stay a theory
        the *idea* superior to actually *going*

Strangely, the mob is no attraction
Being a circus that repels
    in spite of its clowns' acts of genius

Those stampedes now and then remind
    the masses seem to desire death
        a dementia that happens
        with too much *we*

As in
    "We look forward to stealing your mind
    and if you're late to the theft
        there'll be consequences!"

Oh, throngs!   disperse!
Be no more troublesome!
Cease your cravings to *belong*!
No battles will be won or lost if you scatter!

And what Fourth can it be that's not 1776?
What "patriots" repeat is the crack of fire
    all wigs removed and set aside?

There's a dictionary now
    with words left out of Philadelphia's vocab
And engines roaring "man-alive!" intentions
            unimagined in Mozart's century

And that Rainbow?
What species of Oz
    sits in the woods
        in a Marijuana haze
           to squeak a planetary vision
           of "something ain't right?"

How much revitalizing may a zombie accomplish?

Is "tribe" to be ascribed
    to a hippie "be-in"

        pretending *not* to be power-mad
            but whose wayward bodies
                already march
                    disorderly yet intensely
                        to proselytize entropy
                    hurry it along
                            so the bombs that will fall
                            fall sooner?

Daytona!
Round and round!
Faster and faster!   dumber and dumber!
    a threadbare intelligence

You're in trouble if you go
If you're accustomed to worship a "formula"
The open track devoid
        of open-wheel and single-seaters
                so you grouse
                      and pick fights with other idiots

A high-speed wreck
        will surely please the atavistic brainstem
Make it seem so very worthwhile!

Even the clambakes back east back when
        with the late forties finishing up
That feast   too attended with dogs and drunks
The pulp of watermelons
        not enough sweetness to alleviate frictions
The later bonfires failing to truly motivate

And we'll be skipping any rallies
The excuses made for looky-loo density
The audience for *anything*
The togetherness of armies

We'll be avoiding the Olympics
        and who's "best" by a thousandth of a second

And it will be so easy to veto a class reunion
When strangers claim they know you
        and demand a list of your cancers
                since that long-ago chess club

And no countries that are crowds
      as soon as they're entered
Whose citizens have momentum enough
         to end up the only species within its borders

Maybe just the gathering of you and I   *yes*
The two of us cheering and rooting and schmoozing
Our crowd roar to include
      at *least* a consonant or two
         and be the infinite refinement
           of those "Ooh"s and "Aah"s of others

Only Burning Man
But a Burning Man of privacy then
Something owned by our contentment
      and never able to overwhelm or overawe

The playa was *always*
      our very own beach of a lakebed
      and all that's yearly built upon it!

And no matter how populated it gets
      joining in will never surpass
         your hand in mine

Despite those thousands
Alone-together we are
      and besting Orwell's domain of lovely art!

140. LAURA

Note: 'humint' is a recently coined abbreviation for 'human intelligence'

She's Laura
She's the Gate

All the fuss fallen away
      and compressed to one woman's welcome

To Black Rock   to blessing   to Everywhen!

2020's version of 1996
The year every year *after* was somehow
             like a recurring desert dream

Laura's solo
        and her attention *undivided* is
             her RV stickered and lettered nicely

"Plant Something"
"Volunteer"
"Don't Litter"
"Recycle"
"Reuse"
"Playa Patrol"
"Earth-Friendly"
"Make Every Day Earth Day"

There are handprints painted
        looking Amerindian
             prehistory's pictographs
                 mysteries she wants to write

She offers free buckets
       and news of the non-event
      anon   to come   to happen
Like good ideas

There are bold red letters that say
                            "No Fires!"

Laura's sunglassed with boots and blonde hair
     at the end of a cobbled stretch
         that veers from two-laned
            the road from Gerlach
               after the road from Cedarville

The end of human engineering
And the start of a highway as vast as the playa
Every square foot accessible

She's stashed a pennant and hula hoops
With *resolve* she's come

      and she wears a dress
           first fashion conceived
           her apparel just right
She's Mad Max's date in the sun
And believing in the ghost of Larry Harvey

"Wherever you live
        live *here* to like it more!"
           warns Laura
           but only slightly
                with a smile

The drill so well-known it's telepathy
No hard-sell's required
We know about   "that"

Burning Man
      the *homo sapiens*'s long-sought recreation
          all of the mind in play
          as if children are to run the world

The soul to be fully understood
So no Big questions asked and answered

Her Gate
      unlike the other years
          will conduct no inspections
There'll be no search for stowaways
Or any inexplicable delays

Just Laura's short story of sparse arrivals
The sketch of camps and setups
      barely constructed
             unexpectedly ingenious

With a gesture
      she sweeps the pristine cracks of the lakebed
          that will not see those streets and alleys
              pounded to washboard

Nor the tired patrols
      of Rangers
          and law enforcement
              looking to stop travel

                at more than five miles-an-hour

The only admission required's
      a willingness to enter
      and let binoculars be your guide
Scanning the far-flung canceled city
          that's virgin-fresh
              waiting on dust devils
              and *all* the episodes
                    of the sun and moon

Enjoying the wraparound world of granite
          and ancient limestone islands
Those several hot springs
          tracing a fault
              the pioneers would follow
                    to the High Rock Canyon

The Euclidean perfection of Lahontan silts

All is made even
      the playa high-heels optimistic

Hers is a solo welcome
      to global warming's scary preview
          all the time we have left   spread out

And why does "nano" seem to echo
                    in the void of blinding glare?
Burning Man a surprising singularity
      expanding   primordial

There are no controls
There's only Laura

There is no conversation
      that is not about uncertainty
          and the emptiness thrills

Clean-slated
      the first Burning Man's to be reprised
          or the novel's now a haiku you check into
                        like a blank hotel

And just as fantasy's triggered
    by the merest suggestion
        I'm a cat intrigued by vanished thread
            controlled by its owner
            making me pounce

Laura is not admonitive
With the exception of her sign that says "No Fires!"
But even that is moot proscription

Perhaps those crews who fly the UFOs
    who were too shy to come near in '19
        will test land their machines and mingle
           our own forbidden planet to learn
Still evading humint's efforts to fathom Space

In no hurry I ask,
    "Do you want to play *Scrabble*?"
And she answers,
    "The sun's too bright   can it wait?"
I say, "Forever" as if I meant the Black Rock
And   a game begun after all
    the even desert
        with the last tile in place
            declares a tie

It's wrong to say it's a "Rogue Burn" we've come to
All the rest were this same skeleton's clatter
    in praise of outline's theories
Something at the heart of celebration
        that's a wink
        and a nod
            to simplify

Minimal attendance
    to heighten awareness
        of the reason they come
            and can*not* be found
                on the beach called Baker in San Francisco
Nice as those fires had been
        warming the night away

It was always   since the nineties
    the spell of a landscape

Kind of place that makes you admit,
        "I don't know who I am
           so I don't know who is dying"

So Burning Man just got better
        being committed to Nature first
           the moment made an hour's awe

Thus the edgy tutelage of pure op art
Strange adrenalin ensuing
The Coney Inland Island conjured as hologram
        where every motive's untangled
        and parsed for relevance
           in this   the Anthropocene

Tonight
        in the ephemeral city postponed by COVID
           I'll sleep the same as before the virus

The motor memory dreaming of tents and domes
Of electrified horizons
        and fat tires rolling glitter and delight
Of dubstep's culminating noise the night of the Burn
                its overwhelming apotheosis!

Laura's outstretched hand
        is the enchantment of a sudden angel
           who wands like a magician
She's relaxed
And urges straight ahead when you're ready
        making laws for yourself
        that aren't easily broken

There's Old Razorback
The Selenites
        and the distant Jackson Range
Dedans for the tennis we'll play
           for Antonioni in 1966

We have a New Deal called 2020
        though separation's antitrust obtains
An expanded universe of playa
           to let the planes come and go
                without wreckless endangerment

The gravitational pull of villages weakened
All rights in perpetuity
       to bring us   astoundingly   closer
Our go-ahead party a quiet rerun of sofas

Is it Laura could say who she's seen so far
           but she just doesn't want to spoil it?

"Thanks for asking   but I just can't remember"

So what's canceled is further forgotten
Like a single mom's reluctance to wed
      once her independence is known
               for the first time

If you want to see each artist
      you will be able
          as patron-dilettante
In fact   for the first time
      everyone's *name* might be known!

She's offering ice cream   even sorbet
I said, "You're the best!"

She was the mildest intervention
Rewinding the years
      while we stood with the bars from an ice chest
      and gently balanced preludes and finales

The voice that whispered "Come and see"
      though what to see was not to be
The prompt that always seemed
        a weird signal for migration
        or a call to marriage
Whatever self there was that said to stay
      is brought to Laura anyway
      to hear her speak as if in song
        as mellifluous a greeting as Billie Burke's Glinda

I'll be an Arab
      and channel Lawrence long enough
        to cross the great Nefud

                    pretend it's the "sun's anvil"
                              right here and now
With no obligation to battle the Turks

Laura's desert's beflagged with a rainbow
And lyrics that were nearly lost
        what it's like to be "somewhere over"

We're not taking calls   the Internet's torn
And the "real" world lost to "pretend"
There'll be no rent this time
        no tickets or passes
              and knocking on the door of the desert
For it opens before the second knuckle's tried

And Laura
        whose name's so like the sound of the wind
Laura   has proposed an hapax legomenon
        for 2020's novelette
"Make it 'impossible'
                the word said once only
                    as befits what's before us!"

"Agreed   'impossible'
        the word our mirage would refute
              I think I see an artcar!"

"Just maybe," she murmured

Seems only yesterday we all left Africa
Think it was to find Nevada   instinctive flocking

The Anthropocene is a mental state
A hidden passage to End Time concerns
And the migraine of crowding
        and Black Rock
        Is a most outrageously effective
                                    oblivion
                                          all selfishness aside

Think you'd like to meet Laura?
Yes   you would
We'll be smart enough to delete the videos
        lest anyone grow jealous of your sudden delight

If you've broken up with the cities
        and are tired of fighting
                step into the future
                      for a night out on *its* town
The wrong shoes discarded for platform sneakers

Freedom has flatlined
And requires space to recover
        the best medicine possible
                your DNA copied and stored
                      in the mountains
Kept in the care of King Lear
His hospital
        of weathered volcanics with "limestone lensing"

He is "Author of the Moment"
The song Laura sang with her perfect contralto

For now she's Mother Earth
Gracious   unassuming   happy to be of help
                in the broken rock
                and scrub
                      of the Edge
A no-frills nursing station

It'll start   maybe it has
The crazy thing is
        near nothingness is so appealing now
The slate in a state of astounding cleanliness
A mystery as much as the red sun's misdirection

I want Offenbach here
And his "Tales" told to the impressionable
        here in the capitol of slumber

There'll be other times
        and other clouds of fine dust
There'll be noise and confusion
                after COVID concludes

This is our chance for exceptional peace
With history

        that was just the futile projection of power
            halted

Call it Laura's intermission
The *fermata* in some frantic symphony
      when even Marxism dries up and grows hoarse

And   as in "Hoffmann's" coda
      the dancers stepping towards
          that vanishing point of convergence
      the filmed opera's penultimate vision
Perhaps I'll walk with Laura too
Like the fifties ballet says to do

Her guidelines the fantasy of *Opera Comique*

And we will disappear
Into its shrine
      to the nineteenth century's secret places
To be closer to the story
      than you ever thought possible
How truly remarkable to learn
        such a wasteland may be a reward
        or even completion!

How long will it take otherwise?
If extinction is accomplished
      all the lessons are learned
Think big!
Serve notice
      that nothingness
          is a brainstorm worth the lightning

Laura said she will be planting flowers
      known by Latin names she can't pronounce

And I said I could help
      because I once fell in love with a Latin teacher
        and wrote a piano piece for her
          called "Ruinae"
Playing it before High School closed its doors for good

Is it too late to look for a keyboard?

I want to add *my* hands to her camper's collection
Promising to reuse and recycle
      never litter
           and *pray*

But to which deity, Laura?
They're all outdated and well into their dotage
Earth-friendly will mean a lobotomy at least
      for Reality bats last
      and the game of Eden's ended

Laura!   be Psyche!
And live in the house
      that was built for her
           in the wilderness once in September
           before the Trade Towers fell

Psyche who made the mistake
      of glancing at Eros
           and so was sorely banished

You'll be at home in the invisible city
Installed like the art
      and taken care of for the duration
                    lovingly, too

The world
      is left for the next go 'round and reenactment
May there be gaiety
      beyond the means of contrivance

I've heard so much music
           it's become the only language
But with Mozart's speech preferred
                    to multi-ton Wagner

And Laura's voice
      with a crime-stopping cadence
           is solo
The same as the opera that used to be sung
On Saturday   at the End
The torches touching hay for conflagration's sake

Laura's song is music ahead of time

The week still to come
            and all its slang
                        security
                                  and protection
The fulvous desert ranges enclosing

Ere now the frantic caravans would come
Those lumbering hippie vans and wagons
Like the consequence of a natural disaster

But Laura's simplicity
        and knowing where you are is where you live
                      is all the time in the hologram city
                                  of sly intentions

Oh, and did I mention they're hiring?
Yes!   good pay and benefits
        for stewards of fancy
        despite the claims of barter only

Laura's already made a million
But she gave it to the coyotes
                theirs to better spend

The adventures of the sun and moon
        to be told with every step taken out there
        with strangers' sudden friendships accepted

I'll listen closely to their music
Then play it completely for Laura
        the flats and sharps sure to be familiar
Her comfort level a contact serenity
                          and symphony of minuets

Not knowing you're learning you *do*
As the grownup infant you are

Boisterous!
        cribless!

About the Author:

Steve Arntson is actually Stephen Francis Cosgrove, but he never liked that name and decided to use his first girlfriend's last name instead — that way, even though they never married he could kind of pretend they had. Steve grew up in Massachusetts but at age 8 the family moved to Seattle — there was no more growing up after that, although he did attempt the University of Washington. It frightened him, so he dropped out and started selling encyclopedias door-to-door, thinking to get rich. This didn't happen. He went to Colorado and was overcome by the scenery. When threatened with being drafted he joined the Army Reserves to avoid death in Vietnam. He basically wasted a lot of time from '65 till '85 but eventually thought he'd found a group that said it didn't matter all that much — he'd discovered the poetry scene in S.F. Somehow the escapism involved gave him hope and he started making friends. Old Spaghetti Factory, Cafe Babar, Chameleon Lounge and Above Paradise — he's been more-or-less happy ever since and has been scribbling constantly, believing monkeys might in fact be able to write Shakespeare. But when writer's cramp occurs, he plays the piano; his favorite composer is Franz Schubert.

Steve has attended the Burning Man Festival 27 times, including in the Pandemic year when there was no formal gathering.

Other books from this author:

Skylight
(Blue Beetle Press, 1992)

To and From on the Day-for-Night Coast
writing as Stephen Francis Cosgrove
(Regent Press, 2017)

The Year of the Fox
(Regent Press, 2019)

Gypsy and Other Poems
(Last Laugh Productions, 2022)

Hall of Painted Sonnets
with Diane Lee Moomey
(Last Laugh Productions, 2023)

Anthologies:

Horsemen of the Apocalypse
edited by Alan Kaufman
(Cyborg Productions, 1991)

Cuts from the Barbershop:
an anthology of poems & translations
edited by Liz Henry
(Tollbooth Press, 2004)

Other Offerings from Last Laugh Productions

We'll Always Have Stockton, by Steve Arntson

The Worlds According to Loki, 2nd Edition, by Vampyre Mike Kassel

For Whoever Thinks a Piano is Furniture, by Rudy Jon Tanner

The Hall of Painted Sonnets, Sonnets by Steve Arntson, Art by Diane Lee Moomey

Embodied, by Jan Dederick

Gypsy & Other Poems, by Steve Arntson

Armageddon Bootcamp…and other poems (hardcover), by Maria Elizabeth Rosales

Three Kinds of Dark (ebook, hardcover), by Deborah L. Fruchey

Touchstones (hardcover), by Maria Elizabeth Rosales

Priestess of Secrets, by Deborah L. Fruchey

Bat Flower: poems, plays & other perversions, by Vampyre Mike Kassel

Armadillo (ebook, hardcover), by Deborah L. Fruchey

Color Cards & Self Healing, by Jean Luo

The Colors of Sound (companion CD or MP3), performed & composed by Robert Hamaker

A Scandalous Creature, by Deborah L. Fruchey

Mental Illness Ain't for Sissies, by Deborah L. Fruchey & Dr. David Kallinger

The Unwilling Heiress, by Deborah L. Fruchey

Island Journey (Instrumental CD or MP3), composed & performed by Robert M. Hamaker

Island Journey (Narrated Meditation CD or MP3), by Robert M. Hamaker narrated by Deborah Fruchey

Crystal Connections (CD or MP3), by Robert M. Hamaker & Erik Satie *(gymnopodie #1)*

Crystalline Sleep (Binaural Beats CD or MP3), by Robert M. Hamaker

www.lastlaughproductions.org

www.ingramcontent.com/pod-product-compliance
Lightning Source LLC
Chambersburg PA
CBHW081201170426
43197CB00018B/2889